Editing Early Modern Texts

Editing Early Modern Texts

An Introduction to Principles and Practice

Michael Hunter

© Michael Hunter (Michael Cyril William Hunter) 2007, 2009

All rights reserved. No reproduction, copy or transmission of this
publication may be made without written permission.

No portion of this publication may be reproduced, copied or transmitted save with
written permission or in accordance with the provisions of the Copyright, Designs and
Patents Act 1988, or under the terms of any licence permitting limited copying issued
by the Copyright Licensing Agency, Saffron House, 6-10 Kirby Street London, EC1N 8TS.

Any person who does any unauthorised act in relation to this publication
may be liable to criminal prosecution and civil claims for damages.

The author has asserted his right to be identified as the author of
this work in accordance with the Copyright, Designs and Patents Act 1988.

First published 2007
Paperback edition published 2009 by
PALGRAVE MACMILLAN

Palgrave Macmillan in the UK is an imprint of Macmillan Publishers Limited,
registered in England, company number 785998, of Houndmills, Basingstoke,
Hampshire RG21 6XS.

Palgrave Macmillan in the US is a division of St Martin's Press LLC,
175 Fifth Avenue, New York, NY 10010.

Palgrave Macmillan is the global academic imprint of the above companies
and has companies and representatives throughout the world.

Palgrave® and Macmillan® are registered trademarks in the United States,
the United Kingdom, Europe and other countries.

ISBN–13: 978–0–230–00807–6   hardback
ISBN–10: 0–230–00807–0   hardback
ISBN–13: 978–0–230–57476–2   paperback
ISBN–10: 0–230–57476–9   paperback

This book is printed on paper suitable for recycling and made from fully
managed and sustained forest sources.

A catalogue record for this book is available from the British Library.

Library of Congress Cataloging-in-Publication Data

Hunter, Michael Cyril William.
   Editing early modern texts : an introduction to principles and practice /
  by Michael Hunter.
     p. cm.
  Includes bibliographical references and index.
  ISBN 0–230–00807–0 (cloth) 0–230–57476–9 (pbk.)
   1. Criticism, Textual. 2. Editing. I. Title.

P47.H86 2006
808.02–dc22

2006045772

10 9 8 7 6 5 4 3 2
17 16 15 14 13 12 11 10 09

Printed and bound in Great Britain by
CPI Antony Rowe, Chippenham and Eastbourne

*To my co-editors:
from whom I have learned so much*

Contents

List of Illustrations	ix
Acknowledgments	x
Note	xii
1 Introduction	1
2 Manuscripts	14
3 The Role of Print	24
4 Types of Edition	36
a. *Works*	37
b. *Correspondence* and *Papers*	43
c. Archives	52
5 Presenting Texts (1) Printed	58
6 Presenting Texts (2) Manuscripts	72
7 Modernised Texts	86
8 The Apparatus	92
a. Front Matter	92
b. End Matter/Appendices	95
c. Annotation	96
d. Translations	99
9 Indexing/Searching	102

Appendices

1 Alternative Methods of Transcribing a Seventeenth-century Manuscript	109
2 A Confusion of Brackets	118
3 Separate and Combined Versions of a Revised Text – the 1597, 1612 and 1625 Versions of Francis Bacon's Essay 'Of Regiment of Health'	121

4	Unmodernised and Modernised Versions of the Last Section of Chapter 47 of Thomas Hobbes' *Leviathan*	127
5	Peter Nidditch's Description of the Evolution of his Editorial Method	132

Notes   134

Glossary   145

Bibliography   147

Index   163

List of Illustrations

Plate 1:   Royal Society MS 186, fol. 105v (dimensions of original: 155 mm × 100 mm)   113
Figure 1: Disposition of the pages on an octavo sheet   27
Figure 2: Contrasting editorial uses of brackets and other symbols   120

Acknowledgments

The following have kindly read drafts of this book and made invaluable suggestions for emending it; many of them also provided me with helpful references which I hope I have made good use of, even when I have failed to comply with all their ideas for changing the text: Peter Anstey, Iordan Avramov, Peter Beal, Jeremy Black, Jan Broadway, Justin Champion, Nick Jardine, Phil Jeffries, Tim Raylor, Graham Rees, Alain Segonds, Nigel Smith and Alison Wiggins. Among these, I would like to single out Graham Rees and Jan Broadway and Alison Wiggins of the AHRC Centre for Editing Lives and Letters at Queen Mary, University of London, who played an especially important part in the early stages of planning the book. I would also like to record my long-term debt to the late Jeremy Black, who, although concerned with editing material from a quite different period – namely Sumerian texts surviving on cuneiform tablets – joined me in many fruitful discussions of editorial issues.

Various of my current research students kindly allowed themselves to be used as guinea-pigs from the point of view of assessing the useability of the book, and I am grateful to Sue Dale, Gerry Dawson, Marilyn Lewis, Kate Meaden, Matthew Neill and Michael Townsend for their helpful comments. I am also grateful to the following for advice and suggestions: Kate Bennett, Elizabethanne Boran, David Carnegie, Ros Davies, Roger Gaskell, Guido Giglioni, Sarah Hutton, Harriet Knight, Peter Lindenbaum, Charles Littleton, Giles Mandelbrote, David McKitterick, Stephen Pigney, Larry Principe, Craig Walmsley and Paul Wood. Heather Wolfe and her colleagues at the Folger Library, Washington, DC, arranged for me to give a presentation there in April 2003 in which I tried out various of the ideas expressed in this book.

I am grateful to Richard Maber, editor of *The Seventeenth Century*, in which my article, 'How to Edit a Seventeenth-century Manuscript: Principles and Practice', was published in 1995, who has kindly allowed me to reproduce in slightly adapted form the text of the appendix setting out alternative methods of transcribing a seventeenth-century manuscript that appeared there. The quotation from Peter Nidditch in Appendix 5, from volume 1 of the edition of the *Drafts* for Locke's *Essay* published by John Rogers after his death, appears by permission of Oxford University Press.

Plate 1 is reproduced from Royal Society MS 186, fol. 105v, by permission of the President and Council of the Royal Society. The jacket illustration is reproduced by permission of the Trustees of the British Museum.

Michael Hunter
March 2006

Note

For a glossary of terms used in this book, see pp. 145–6.

The notes appear at the end of the book on pp. 134–44.

All books and articles are referred to in the notes by author's surname and short-title. For the full title and publication details, see the Bibliography, pp. 147–62. CD-ROMs are also included in the Bibliography, as are specific articles accessed through websites. However, editions and websites accessed online by URL are not: these are cited piecemeal in the notes. All such URLs were last accessed in March 2006.

1
Introduction

Editions of key texts are central to scholarship. Editions bring together disparate materials. They make the inaccessible accessible. And, through them, users benefit from the expertise in elucidating and interpreting complex texts of the editors who produce them. Almost all who work in the humanities, and particularly those working on periods remote from the present, use editions on a regular basis. They should therefore think carefully about their rationale. Moreover, though few themselves become editors on a large scale, many dabble in editing to the extent of transcribing from manuscript original documents on which they wish to base an argument. Hence they should reflect on the tradition in which they participate in doing so.

Yet the theory and practice of editing are often taken for granted, for various reasons. Though most scholars have at least a vague awareness of the formidable technicality which editing can involve – for instance, in the case of the text of certain Shakespearean plays – the task often seems straightforward to the extent of being self-evident. Given a single copy of a single document, what is needed other than accurately to convey what is in front of the editor with the minimum of obtrusiveness? In fact, as anyone who has attempted the simplest piece of editing will be aware, even an ostensibly straightforward task necessitates decisions being made, and the longer and more complex the text, the more such decisions will be involved. As with any such set of choices, the quality of the ultimate outcome will often be enhanced by consideration of alternative strategies used by others in comparable situations and the choice of the one that seems most appropriate. Yet all too often the editorial challenge evokes a kind of libertarian streak in scholars, a sense of self-sufficiency in the face of an ostensibly straightforward task which in turn has led to a proliferation of differing practices, some of which are clearly preferable to others.

This sense of self-sufficiency is no less marked in those heavily involved in the editorial task, who often seem prone simply to want to get on with the job rather than to waste time discussing the principles underlying it. This is partly because the principles underlying an edition are typically decided relatively early in its execution, much of the time thereafter being spent in implementing rules which it is easier to retain than to change and which there is therefore a disincentive to reconsider. In fact the planning stage, when an appropriate editorial strategy is adopted, is perhaps the most critical point in the entire editorial process, at which crucial decisions have to be made as to what is appropriate and what is not. Yet most editions say less about these decisions than they might: though the editorial principles that have been applied in them are expounded, this usually takes the form of a curt, descriptive statement rather than an exposition of their underlying rationale. As publication approaches, it is in any case too late for modifications to be made, and this also often inhibits discussion in the form of reviews: when a scholar has spent years of his or her life preparing an edition, it seems rather churlish to question its rationale rather than to celebrate its content.

As a result, such cumulative development as the practice of editing has shown has often been the result less of an interchange of views than of a kind of osmosis. To a large degree, editors have been self-taught, making their own decisions about the problems that confront them in their chosen tasks. The result has been a marked divergence in practice between different editions. Insofar as this reflects a proper respect for the specific problems of the text that is being edited, it is commendable: the individual characteristics of each text should be the primary arbiter of the editorial treatment that is deemed appropriate to it. Yet decisions concerning the needs of a particular text are almost invariably enhanced by fuller awareness of methods tried elsewhere, while discussion of the pros and cons of different treatments can often lead to an improved understanding of the principles underlying editorial work. The aim of this book, therefore, is to stimulate reflection on such matters. My objective is to induce thought about how meaning is best conveyed and how an edition can be made as intelligible and helpful to its readers as possible, while retaining fidelity to the original on which it is based. It is hoped that even those already committed to the editorial task will benefit from this, but I am more optimistic about influencing those who may produce editions in the future, if only to the marginal extent mentioned in the opening paragraph. Most of all, the book is aimed at users of editions, indicating to them the problems that editors face, and the advantages and disadvantages of different approaches to these, with a view to encouraging a greater sensitivity to such matters which, it is hoped, will ultimately feed back into editorial practice itself.

That such a book might be necessary at all may seem to some surprising, and it is therefore appropriate to say a little more about its rationale. The craft of editing has a long history. Its roots are to be found in the activities of Renaissance humanists who sought to achieve an accurate text of writings from classical antiquity: here, the emphasis was on an attempt to counter the problems of corruption during manuscript transmission, either by conjectural emendation, or through detailed studies of the different extant manuscript versions of classical texts. These two traditions emerged in Italy in the late fifteenth and early sixteenth centuries, and the man who brought them together and did more than anyone to establish the principles by which lost archetypes of texts were postulated was the late sixteenth-century scholar, Joseph Scaliger.[1] Thereafter, the synthesis that he evolved rose to new heights in the work of eighteenth-century scholars like Richard Bentley and Friedrich August Wolf and nineteenth-century ones like Karl Lachmann and A.E. Housman, and it has continued to flourish to this day.[2] A parallel tradition developed in terms of biblical textual criticism, involving some of the same figures – notably Bentley and Lachmann – and such other scholars as Johann Jakob Griesbach.[3] Today, as earlier, classical and biblical scholars are in the forefront of constructing complicated 'stemmata' in which distinctive traditions of the descent of a text are postulated on the basis of common variants, a technique which has subsequently been borrowed by those tracing the descent of vernacular texts in manuscript form, and which will therefore be briefly described below.[4]

A more significant tradition in terms of texts of the kind with which we will be concerned here, however, was the tradition of editing of literary texts which originated with students of Shakespeare like Edward Capell in the eighteenth century and which reached a climax in the work of such English scholars as R.B. McKerrow and W.W. Greg, who devoted extensive attention to English Renaissance texts in the early years of this century, most notoriously the quarto and folio editions of Shakespeare's plays.[5] The principles devised for dealing with such works were then extrapolated more widely, both by McKerrow in his *Introduction to Bibliography for Literary Students* (1927), and above all by the American scholar, Fredson Bowers, who not only continued to refine such principles in relation to Renaissance authors, but also extended them to literary works of the nineteenth century, especially those of American authors.[6] The result was that the latter part of the twentieth century saw a whole tradition of editing of works of this kind according to the rules that such scholars had devised, much of it under the auspices of the Modern Language Association's Center for Editions of American Authors, succeeded in 1976 by the Center for Scholarly Editions, which produced guidelines for such work and followed this up by awarding a seal of approval to editions which met their standards.[7]

The principles underlying such activity derived to a significant extent from a classic paper by W.W. Greg, 'The Rationale of Copy-Text', published in the journal founded by Bowers, *Studies in Bibliography*, in 1950, which sought to establish principles according to which the 'substantive' elements of a text could be distinguished from its 'accidentals', and this has been the subject of extensive discussion ever since.[8] Indeed, it is a tribute to the vitality of the field that, since the 1980s, the entire terms of reference of this school have come under attack by revisionist scholars, leading to new thinking on the way in which texts should be presented, which in turn has been reflected in novel editorial strategies. A key work was Jerome McGann's iconoclastic *Critique of Modern Textual Criticism* (1983), while equally important was the rethinking based on studies of printing house practice associated particularly with D.F. McKenzie, which has led to greater emphasis on the actual characteristics of extant books rather than on the reconstruction of ideal archetypes.[9] The result has been to lead to a more historically sensitive view of how texts developed and were transmitted, which forms the basis of the state of affairs which this book largely takes for granted.

On the other hand, both before and after this, this field has produced a sizeable and complex theoretical literature. Indeed, in recent years various journals have emerged which direct their attention either wholly or in part to issues of this kind, such as *Text*, inaugurated in 1981. There are also a number of books which seek to set out the principles of textual editing, informed by a similar rationale.[10] Such writings certainly demonstrate the intensity of the debates which have arisen in the field, but for non-specialists they have two disadvantages. In the first place, the literature which has arisen is one which many readers of this book will find rather arcane and theoretical, only in isolated cases bearing much relation to the practical issues involved in editing from which this work has emerged and to which it will stay fairly closely anchored.[11] This has therefore been a disincentive to outsiders to read it. Secondly, it has tended to encourage a search for universal principles, applicable to all texts in all times. Yet it is far from clear that principles applicable to the age of the typewriter or word-processor will be appropriate to that of the scribe.

There is also a well-established tradition of editing historical documents, which has engaged the attention of scholars and antiquaries since the eighteenth century, reaching a climax during the nineteenth and early twentieth. Such activity stimulated the setting up of a joint Anglo-American committee in 1921 in conjunction with the founding of the Institute of Historical Research at the University of London in that year, which issued helpful guidelines over the next few years, dealing respectively with medieval and with modern (meaning mainly eighteenth- and nineteenth-century) material.[12] These were followed by a set of 'notes' to editors issued by the British Records Association in 1946, while more recently these have been succeeded by R.F. Hunniset's valuable handbook published by the same body in 1977, and by P.D.A. Harvey's *Editing Historical Records* of 2001.[13] On the other side of the Atlantic, comparable activity devoted to editing the *Papers* of major figures in American history of the eighteenth and nineteenth centuries under the auspices of the National Historical Publications Commission was codified in the post-war years by such works as Clarence E. Carter's *Historical Editing* (1952) and then more fully in Mary-Jo Kline's *A Guide to Documentary Editing*, initially published in 1987 and republished in revised form in 1998.[14]

On the whole, this tradition has always been less theoretically oriented and less self-conscious than the tradition of literary editing. It was partly for this reason that in the years around 1980 there was something of a confrontation between the 'literary' tradition and this one, stemming from an attack in 1978 on the record of the NHPC (by then renamed the National Historical Publications and Records Commission) by a man nurtured in the Bowersian editorial tradition, G. Thomas Tanselle. He cast his critical eye over the work of such editions and took them to task for what he saw as a lack of rigour in their editorial principles, and it is true that editions of this school had sometimes been slightly casual about the way in which texts were presented, as if this was rather trivial compared with their content. This led to extensive controversy in which the rationale of such editions was discussed, which ultimately resulted in Kline's *Guide to Documentary Editing*.[15] Indeed, this is one of the few occasions when the traditions of editing outlined here, which have otherwise tended to remain rather discrete, have had a mutual influence on one another.

There is also a further tradition of editing which needs to be considered, which falls somewhere between the traditions of 'documentary' and 'literary' editing. It is less well known, because scholars involved in this have been as prone as 'documentary' ones simply to get on with the job rather than to agonise over its rationale. Here I refer to the extensive activity that has occurred over the past few decades in editing texts by philosophical and scientific authors such as Francis Bacon, Robert Boyle, Thomas Hobbes, John Locke and Isaac Newton: this is the English brand of an international tradition with a longer history, involving attention to the writings of authors like Descartes, Galileo, Leibniz and Huygens.[16] Indeed, it is from this background that I myself come, having been responsible for editing *The Works of Robert Boyle* (with Edward B. Davis) in fourteen volumes in 1999–2000, his *Correspondence* (with Antonio Clericuzio and Lawrence M. Principe) in six volumes in 2001, and more recently his 'workdiaries' – the record of experiments and observations that he kept for much of his career – and other ancillary sources.[17] The issues that have been confronted and the practices that have emerged in editing texts like these seem as worthy of consideration as those arising from the treatment of works by authors forming part of the literary canon, and many of the examples used in this book will be taken from such editions. Yet there has been much less discussion of texts of this kind and the issues arising from them. Occasionally, those concerned primarily with literary editing have cast a watchful eye in this direction: for instance, the 'Conference on Editorial Problems' held at the University of Toronto since 1965 has devoted occasional sessions to the editing of non-literary texts.[18] Yet arguably those responsible for editing texts like these deserve a fuller place in dialogues about the principles of editing than they have had hitherto, since it is far from self-evident that literary editing should always set the standard in the field.

Even more important to the rationale of this book is its restriction to the early modern period. All too many of the disquisitions on editing that have already been referred to concentrate almost entirely on texts dating from the nineteenth or twentieth centuries, or those of medieval date. This is as true of the discussions of documentary editing that have already been referred to as of those of literary texts: thus, the early modern period was left as something of a no man's land between the guidelines for medieval and modern texts published by the IHR committee of 1921, and this has remained true of the more recent manuals emanating from that school. With literary editing, too, despite the continuing vitality of the editing of dramatic texts of the Shakespearean period, the centre of gravity has otherwise very much shifted to the nineteenth and twentieth centuries, perhaps reflecting the trans-Atlantic nature of the tradition. In contrast, this book is explicitly focused on the early modern period, in other words the period from *c*.1550 to *c*.1800. In this, the book follows on from a paper I published in 1995 discussing the rationale of editing, with particular reference to manuscript texts of the early modern period.[19] This stemmed from my awareness, while editing seventeenth-century texts from the 1980s onwards, of the neglect of the early modern period in discussions of editing: I came to feel that the more chronologically specific a discussion was, the more likely it was to be helpful to those dealing with texts from the period in question, and the 1995 article arguably benefited from addressing such issues in an early modern context largely to the exclusion of texts of other periods. Subsequently, I have extended my thinking on such matters in connection with the Boyle editions and in various review-essays and the like.[20]

Texts of this period deserve separate attention from those of either earlier or later date because of the distinctive problems they present. They are close enough to us to be relatively intelligible compared with texts emanating from the Middle Ages, yet distant enough for this apparent familiarity to be often deceptive. To some extent this is a matter of language, vocabulary, and the like, but it also has a more immediate and technical dimension, relating to the means by which texts were presented. It is obviously a commonplace that the introduction of printing marks off the early modern period from the Middle Ages. But it is equally important to see that the first age of print, prior to the onset of mechanised printing, was more distinctive from our own than is often realised. It is now clear that, in the first instance, the changes that print entailed were less complete and less revolutionary than has sometimes been thought – that manuscript circulation remained important, and that the relationship between print and manuscript remained complex. In addition, early printers retained various practices which represented a direct hangover from manuscripts, for example including sections in red in texts otherwise printed in black, which posed a challenge to printers' ingenuity.[21] More generally, it is clear that the nature of the impact of print has been misunderstood by those who transposed presumptions from the machine-press era back to the age of the hand-press, and that a distinct understanding is required of printing in the period of the hand-press, and hence of the texts produced by it, due to the small scale of production, the ease with which corrections could be made, and the way in which work was organised.[22]

If this is true of print technology, it is no less true of the way in which texts were presented in printed format. The introduction of the printing press was itself accompanied by cultural shifts in the presentation of texts, yet not all of these led as directly to modern practices as might have been expected. To some extent, this is due to the hangover of manuscript traits in print, such as the use of the long 's', a feature of printed books of the early modern period which lasted till around 1800. In addition, the early modern period saw the rise and fall of characteristic practices in the presentation of printed texts which have been as unfamiliar since as they were common then, particularly a distinctive style of punctuation and the heavy use of capitalisation and italic. And if this distinctiveness is true of early modern printed texts, it applies equally to manuscript ones. Handwriting of the early modern period, though noticeably different from that of the Middle Ages, nevertheless retained many medieval hangovers, particularly in terms of the use of contractions and other means to increase speed of composition which are unfamiliar to modern readers and which often cause confusion. The details of such practices will be expounded at greater length in Chapters 2 and 3: these should at once underline the distinctiveness of the early modern period from what went before and from what has occurred since, and also indicate the essential homogeneity of many of the practices that characterised it, notwithstanding such changes as occurred, which will also be dealt with. Indeed, although each text and each author may be unique and hence the problems that they present and the solutions that these necessitate *sui generis*, knowledge of practices that were widespread at the time will help both those creating and those using editions better to understand many features of the texts that they are confronting.

It is also worth noting here that the coverage of this book is primarily restricted to Britain, since this is the area where my own experience has mainly been focused. On the other hand, much of what I say is of wider application: printing practice in the hand-press period was similar throughout Europe, though there were distinctive national traits which are often revealing in themselves, and this is equally true of various of the practices in the composition of manuscripts which are also here referred to.[23] Indeed, I have sometimes instanced editions of texts emanating from elsewhere in Europe and from America where this has seemed appropriate, particularly editions of correspondence and the like, though a different and longer volume would be needed to do justice to regional variations in a systematic way.

It is appropriate to end this Introduction by commenting on perhaps the most significant development that has occurred in relation to editing in the past decade in the form of the onset of digitisation. Of course, this applies not only to early modern texts but to texts of all periods, but it is with its impact on early modern scholarship that we will be primarily concerned here. Anyone living in the twenty-first century is aware of the extent to which computers have transformed our lives, and editing is no exception to this. Indeed, electronic media offer new solutions to editorial challenges that have long confronted scholars, both in terms of how data is organised and analysed, and in making it possible for material to be presented in ways which transcend the capacities of the printed book. The onset of electronic media has sometimes been compared to the impact of print, and there is some truth in this, particularly in the light of the evidence for a long transitional period following the introduction of printing that has already been referred to. It is therefore appropriate to give a little background here to the discussion of the implications of digitisation which will recur throughout the later chapters of this book.

Computers first started to be widely used in the humanities in the late 1980s, and at that point their potential for editorial purposes became apparent. Two pioneering projects may here be singled out in this connection, the *Canterbury Tales* Project, and the Hartlib Papers Project. Of these the earlier was the Hartlib Papers Project, inaugurated in 1987 and devoted to producing a digitised text of the archive of the intelligencer, Samuel Hartlib (*c*.1600–62), now in Sheffield University Library.[24] In this case, the principal implication of the use of computers – which was typical of the earliest phase of the use of information technology in the humanities – was to create a textual database in which material could be electronically searched and retrieved (it also made available a complete set of images of the transcribed documents, another facility made possible by electronic media). The ability to conduct systematic and complete searches by electronic means obviously made this corpus completely different from any previous text in printed form, and it remains one of the chief virtues of digitised texts. The *Canterbury Tales* Project began a little later, in 1989, initially as an experiment with the use of computer collation programmes. From 1992 onwards, however, it was systematised to provide a full collation of manuscript versions of various of Chaucer's writings, a work still in progress. In this case, computer technology was used to link together different versions of the text on a scale which manual collation could never have achieved, so that users were enabled to access and compare these at will, at the same time adding digital images, collations and analysis including computer-aided stemmata.[25]

Insofar as the *Canterbury Tales* Project displayed a greater degree of sophistication than the Hartlib one, it was because it was the beneficiary of rapid developments in digital technology, particularly in terms of standardisation and dissemination, that did much to transform the field in the 1990s. These built on initial steps taken in an academic context in the 1980s, though in other fields their roots go back further still. Already in the 1960s in government and business circles, particularly in the United States, people had become aware that proprietary softwares were often not interchangeable, and that what was required was a common markup language which would allow the exchange of information between different systems. This led to the development in the 1970s of Standard Generalised Markup Language, or SGML, which aimed to capture the meaning of data rather than its appearance by establishing a common set of encoding procedures which transcended those specific to particular softwares.[26] In terms of the application of such ideas to the humanities and to editing, the key initiative was the establishment in 1987 of the TEI (Text Encoding Initiative), which sought to establish guidelines for encoding texts in SGML using a common language of tags with universally agreed meanings and attributes; this has been the subject of a continuous process of evolution ever since.[27] The principles involved are now generally accepted since they have obvious advantages. Not only does such standardisation assist the interchangeability which was its initial aim through assuring the mutual compatibility of such files and hence their longevity: in theory they should be valid indefinitely. In addition, such markup also has intellectual merit, since it leads to a level of 'parsing' that goes beyond more traditional forms – so that, for instance, book-titles are uniformly coded as 'citations', rather than being marked in a specific way – while it also encourages greater consistency in treating material at different levels, since otherwise the encoding fails to operate.

A further corollary of coding of this kind is that it makes it possible to embed into texts a myriad of links which can be activated at will, and which provide the means by which a range of connections can be available in an edited text that is far beyond the capabilities of a printed one. This is the essence of the concept of 'hypertext', which is crucial to the way in which electronic editing has developed in the past decade. Hypertext makes it possible for the user to move in a text in a much wider range of directions than would otherwise be possible. It has been visualised as 'a non-centralized structure of complex relationships', comparable to a library in the way in which it can be exploited by the reader, and in the way in which it is capable of indefinite expansion.[28] As in the case of Chaucer, it can form the basis for the juxtaposition of far more versions of the text of a work than would ever be possible in printed form, while it also means that links to glossaries, notes, bibliographies and the like can be embedded in the text so that they can be activated at will, as can access to facsimiles of original manuscripts or even tunes, in the case of words with a musical accompaniment.

Equally crucial was the development in the early 1990s of the World Wide Web. Again, this stemmed from earlier developments, notably the introduction of electronic mail and Telnet in the 1970s, while the mid-1980s saw the development of the NSFnet, which came to be known as the Internet. The number of host computers using this grew from 1,000 to over 60,000 between 1984 and 1988, thus providing a foretaste of the exponential growth in access that has occurred ever since.[29] This in turn led to the development of rival browsing engines, initially Mosaic, the earliest widely-used browser, which was superceded by Netscape, while a later arrival was Internet Explorer. Communication and access rapidly led on to publication, in that it became possible to set up electronic archives on the Net, including such pioneering enterprises as the Perseus Project, initially devoted to providing a wide range of classical sources.[30] In terms of publishing on the Web, matters were transformed by the onset of HTML (Hypertext Markup Language), a simplified subset of SGML which bypassed some of the complications of the original system, and which therefore made it much easier to encode material for Web use. A further sub-set of SGML is XML (Extensible Markup Language), which has now taken on a life of its own.

In fact, SGML and XML have now become dominant in preparing electronic texts, largely due to the spectacular take-off of the Web, based as it is on HTML. But this was not as inevitable as it might in retrospect appear: SGML was never much used commercially because it was so costly to implement properly, and in the late 1980s and early 1990s there were other competing technologies – for instance HiDES/Microcosm at Southampton, which held the text in RTF (Rich Text Format) and the links in a separate linkbase – though these have now fallen by the wayside.[31] Indeed, it seems likely that electronic technology will continue to develop in spectacular and not always predictable ways, and, partly for this reason, this book will eschew undue technicality in this area, since treatments of such matters are prone to date very quickly.[32]

Most of those confronted by electronic technology initially experience a mixture of excitement and bewilderment. The possibilities that such media open up – in editing as in other fields – are amazing. On the other hand, the means by which these are achieved often require a technical expertise beyond that of most scholars with a traditional humanities background. Moreover, though technical issues obviously need to be discussed in appropriately precise and well-defined terms, some devotees of computer technology are prone to express their ideas in unduly complex language which is discouraging to those new to the field – though there are notable exceptions to this.[33] It has also now become apparent, after the initial euphoria over electronic media in the years around 2000, that information technology needs to be used intelligently in relation to broader goals, and it is crucial to understand just what level of use of such tools is appropriate to any particular editorial task. Online publication is not necessarily suitable for all editorial projects, involving as it does the need for both continuous access to the Internet at a high frequency and longterm maintenance; for other purposes CD-ROM publication (as used both by the Hartlib Project and the *Canterbury Tales* Project) may be more effective, as may the online publication of texts in the form of PDF (Portable Document Format) files which are not text-encoded. In passing, it may be pointed out that tagging a text so that hypertext links can be created is potentially extremely time-consuming. Indeed, there could be cases where digitisation proved as useful in preparing data for editions which were ultimately published in printed form as in the creation of electronic editions. It is also worth noting the extent to which the increased availability of data in electronic form has altered the role of the editor: for instance, in the context of the early modern period, the widespread availability of Early English Books Online means that multiple copies of many key texts can be accessed from individual scholars' computer screens.

Hence much of the challenge of digitisation is in deciding which tools to use and in which context, and I hope to offer advice on such matters in the chapters that follow. Here, I can draw not only on my experience as a consumer of electronic editions produced by others, but also on my experience in helping to create one, in the form of the edition of Boyle's workdiaries, initially published with the help of Charles Littleton on the Boyle website in 2001 and since republished in greatly improved form in conjunction with Alison Wiggins and Jan Broadway on the website of the AHRC Centre for Editing Lives and Letters.[34] This exemplifies various facets of electronic editions which have become increasingly common: the ability of readers to switch between various versions of a text, diplomatic, editorial or printer-friendly; the use of hypertext links to enable users to access an apparatus in the form of biographical and other compendia; and the provision of full-colour digitised facsimiles of the original manuscripts in juxtaposition with transcripts of them. Though it does not make use of all the potential tools that digital media can provide – for instance, it does not provide links between multiple versions of a text, as exemplified by the *Canterbury Tales* Project – I believe that my involvement with a project of this kind and my experience of others places me in a strong position to offer guidance on the implications of the onset of electronic media for editing. Yet the fact that I already had lengthy experience of more traditional forms of editing makes it possible to place this in the context of the broader issues which all editors have to confront, whether the outcome of their efforts is electronic or printed.

The structure of the book is as follows. It begins by considering some of the basics underlying editing, in the sense of the technologies of producing manuscript or printed texts in the early modern period, including the ways in which these changed over the centuries, since many of the editorial issues that subsequently emerge relate to the most effective ways of dealing with these. This will also involve considering the different modes of circulation that were available, and the extent to which authors were complicit in the published format of their works when these appeared in print (Chs. 2–3). From there, we will move on to consider certain established genres in editing and their rationale, particularly 'Works', 'Correspondence' and archival projects of various forms (Ch. 4). Then, we will look in more detail at the outputs that editors aspire to produce, considering in turn how printed and manuscript texts are appropriately dealt with, whether they survive in single copies or in multiple and revised forms. This will involve considering the proper balance between presenting the text in as authentic a form as possible and serving the requirements of readers, and in this connection consideration will also be given to the issue of the provision of modernised texts (Chs. 5–7). Lastly, we will consider the rationale of the apparatus with which scholarly editions should be provided, and the function of indexes and searching facilities (Chs. 8–9).

As will be seen, at each point issues will arise concerning what editors are trying to do, and how this should relate to the intentions of authors or the needs of the users, matters which require careful consideration whether electronic or more traditional means are used to achieve these goals. Though the consideration will be almost exclusively of texts of the early modern period, comparative examples from other periods will occasionally be introduced where this seems helpful. The aim is not to write a definitive account of editorial practice, but to offer a consideration of the issues involved in editing texts specifically of the early modern period which is wide ranging and balanced but nevertheless fairly brief. I want to make people think about editing, to encourage putative editors to consider what it is they hope to achieve and how best to achieve it and, more important, to encourage users of editions to reflect more carefully on the rationale of the texts they study. The aim is not to lay down the law, even in relation to early modern texts: as we will see, no two authors, or corpora, are identical. But understanding of the decisions involved in producing editions of such texts will undoubtedly be enhanced by careful consideration of the issues raised in this book.

2
Manuscripts

There is something almost visceral about handling a manuscript dating from the early modern period. Such documents arguably bring us as close as we can ever get to the early modern authors and scribes who created and transmitted the texts that have come down to us, their hesitations, errors and second thoughts. Indeed, until the invention of, first, the typewriter and then the word-processor, all texts were invariably initially written by hand: only after that might they be set in type and printed. Of course, they might have had a now lost prehistory in oral forms, which might continue in parallel with written ones; ideas might also initially have been inscribed in temporary form on 'writing-tables', in which various scholars have recently become interested.[1] Insofar as texts have come down to us, however, they almost always existed in manuscript before they were printed (works set straight in type with no manuscript prehistory are rare, virtually the only exceptions, then as more recently, being in the world of journalism). Moreover, many texts survive in manuscript, including many that have never been printed as well as some that subsequently were.

The study and understanding of manuscripts is therefore central to textual scholarship. Many of the most exciting opportunities both in editing and research derive from making material that has hitherto survived only in manuscript form more widely available through publication. In addition, an important factor in analysing printed works from the early modern period has derived from hypothesising the former existence of a manuscript version of the text in question, and trying to work out how the printer might have treated it, in terms of misreading ambiguous letter forms and the like.[2] Hence an understanding of manuscripts, and the techniques by which they were written, composed and circulated, is crucial to understanding early modern texts. This therefore seems a natural place to start.

Even the technology of early modern writing is unfamiliar in the age of the ball point pen and the computer keyboard.[3] The pen was a quill, made from the feather of a goose, preferably from the middle feathers of the left-hand wing. This was cut and shaped with a knife to form a nib, the shape depending on the type of handwriting for which it would be used; it was then kept in good shape by trimming, and the changes in the appearance of an individual's handwriting caused by such trimming may be in evidence in the course of a single manuscript. The manuscript may also show differences in the ink that was used. All ink had to be mixed manually, either by the user or by a supplier, and hence noticeable differences in colour and texture may be in evidence. The most common type of ink was made by mixing galls (the excrescence of gall flies on oak trees) with iron sulphate, and then adding gum arabic. The usual proportion was five parts of galls to three of sulphate and two of gum, but variants are known and extra ingredients were sometimes added, while there were also shortcuts like making ink from powdered burnt wool mixed with water or vinegar. The result was to lead to a variety of appearances, while the wrong formula could sometimes lead to acid damage to the paper to which the ink was applied, which is prone to make manuscripts difficult to read, if not to cause them to disintegrate. Occasionally, as an alternative to ink, other media might be used, such as a pencil made of black lead, or a crayon made of coloured chalk; note will naturally need to be taken of these where they appear.[4]

The aspect of manuscripts which is most obviously susceptible to analysis is the handwriting used in them.[5] Handwritings are individual, and can be used to identify the authors responsible for them, almost like a finger-print: but they also fall into broad chronological and other patterns. All of the scripts used in the early modern period basically derived from classical antiquity, but they developed in quite distinctive ways, reflecting a tension between a pursuit of elegance and the desire to be able to write quickly. In particular, the Middle Ages had seen the development of various cursive or running hands, notably that known as 'court hand' or 'anglicana', and that known as 'secretary', both of which enabled a scribe to write much more quickly than was the case with more classical letter forms. However, in the Renaissance such hands were challenged by a revival of italic, and by the seventeenth century secretary gradually died out, being replaced either by italic or by round or mixed hands, characterised by more rounded and looped letter forms. This means that, increasingly as the early modern period progressed, quite a wide range of hands was in evidence, thus often providing significant evidence of authorship on which a student of manuscripts can draw.

In addition, the handwriting even of specific individuals might vary. Thus some were capable of more than one hand, one neater and more formal, the other more rapid.[6] It also seems likely that the handwriting of individuals varied in the course of their lives, and in some cases – for instance, Isaac Newton – elaborate claims have been made by certain scholars for their ability to differentiate his writing at different stages in his career, though others have expressed scepticism about the reliability of such techniques.[7] It certainly stands to reason that handwriting would change as people aged – though there has been surprisingly little systematic study of this topic – but the disagreement over Newton reveals the difficulties involved, particularly when factors like the sharpness of the nib, the quality of ink and the space available are taken into account, and this is an area where it is advisable to tread with caution.

It was not only through the use of cursive scripts that speed was achieved in manuscript composition. In addition, since the Middle Ages extensive use had been made of abbreviations and contractions as a means of conveying meaning in a more succinct manner. These can be divided into two groups: on the one hand, abbreviations by suspension, on the other abbreviations by contraction, the former consisting of suspending the pen after the initial letter or part of the way through a word, with a full stop or special sign to indicate the omission (as in 'A.D.' for 'Anno Domini', or 'ei^9' for 'eius'), the latter giving the first and last letters of a word (and sometimes an intermediate one), as in 'dñs' for 'dominus'. It was in court hand that the use of contraction and abbreviation reached its peak.[8] However, contractions continued to be deployed in secretary, and to a lesser extent in the hands that succeeded it in the seventeenth century. In particular, we find the use of the tilde to denote that the second of two identical letters had been omitted, as in 'añounce' for 'announce', and the use of superscript to present an abbreviated form of a word, as in 'w^{ch}' for 'which'. In addition, the Anglo-Saxon thorn long remained in vestigial use to denote the sound 'th', transmogrified so that it was indistinguishable from the letter 'y', often in conjunction with a similar use of superscript to denote abbreviation, as in 'y^e' for 'the'. The extent to which these were used in any part of our period varies: they were commonest early on, and increasingly archaic by the eighteenth century, but in the mid to late seventeenth century there is extreme variation as to how far they were used by different individuals.

The student of manuscripts also needs to be aware of the methods commonly used to make or cancel revisions to a text. It is fairly obvious that words might be removed from a text once it was written by crossing through them, either by deleting a word or words within a line, or by crossing through a whole section, while additions to a text once written could only be made by inserting words between the existing lines, or making an addition in the margin or on an adjacent page, keyed to the relevant place in the text with a symbol. But other accepted conventions of the period are less familiar, and sometimes even puzzle scholars, for instance of indicating that the order of two words was to be changed by marking them '2' and '1' to indicate that the second word should precede the first, or by a variation of this in the form of two contrasting symbols.[9] It was even commoner to indicate that a passage which had been struck through should be reinstated by placing a row of dots underneath it. In addition, it is often possible to distinguish changes made in the course of composition from those made retrospectively, in that, if an author had second thoughts about a word and replaced it as soon as he or she had written it, the replacement word would appear on the line following the deleted one, rather than being inserted above the line. These are the kind of clues to which editors need to be alert, and which editions need to find means of denoting.

As for the material on which people wrote, parchment had been widely used for manuscripts of all kinds in the Middle Ages, but by the early modern period it was rarely used except for legal documents, a usage that was to continue for centuries due to the added durability it was thought to give: thus deeds, wills and other types of document were often written on parchment, often on membranes of a size that required multiple folds for purposes of storage. For almost all other purposes, on the other hand, paper was used, much of it imported until surprisingly late as far as England was concerned: until 1670, almost all of it came from France, especially from Normandy, after which it mainly came from Holland, either from Dutch mills or from French mills using Dutch ports for export. In the late seventeenth century, however, English papermaking got under way on a substantial scale, and it increased in scale until by the mid eighteenth century foreign imports had almost ceased.[10]

Paper was made from the pulp from linen rags, which was poured into a pair of rectangular frames with brass wires forming a sieve through which the water drained away, prior to the paper being sized, pressed and hammered. Often, paper was provided with a 'watermark', comprising letters or distinctive patterns executed in wire and fastened to the surface of the wires on the frame: these acted as a kind of trademark for the manufacturer, thus providing clues to the source of the paper used, and hence to the date of a document written on it. Various standard reference books exist which illustrate such watermarks, and these can be used to identify the watermarks on extant documents.[11] On the other hand, watermarks are not necessarily easy to identify, and neither do they provide the kind of exact dating evidence that archaeologists derive from tree rings. Many manufacturers used similar marks, so great care has to be taken in matching them, while not all paper was watermarked, and, even when a watermark appears, it is to be found only on part of the sheet on which it was impressed. However, in certain instances the key evidence provided by such analysis can justify the expenditure of time and expertise that it necessitates. For instance, in order to elucidate the manuscript descent of John Donne's poems a new taxonomy of such marks has been devised, while in the case of Newton, it has proved possible to identify batches of paper with a common watermark which he used over a fairly limited period before moving on to a different batch with a different marking.[12]

A more straightforward point arising from the way in which paper was made is that the frames used were of fairly standard sizes, meaning that so, too, were the sheets of paper that they produced. In particular, much of the paper used was of what was described as 'pot' or 'foolscap' size (both so named because of one of the components of the watermarks they showed), the former about 30 by 40 centimetres, the latter a few centimetres larger in each dimension, though there was variation even in these sizes – as is revealed, for instance, by an extant inventory of paper dating from 1674.[13] In addition, the overall sizes of these types of paper gradually grew during the early modern period, while by the eighteenth century the commonest paper size was demy (from the French for half, since it was half the rarely used 'imperial' size), which was slightly larger still. Allowing for these variations, this means that those who used paper started with a basically similar unit, which they could deploy in various ways. It was possible to write across the surface of an entire sheet, but on the whole this format was rather cumbersome and was rarely used. Instead, people folded the sheets, either once, forming a bifoliate, or more often, forming a group of four, eight or more leaves.

Manuscripts of the period display a fairly standard range of formats, derived from such sub-divisions of sheets of paper and reflecting the purposes for which they were produced, along with the taste of the compiler. Thus letters were frequently written on bifoliates, of folded pot size for lengthy letters or of smaller size – formed by cutting a bifoliate in half and folding it again – for shorter ones. This had the advantage of providing an ancillary sheet which could be used as a cover on which the address of the letter could be written prior to the whole being folded up and sealed. For longer manuscripts, the format selected depended on a similar mixture of functionality and taste. Often, folded pot sheets were used, which could be placed one inside the other and stitched together to form a book. Alternatively, a smaller booklet, formed by folding each sheet a greater number of times, could be used; again, these could be stitched to keep the leaves together and the edges of the leaves slit open to gain access to them. Indeed, from a surprisingly early date it was possible to buy such books of paper ready-made.[14] Obviously, different formats were appropriate for different purposes. A learned treatise, written in the study and intended to be perused by others in similar settings, might well be in the largest format, thus giving the greatest page size and minimising the number of leaves required for a lengthy text. At the other extreme, for a memorandum book meant to be carried around in the pocket a much smaller format was appropriate. Intermediate sizes might be deployed for manuscripts of intermediate function, for instance devotional manuscripts, for which a large format might be impractical, but which might be too long to be conveniently encapsulated in a tiny pocket book.

Archives often contain manuscripts in a variety of formats, reflecting these different purposes. For instance, John Locke's papers, now in the Bodleian Library, Oxford, comprise volumes of a range of sizes reflecting the kind of criteria outlined here, and much the same is true of the archive of the Rye merchant and astrologer, Samuel Jeake (1652–99).[15] Thus in Jeake's case, the ledger in which he entered his accounts was an impressive vellum-bound volume of folded pot sheets, and he also used this format for the most elaborate of his astrological disquisitions, and particularly discussions of the application of the principles of astrology to his own life, as in the analysis of his own 'Nativity' on which he was working when he died. But he also used smaller formats: thus his list of astrological 'directions' – deductions from analysis of his horoscope as to favourable aspects of the planets – are contained in a small pocket book. For items which he thought might have a wider readership – for instance, his expositions of astrological principles, or his analysis of his wife's horoscope – he used an intermediate size of manuscript, about half the size of his ledger. Yet another example is provided by the Stratford-on-Avon physician, John Ward, who seems to have had a penchant for small notebooks in which to write down memoranda, and a whole series of these, spanning many decades, survives in the Folger Library, Washington, DC.[16]

When studying either individual manuscripts or the assemblages of manuscripts that have come down to us from the early modern period, the student should be alert to such aspects of their physical appearance, from which it should be possible to generalise about the compositional habits of different authors. To some extent this was evidently mainly a matter of taste, but in other cases financial considerations may have entered. In particular, it is important to bear in mind that paper was quite expensive: in the 1674 inventory, a ream of foolscap or pot cost around five shillings.[17] This, too, was almost certainly a factor in dictating how people composed their manuscripts, meaning that, though some wealthy figures could afford to be lavish in their use of paper, others had to be parsimonious with it. Quite apart from issues of format, this might also influence the size of people's handwriting, which obviously affected the number of words they got onto each page. In addition, particularly in provincial locations, the supply of paper was sometimes a problem. The result was to encourage the reuse of paper, leading to juxtapositions which can be either puzzling or revealing in themselves.

So far, manuscripts have been described in relation to the individuals with whom they originated, and of course manuscripts are potentially wholly private documents – perhaps the quintessential example of this being the personal diary, a genre which flourished for the first time in the early modern period.[18] Another typically 'personal' genre which has received extensive study in recent years is the 'commonplace book', in which readers made notes on books that they read.[19] In addition, manuscript was obviously the prime means by which people communicated with those with whom they did not have oral contact by using letters, and these, too, could also be essentially private, in the sense that they were intended only for the eyes of the recipient to whom they were addressed. On the other hand, to see manuscript as a quintessentially 'private' medium – as some have done, with implications to be considered in Chapter 6 – is certainly incorrect, particularly in the context of the early modern period. It is clear that manuscripts were widely circulated in the contexts of domestic and other coteries. Even diaries often presuppose readers other than their compiler, and the same is true of almost all other types of document that people compiled at the time.

Certain such genres survive from the period on a large scale, and a few may be itemised here because they have become well known in recent years through scholarly study of them. One is of recipe books, frequently shared by many members of a household, and often passed down from one generation to another. These are of interest for various reasons. In part, this is because the collection and circulation of such data does seem to have taken place through manuscripts to a large extent, though various printed anthologies were published at the time. In part, it is because women seem disproportionately to have been involved in creating such compendia, the recipes involved often being culinary, though these were frequently interspersed with medical ones. Through such collections, it is possible to observe people copying recipes, trying them, sometimes refining them and adding their comments, and then passing them on to others in a kind of microcosm of the social system of the period. The potential of such collections in terms of tracing the descent of recipes and understanding the rationale of different collectors is now just beginning to be realised.[20]

Another genre is of verse miscellanies. Such authors as Arthur Marotti, Mary Hobbs and Henry Woudhuysen have devoted particular attention to these, indicating the social milieux in which they were created and circulated, including the family, the universities and – as with recipes – women. As Woudhuysen puts it: 'the attraction of manuscript circulation lay in the medium's social status, its personal appeal, relative privacy, freedom from government control, its cheapness, and its ability to make works quickly available to a select audience'.[21] Certain kinds of composition were particularly prone to be circulated in this manner, most notably obscene verse and items with political subjects, but such anthologies could also range much more widely to include poetry of a variety of types. They also varied greatly in their manner of presentation, from casual collections to carefully scribed anthologies. Modern studies have revealed various characteristics in compendia of this kind, including an extreme degree of textual instability, and a relative nonchalance towards authorship by comparison with printed collections. Again, much can be learned from studying such compendia about the way in which the roles of author, scribe and reader overlapped, a poem often being invested with significance through its juxtaposition with others which can be revealing in its own right.

Manuscript circulation could also clearly serve significant functions for authors, as Henry Woudhuysen has illustrated especially clearly in relation to the circle of Sir Philip Sidney, since it turns out that almost all of Sidney's literary output was initially 'published' by such means prior to its appearance in print, giving restricted circulation to compositions over which the author wished to retain control.[22] A related state of affairs existed with antiquarian writings. Though some works were published at the time, such as William Lambarde's *Perambulation of Kent* (1576) or Sir William Dugdale's *Antiquities of Warwickshire* (1656), the distribution of manuscript copies among authors' gentry peers was the norm, and a whole genre of compilations of this kind circulated by such means, remaining unprinted until the nineteenth or twentieth centuries. In the preface to his *Breviary of Suffolk,* written in 1618, for instance,

Robert Reyce took this for granted by referring to the work as 'this course and homely manuscript'.[23] In other cases, manuscript might be used as a medium for special copies intended for presentation to a patron or other grandee whom the author wished to influence: thus Francis Bacon produced a copy of his *Essays* for presentation to Henry, Prince of Wales, while a carefully scribed version of Hobbes' *Leviathan* was probably destined for a comparable royal recipient a generation later.[24]

Equally revealing is the extent to which it has become clear from recent studies that 'publication' in manuscript form was widespread in the early modern period, in the sense of the existence of scriptoria which produced 'editions' of works in virtually identical form on a quasi-industrial scale. Again, this was particularly common for particular types of texts, perhaps especially newsletters and 'separates' (copies of parliamentary speeches and the like), where rapid access to reliable information was at a premium, and where those who could provide this built up a network of customers who paid for such services by subscription.[25] In addition, verse might be circulated in such ways, and evidence has come to light for scriptoria which specialised in the production of copies of topical poetry, a particularly notable case of this being documented in the 1690s.[26] Indeed, quite apart from sensitive material or material of limited interest, manuscript publication provided a perfectly viable alternative to print in that the unit costs of production were low. The benefits of print in reducing unit costs for the production of large quantities of copies, which we will consider in the next chapter, were offset by the fact that the initial investment in typesetting was high, so that (in the view of D.F. McKenzie) 'anything under a hundred is hardly economical': here, therefore, manuscript production had distinct advantages, being able to furnish as many or as few copies as were required.[27]

Transmission either through private circulation or by such more commercial means raises a further issue relating to manuscript texts, and this is the history of their transmission. Since every manuscript text has to be written individually, each of them creates a piece of textual history (in contrast to the relative uniformity of a printed edition). Hence, through detailed scrutiny of all manuscript versions of a text, a detailed history of its dissemination can be built up. This is the study of 'stemmata' which was initially pioneered in relation to biblical and classical texts by scholars from the sixteenth century onwards, but it is equally relevant in relation to texts that were widely circulated in manuscript in the early modern period. The point is that each new manuscript copy of a work is created by copying an existing one, and the scribe who makes it will reproduce the bulk of the characteristics of that, while also almost inevitably introducing a few modifications of his own. Insofar as his copy is then transcribed by others, they will follow the same pattern. In addition – and particularly with the circulation of authorial manuscripts already noted – the author might revise the text between copies, or create different manuscripts for different recipients. Through painstaking study of all existing versions of a work, these can therefore be grouped together and the transmission of the text traced back through various exemplars to the original from which they were derived. In cases where such a pattern of transmission occurred, it is as appropriate that this should form the subject of study for an early modern text as for classical authors, and, where this was the case, it should therefore form an integral part of the preparation of an edition of the work in question.[28]

Hence it behoves anyone interested in early modern texts to be aware of many facets of their history in manuscript form – perhaps more than would be the case at a later date. We will recur to the implications of a number of the points raised here in later chapters when considering issues to do with how manuscript material should best be edited.

3
The Role of Print

The printing press has been acclaimed as one of the great innovatory agencies in early modern Europe, and the claim has been hotly contested.[1] Looked at dispassionately, it is hard to deny the significance of print, particularly in terms of dissemination. Its impact is demonstrated by two statistics. In about 1466, when the Florentine humanist, Leon Battista Alberti, heard of the invention of printing, he learned that by means of the new technology, three men could make 200 copies of a book in 100 days. By comparison, when Cosimo de' Medici decided to equip a library at Fiesole with books, it took forty-five scribes two years to produce 200 texts. Of course, the latter were different books (though producing this number of copies of the same one by scribal means would not have saved very much of the time involved), and a compositor was required as well as pressmen. But this is indicative of the change in speed of distribution which printing brought in its train.[2] Moreover, once the new invention became established, it has been calculated that a single pressman could produce 250 sheets per hour, a strikingly high figure that thereafter remained constant for a surprisingly long period.[3]

Claims have also been made for the significance of print in giving 'fixity' to texts, and hence in encouraging a cumulative growth in accuracy. Insofar as such claims go beyond the truism that copies of a single impression of a text were more uniform than would have been the case with scribal copies, they have proved more controversial; they are in any case somewhat at odds with what we now know about printing house practice, as we will see below.[4] There seems little doubt that the degree of standardisation was increased, with a cumulative impact on various aspects of the presentation of texts, some of which we will consider later in this chapter. But there was nothing automatic about the superiority of printed texts from the point of view of accuracy, since in fact print was as capable of disseminating bad texts as good ones. What is most crucial is that, because of its effectiveness as a means of distributing texts on a massive scale compared with manuscript circulation, and despite the continuing vitality of scribal publication noted in Chapter 2, print became the primary medium for the dissemination of texts from the sixteenth century onwards.

Not only were massive quantities of books produced in the period; the range of kinds of books produced in England as in other countries was also vast, in both Latin and English, and covering a myriad of subjects, which have been the subject of various attempted surveys over the years.[5] They also appeared in a wide range of formats, deriving from the same sized sheets of paper which we encountered in the previous chapter, since, when folded fewer or more times, these gave rise to standard formats which were named in connection with the size of books in which they resulted. The commonest sizes were folio, if the sheet was folded once to form two leaves; quarto, if it was folded twice to form four; octavo, if it was folded three times to form eight; or duodecimo, if it was folded once more to produce twelve leaves. Obviously, as with manuscripts, a mixture of utility and taste dictated what formats were deemed suitable for different types of books, and contemporaries clearly had a sense of this, though the subject has received little systematic study. A vignette is provided by the eighteenth-century didactic writer Lord Chesterfield, who wrote:

> I converse with grave folios in the morning, while my head is clearest, and my attention strongest; I take up less severe quartos after dinner; and at night I chuse the mixed company and amusing chit-chat of octavos and duodecimos.

If extended to include the extent to which market forces dictated smaller and cheaper formats for works aimed at those of lesser means, this gives some sense of the associations that the different formats had.[6] On the other hand, there were certain changes during the period, partly due to the increase in paper sizes referred to in the previous chapter. Initially, this led to more frequent use of double columns for folio books, but increasingly it seems to have resulted in the popularity of smaller formats for types of book that might once have been presented in folio: a case in point is provided by the collected editions of literary authors, which, having typically appeared in folio in the seventeenth century, were increasingly produced in editions of smaller format in the eighteenth.[7]

The basic technology of printing changed relatively little over the early modern period. It is symptomatic that, in his *New Introduction to Bibliography* (1972), Philip Gaskell has two eras, 'the Hand-Press Period

1500–1800' and 'The Machine-Press Period 1800–1950'. We are concerned only with the former, and the basic techniques involved do indeed seem to have remained relatively static over a surprisingly long time. Indeed, if anything, the revisionist findings of D.F. McKenzie and others have reinforced this, illustrating just how conservative press practices were around 1700, which McKenzie was able to study in detail not least due to the survival of extraordinarily full records for the working practices of Cambridge University Press in its early years.[8] The basic pattern was as follows.

Each letter was formed from a separate piece of type, comprising a reverse image of the letter in question on a long shaft: the compositor took the pieces of type from a case, in which letters were placed in compartments of different sizes arranged in a standard way which approximately reflected the frequency of use of the various letters. Of course, a large quantity of type was required even for a fairly short book, and if a long one was involved – or if a printing house was using the same fount of type for more than one book at a time – shortages sometimes arose, which might be dealt with by using letters of a different fount or (for instance) by using italic type instead of Roman. The letters were composed together line by line to form the words and sentences required to form a mirror image of the text that was being set, with the spaces between words formed by short pieces of type with no letter on them; spaces of various sizes were available, and at the end of each line and then at the end of each page the compositor adjusted these to 'justify' the lines, while in addition they might be 'leaded' by adding thin strips of metal between them.

Once the pages that were to be printed together on a sheet had been composed, these were placed together in a rigid iron rectangle called a chase, with the spaces between and around the pages filled up with pieces of wood called 'furniture'. This was laid flat and locked tightly in place. Then, when the printer was ready to print from it, the type was inked, and a press used to impose sheets of paper onto the type so that the sheet received an impression of the text of the group of pages that had been composed in this way. The ink used for printing was different from the ink used for writing manuscripts, comprising a mixture of varnish and colour: the latter, usually black, was derived from lampblack, while the former, usually linseed oil, acted as a liquid medium which dried after conveying the colour to the page. Almost invariably, books were printed on both sides of the sheet, and the printed sheets therefore needed to be left long enough for the ink to dry before the other side of the sheet was printed. If a printer had more than one press, the reverse side of the sheet could be printed almost immediately, but, if not, the one-sided sheets might be kept for some time, a practice also encouraged by setting 'by formes', when a compositor set all the pages for one side of a sheet and sent them to be printed before the other side of the sheet was set.

Whatever the period that elapsed before the second side of the sheet was printed, however, it was obviously crucial for the text to be imposed so that the pages came out in the correct order when the book was assembled, with the correct page appearing on the reverse of the page that was immediately to precede or follow it (see Figure 1). The number of pages that were printed at a time depended on the size of the final book and hence the number of times that the sheet was intended to be folded to form its individual pages. To print a single sheet of an octavo book, for instance, sixteen pages of type needed to be set, eight for one side of the sheet and eight for the other (if setting was done by formes, obviously only half as many had to be set at a time). Moreover, the type had to be kept locked in chases in this way until as many copies of the sheet in question had been printed as were required. Time had to be allowed for either the author of the text or a proxy to check a preliminary version in the form of a specially printed-off 'proof' to ensure that the text had been printed correctly, and only after that could the multiple copies intended for the final book be printed. The same process had to be gone through for all of the other sheets of the book. Once this had been done, the sheets could be folded, assembled, pressed and stitched to form the finished book.

Within this standard pattern, various potential complications arose, which the editor or reader needs to be cognisant of. One was the practice of multiple printing. In order to speed production, and/or to spread the pressure on the stock of type of any particular printing house, parts of a book might be printed by more than one printer concurrently. This was assisted by the ability of skilled compositors to 'cast off' a manuscript text

Figure 1: Disposition of the pages on an octavo sheet

Recto, left to right:

ς	ZI	6	8
4	13	16	1

Verso, left to right:

ʟ	0ʟ	ᴉᴉ	6
2	15	14	3

Note: on each side of the sheet, the text of the lower set of pages is printed the opposite way up to the upper set, so that they come out the same way up when the sheet is folded.

and estimate how many printed pages it would require; this could then be subdivided so that a certain number of entire sheets could be printed separately from others, not necessarily in the order in which they were to appear in the book, and not necessarily even in the same printing house. Often this worked so well that it is difficult to detect; but it sometimes went wrong, resulting in an error in the book's pagination, or in type being set abnormally tightly or abnormally loosely to fit into the requisite number of pages (such defects might also be the result of setting by formes, as described on pages 26–7).

A further common practice to which editors and readers need to be alert is that of 'stop-press correction'. Although it seems normally to have been the case that a proof was printed and checked between the type being set and the main run of printing being begun, it was quite common for further changes to be made as errors were noted while printing was in progress. This necessitated stopping the press, loosening the chase and altering the type, prior to tightening it up and continuing to print copies. This could happen a number of times during the printing process, and it meant that copies of the sheet in question printed subsequently would have a different reading from those printed before the correction had been made. As early as 1862, W.A. Wright noticed discrepancies of this kind in copies of the 1625 edition of Bacon's *Essays*, and it is now apparent – in contrast to presumptions of the uniformity of the products of the printing press made by early bibliographers – that contemporaries almost took it for granted that different copies of a book would vary in this way.[9] Hence it is prudent for an editor to collate multiple copies of an early modern printed book to check for such changes made during printing, particularly in the case of a definitive edition of a complex text, though discretion needs to be used as to how far to take this, especially if initial sampling fails to reveal that a book seems to have been subject to revisions of this kind. In addition, alterations might be made even after the book had been printed. The commonest way in which this was achieved was by adding a list of 'errata' at the start or end of the book, but alternatives included 'cancelling' a leaf – in other words, cutting out a leaf and pasting in a corrected substitute – or making manuscript corrections to individual copies, or pasting in corrections on slips of paper: all of these changes might or might not be systematically executed in all copies of the book, so scrutiny of multiple copies is again required. Clearly, pitfalls await editors and others who ignore such characteristic practices in book production of the period.

In addition, if the type from which one or more of the sheets which a book comprised had been printed was distributed before all the copies that were required had been provided (all the more likely if type ran short in the printing house), it might be necessary to reset the sheet in question. Usually, an attempt would be made in such circumstances for the reset section(s) to look as similar as possible to those that they replaced. But, almost inevitably, minor variants would occur, to which the editor needs to be alert. The same might be true of the book as a whole, if demand exceeded the expectations of sales on which the initial print-run was predicated. It is not uncommon for two distinct versions of a book to exist, ostensibly the same edition of the same work, but representing two completely different settings of type. That this is as common as it is is partly due to the fact that, as part of the rather paternalist industrial legislation of the Elizabethan period, it was laid down that the maximum number of copies of a book that could be printed from one setting of type was 1,500, so in theory any book that sold more copies was supposed to be reset, though in practice it seems likely that this ruling was observed as much in the breach as the observance.[10] On the other hand, if a book sold badly, it might be reissued, with the pages as originally printed given a new title-page, while, with multi-volume works in particular, sets might be made up partly of such reissues and partly of original impressions.

Thereafter, discrete editions – explicitly so described – might be produced. These might be simple reprints of the original edition, or they might be revised or extended. Obviously, it was in the publisher's interest to encourage sales by implying that the new edition superseded the old one, whether or not this was actually the case. Hence all subsequent editions clearly need to be carefully scrutinised in studying any work, and careful thought is required as to whether an edition should follow the original edition or a revised one, and, if so, for what sections of the work. In this, the criterion most usually deployed by editors is that of evidence of authorial intervention in the changes that were made, thus raising complex issues about 'copy text' to which we will revert in Chapter 5.

When a text was transferred from script to print, various changes were made to it which we need to consider in detail here. Indeed, these merit attention not least because it was in these aspects of book production, more than the basic practice of printing, that significant changes were in evidence during the early modern period. Most obviously, the text was the subject of the standardisation involved in transforming the letters and words from the individual handwriting of the person who wrote it to the mechanised form of type. As already noted, typesetting involves composition in the form of the juxtaposition of standard, separate letter-forms. This therefore had the effect of obliterating the extent to which letters were linked to one another in script to prevent the pen being taken off the paper, or to which their shape varied according to the adjacent letter with which they were juxtaposed. In this respect, print had an inescapable 'mechanising' effect on texts, rather akin to that involved more recently in typewriting or word-processing (which also involve the encoding of text in sequences of discrete, individual characters), and this has important implications for the editing of manuscripts to which we will return in Chapter 6.

Somewhat more gradually, print came to eradicate the tricks aimed to speed composition that characterised manuscript texts, in particular the use of standard abbreviations and of tildes and superscript letters. Books printed in the first century of printing use quite a wide range of contractions, perhaps particularly for syllables beginning 'p' or 'q'. In addition, there was a widespread use of tildes and superscripts.[11] Increasingly, however, these practices were abandoned, as if printers came to realise the true implications of the transition to mechanised letter forms, and gradually all of these abbreviations became obsolete. Thus, in contrast to the Elizabethan period, when the use of such abbreviations persisted, by the late seventeenth century they had almost entirely died out, being used (if at all) only when space was short, either because of a miscalculation in casting off, or due to text being added at the proof stage. Moreover, their use was regarded as reprehensible by the elite of typesetters: as Joseph Moxon said of such contractions in his *Mechanick Exercises on the Whole Art of Printing* (1683–4), 'They have been much used by Printers in Old Times, to *Shorten* or *Get in Matter*; but are now wholly left off as obsolete.'[12] More gradual still was the abandonment of the long 's', an echo of manuscript usage in which the initial or medial use of the letter was differentiated from its use at the end of a word. This remained in standard use right through the early modern period, only being abandoned in the late eighteenth century, starting with pioneers in the years around 1750 like Joseph Ames and Edward Capell and becoming universal almost overnight in 1800.[13]

On the other hand, from quite an early date, compositors seem to have been in the forefront in championing the differential use of letters for vowels and consonants. This particularly applies to the letters 'i' and 'j' and 'u' and 'v', which had been used interchangeably in medieval manuscripts. The consistent use of 'i' and 'u' as vowels and 'j' and 'v' as consonants originated with Italian printers in the early sixteenth century. In the later sixteenth century it was adopted by French authors and printers, and was particularly championed by the intellectual reformer, Peter Ramus, so that such letters were sometimes called 'consonnes Ramistes'; its early spread in England was evidently associated with the influence of his ideas more broadly. The new practice first appears in English books from the late 1570s onwards, becoming increasingly widespread so that by about 1630 it was universal.[14] An ancillary development was the use of the letter, 'w', as against 'vv', while another change in usage that became adopted at the same time was the replacement of the initial 'ff' by a capital 'F'. Again, the earlier usage is hardly in evidence in printed books after the early years of the seventeenth century.

Compositors also played a major role in transforming punctuation. Punctuation in medieval manuscripts appears to have been restricted to marks indicating the pauses that should be observed when reading out loud, and had been limited to the use of the virgule (/), colon (:) and point (.). With the advent of printing, a more nuanced system of punctuation, aimed at achieving clarity in presenting the text, began to come into being (and, having started in printed books, was then increasingly adopted in manuscripts). The comma was introduced in English printed books (following Italian precedents) in 1521, and increasingly replaced the virgule. The question mark originated at a similar date; the semi-colon, although first used almost equally early, only became common from c.1580. The exclamation mark, apostrophe and hyphen date from the later years of the sixteenth century, as do brackets as commonly used today. Drawing on this wider range of markings, punctuation became increasingly complex in this period, often involving intricate sentence structures which are unfamiliar to a modern reader, while associated with this elaboration of punctuation was an increasingly systematic and extensive use of capital letters. It now became the norm for sentences to be begun with a capital letter (i.e., following a 'period', though the concept of a point forming a 'semi-period', which did not therefore need to be followed by a capital, continued vestigially into the late seventeenth century).[15] In addition, capitals were increasingly used for proper names, while they were commonly also used to denote personifications, titles and terms of address, and for emphasis. Grammars and similar texts of the period often tried to provide a systematic rationale for such capitalisation, which at no point became universal for all nouns or concepts, but an element of inconsistency persisted despite their best efforts.[16]

Print also encouraged standardisation in spelling, although it did so less consistently than was the case with punctuation and capitalisation, and it is important to stress that it was not the only factor in the linguistic changes involved: a similar attempt to simplify spelling had been associated with late medieval scriveners, while more radical proposals were put forward by a number of spelling reformers, though they were usually well ahead of the kind of consensus that compositors reflected.[17] What is clear is that – as with punctuation and capitalisation – compositors felt that they had a responsibility to alter their authors' usage to match what they perceived to be preferred usage, and this entailed the removal of redundant final e's and doubled consonants serving no linguistic function.

Other facets of the effect of the transition to print were less inevitable, but none the less real. Within print, there was a choice in type styles, either for entire texts or for components within them, which had implications which we need to understand. The earliest printing types were black letter, derived from the cursive scripts of the late Middle Ages, and these remained in use for publications intended for a wide readership, evidently because many elementary readers found them easier to decipher than Roman type.[18] However, for books aimed at a more literate audience, Roman and italic type quickly established themselves as more normal, and a fashion early arose for a combination of the two, with italic type being used to demarcate specific sections of a book – such as its dedication or preface – and to give emphasis to individual words within the text. In particular, italic was used for the kind of words that were also capitalised – proper names, personifications, and the like – while it was also used to denote quoted material. However, this is an area where fashions changed during the period, and these changes are also worthy of note. A reaction against the use of italic for lengthy passages of text set in as early as the sixteenth century in France, leading to the introduction of inverted commas (or Guillemets, after their originator) as an alternative way of denoting reported speech. By the eighteenth century, the use of italic interspersing a text otherwise set in Roman type was increasingly seen as unnecessarily fussy. John Smith, in his *Printer's Grammar* of 1755, was disdainful of it, and this reflected a changing taste that was more general.[19]

A few further aspects of the format of printed books may be mentioned more briefly. The title-page became almost universal from *c*.1500, having been rarely used either in medieval manuscripts or incunabula (though, as so often with script and print, there was then a cross-fertilisation, and early modern scribes are often to be found giving manuscripts title-pages which aped printed ones). Thereafter, printed title-pages saw significant development; indeed, Moxon noted how 'the mode of ordering *Titles* varies; as may be seen by comparing the *Title Pages* of every twenty years', and there is a good deal of truth in this perceptive remark.[20] The elaboration of text, whereby title-pages were used as a 'puff' for the book, probably because they were printed off separately and used for promotional purposes, reached a climax in the Elizabethan period. In the seventeenth century, a greater brevity in wording becomes the norm, often in conjunction with the use of pairs of rules to frame the title-page, together with rules separating its component parts: such a layout became *de rigueur* in the years on either side of 1700. In the eighteenth century, on the other hand, there was an increasing abandonment of ornament of any kind and a pursuit of a kind of classical plainness which reached its climax at the end of the period.[21]

Pagination in Arabic numerals became common from the late Elizabethan period, and it was at this time that the practice emerged of differentiating the preliminaries of a book, either by giving them a separate numeration in Roman numerals, or dispensing with pagination altogether.[22] It was possible to dispense with pagination because this was duplicated by a further set of references to the make-up of the book in the form of its 'signatures', in fact intended to identify the order in which sheets should be bound, but which also had the effect of providing an alternative notation of page order for users of the book. This meant that the recto of each leaf in the first half of each gathering was given a distinctive marking in the bottom margin, in the form 'A' (for the first leaf in the gathering, hence usually referred to as 'A1'), or 'B2', or 'c3' or the like: letters might either be capital or lower case or a mixture of the two, and the numbers might be Arabic or Roman. Continuity was also assured by the use of 'catchwords', which gave the first word of the following page at the bottom of the previous one: these began to disappear only in the later years of the eighteenth century.[23] On the other hand, the practice of providing books with 'running heads' indicating the content of each of their component parts became more, rather than less, common as the period progressed.

All this has presented the printed book as a kind of great automaton, carrying all before it, and it does indeed seem to be the case that printing house styles were decisive in bringing about many of the changes described in the previous paragraphs. On the other hand, this raises an important issue for anyone interested in texts of the period, and particularly for those responsible for modern editions of them, namely of how far authors were willing accomplices to the styles which printers imposed on their work. That compositors of the period were capable of being quite doctrinaire in expanding contractions and in imposing patterns of spelling, capitalisation, italicisation and punctuation on works that passed through their hands is clearly revealed by cases where the manuscript copy of printed books survives and one can compare the two.[24] But how willingly did authors accept the changes that were made to their texts when they were printed, and, in particular, the way in which 'accidentals' – spelling, capitalisation and the like – were imposed on them by compositors? This has been a matter of controversy among modern scholars, not least because of its significance in relation to the theory of copy text, in which 'accidentals' are seen as trivial.

Many examples can be found of authors acquiescing in the way in which their works were treated at the press.[25] (In this connection it is perhaps worth noting that, where it has been studied, a similar state of affairs seems to have prevailed with scribally copied manuscripts. Thus Francis Bacon seems to have taken it for granted that his amanuenses would copy-edit his work, inserting accidentals which he presumed should be present but which he did not have time to insert himself: Bacon was thus sparing in punctuating the text of his compositions, evidently in the expectation that his scribes would add further marks and he also seems to have expected them to emend his spelling and capitalisation.[26]) On the other hand, it was clearly expected at the time that authors should give the printer some indication of how a work was to be presented, in terms of 'marking words which are to be in italic letters, or with capitall letters', as one contemporary put it when delegating the matter to a colleague.[27] Some authors were fastidious in correcting what might seem minor matters of italicisation and capitalisation in the printed copy of their works, like Matthew Prior or John Locke, who went to particular lengths in this respect.[28] There are also some examples of authors who seem to have insisted that particular archaisms were retained in their printed copy, as with Edmund Spenser.[29] In other instances, on the other hand, authors seem to have had a kind of symbiotic relationship with the printers in the evolution of the text from manuscript to printed form, as in the case of Alexander Pope.[30] It seems likely that the attitudes of authors to such matters need to be assessed on an individual basis.

To this is linked the issue of the extent to which the author had any control over a work once it had passed into the hands of the printer. It is certainly the case that landmark decisions in the eighteenth century, from the Copyright Act of 1710 onwards, gave more rights to authors, and that men like Pope capitalised on this. By comparison, the sixteenth and seventeenth centuries may have been more of a free for all, and so they have often been depicted by historians in the past.[31] On the other hand, generalisation is again premature. Though it is not difficult to find hostile remarks about booksellers and their cavalier treatment of authors from the period (usually from authors who perceived themselves victims of such practices), evidence is also coming to light for the presumption of a kind of moral right of authorship even in the dark days of the seventeenth century.[32]

Moreover, though the evidence is again patchy, instances are known in the early modern period of authors playing a part in planning their books, either in conjunction with booksellers – probably reflecting the provision of a financial contribution towards the publishing costs on the author's part – or sometimes wholly independently. A case of the latter which has received recent attention is that of the astronomer, Tycho Brahe, who went so far as to set up his own printing press, while an English example is provided by the antiquary, Sir William Dugdale, who took a direct interest in the publication of his own works, raising the capital required to finance them, purchasing the paper on which they were printed, organising the engraving of their plates, and taking responsibility for their distribution.[33] Subsequently, starting in the seventeenth century but increasingly commonly in the eighteenth, we find authors attempting to get into print works which might not otherwise have been viable by arranging for the cost of publication to be borne by subscribers, and publishers also found this a useful means of supplementing purely commercial distribution.[34] Even before this, however, a partial analogy is to be found in the clear evidence that exists that the distribution of printed works, like manuscripts, formed part of a social network of gift-giving, with authors taking a direct interest in readers' responses to their work.[35]

Once again, therefore, we come to a degree of overlap between print and manuscript publication which acts as a warning against exaggerating the distinction between the two. In fact, for all its power, the printing press did not carry all before it in the early modern period to the extent that was to be the case in the nineteenth and twentieth centuries. This, too, needs to be taken into account in approaching books of the period if they are to be properly understood, not least concerning the editorial decisions that need to be made in relation to them.

4
Types of Edition

Armed with the knowledge of how texts were actually produced in the early modern period that has been provided in the previous two chapters, let us now turn to issues relating to how these texts should be treated by modern editors. At the outset, it is worth asking: what is an edition for? The answer surely is that it has to provide something that would not otherwise be available. This may be done by giving access to an otherwise inaccessible text – for instance, by putting a manuscript into print. Alternatively, or in addition to this, it may provide a version of the text that would not otherwise exist, for instance by collating multiple versions that survive in a various forms – whether both manuscript and printed, or different versions of a printed text – or by providing a commentary on the text and its subject-matter (a simple reprint of a printed text that survives in a single witness would hardly constitute an edition, particularly now that so many early modern works are readily available in digital form through Early English Books Online, and even an unannotated transcript of a manuscript is on the periphery of the genre).

Hence, an edition of a single text or document may be a free-standing entity, and some of the most important editorial activity has taken the form of producing editions in this kind. Equally, however, the rationale of an edition may lie in bringing together in organised and systematic form a collection of such material – the *Works* of an author, for instance, or their *Correspondence*. In this chapter, we will consider the types of larger-scale edition that modern editors have commonly produced – indicating the characteristics of such genres, and in some cases the complications and difficulties associated with them. By considering the units or groupings in which texts have tended to be dealt with, it will be possible to understand what types of corpus are appropriate for what kind of editorial treatment, and what methods should be used in handling them. Some of these issues are less straightforward than they may seem at first sight, and they therefore merit careful scrutiny. In addition, the use of electronic technology has opened up fresh possibilities which need to be considered in each case.

a. *Works*

As already noted, one of the commonest types of edition is of what we might call a single 'work', in other words a discrete book, pamphlet or other publication, or its manuscript equivalent. The selection of such items for publication is straightforward, leading almost immediately to detailed questions as to how the text should be prepared and presented that will be dealt with in subsequent chapters. At this point virtually the only issue that arises is of completeness: it seems axiomatic that a work should be published as a whole or not at all, since any partial edition is almost bound to give a misleading impression of it. This may be illustrated by a single example, the fascinating treatise, *Generall Learning*, written by the scholar and cleric, Meric Casaubon, in 1668, which survived only in manuscript until modern times. In 1981, Michael Spiller included as an appendage to a monograph on Casaubon an edition of part of the text which illustrated precisely why such partial editions are to be avoided, since his criteria of selection gave a misleading view of Casaubon's preoccupations by omitting much of the material illustrating the role of the learned traditions by which he set such store. Fortunately, however, it is possible to report that the defects of Spiller's version have now been more than rectified by a model edition of the work in question by Richard Serjeantson.[1] Obviously in an anthology of texts for student use, selection may be inevitable (though even here it is potentially open to comparable objections): but part of the point of an edition is to present an entire text as an object of study, and the reader must be able to rely on it from this point of view. A partial edition is therefore wherever possible to be avoided.

With some authors, there may be problems in defining just what a work constitutes. In some cases, the collation of different printed versions or of printed and manuscript ones may reveal such marked variations between these that it may be desirable to print more than one as a discrete text in its own right, and the appropriate strategies in such cases will be considered in Chapter 5. Equally problematic is the question of the boundary of the work, particularly when the unit of production is small, as with genres like poetry, and here the problem is more complex. A starting point is provided by retaining groupings that were used at the time – most obviously, collections of poems by individual authors, but also anthologies of the work of various authors which were compiled at the time either in manuscript or printed form, and which therefore have a contemporary mandate. On the other hand, the relative nonchalance about authorship displayed in manuscript collections means that the two considerations may pull in different directions, thus presenting a challenge to the editors of material of this kind.[2]

A different issue arises with certain manuscript compilations such as John Aubrey's *Brief Lives*, since this appears to have overlapped with other collections of data that he compiled, which earlier editors selectively raided for biographical material which has hence become accepted as part of Aubrey's biographical 'work'. Indeed, this tendency would have been taken to an extreme by an edition which Oxford University Press considered publishing in the early 1970s, which would vastly have extended the work by including biographical information from virtually all of Aubrey's other writings, though in the event this proved abortive.[3] Here, the best solution is to publish the actual manuscripts that Aubrey thought of as his *Brief Lives* on their own – namely nos. 6–8 of the Aubrey manuscripts in the Bodleian Library, and perhaps also MS 9, 'The Life of Mr Thomas Hobbes of Malmesburie', and MS 23, Aubrey's biographical-astrological 'Collectio Geniturarum' – even though this means omitting certain nuggets of information which many users presume form part of the *Lives* because of their appearance in more inclusive editions. Such an edition should be accompanied by a prominent acknowledgment of the fact that the *Lives* form part of a larger corpus of works by Aubrey which also contains much material of biographical (and broader) interest and which deserves publication in full. This includes Aubrey's correspondence and such other works by him as his innovative *Monumenta Britannica*, a pioneering collection of archaeological and related data, which should be published separately even though there is a marginal overlap between *Monumenta Britannica* and *Brief Lives* – in that memoranda for the *Monumenta* are interspersed with the manuscript of the *Lives* – while Aubrey's letters to Anthony Wood contain biographical material which is often hard to distinguish from material that actually reached his own biographical compendium.[4] This strategy would mean that those mainly interested in biographical data could be satisfied by cross-referencing, while Aubrey's more varied writings would gain the attention they deserve in their own right.

In effect, the result would constitute a complete edition of Aubrey's writings – something which is long overdue – and the commonest larger category for an edition of a person's writings is that of their *Works* or *Collected Writings*. The idea of a collected – often ostensibly 'complete' – edition of the works of an author is now so enshrined in our scholarly consciousness that we do not pause to question its pedigree and rationale as much as might be desired, though (inspired by Foucault if no one else) we perhaps should.[5] What is such an edition for? The principal advantage is arguably one of convenience. Particularly for authors with a large and diffuse *oeuvre*, it is obviously useful for their works to be available in a reliable version in collected form. Such editions have the advantage of providing a standard, accessible text to which reference can be made by volume and page number – preferably in combination with a helpful apparatus, though this is less crucial. Essentially, the genre seems to be an invention of the great humanist printers of the sixteenth century, who produced such editions both of classical authors like Aristotle and of the great scholars of their own time (the role of such editions in providing a system of referencing is perhaps symbolised by the case of Aristotle, since, although the early modern collections of his writings have long been superseded, references to his work are still given according to the page numbers of the standard edition produced by Immanuel Bekker in 1831).

Such editions were most commonly in Latin, the *lingua franca* of the learned world at the time, and they continued to be produced throughout the seventeenth century, especially in continental Europe, while from around 1600 one begins to find comparable vernacular collections, not least in England. Initially, and most commonly, these were of the writings of popular divines, such as the famous Puritan preacher, William Perkins, but from around the same period one also starts to find collected editions of literary texts, as in such well-known examples as Thomas Speght's edition of Chaucer of 1598, or Ben Jonson's self-consciously entitled *Workes* of 1616. By the late seventeenth century, many such collected editions of an author's works were produced, sometimes by the author himself, sometimes as a posthumous act of piety by his disciples. The authors involved ranged from men like the Elizabethan ecclesiastical polemicist, Richard Hooker, to the mathematician, John Wallis, and editions of the writings of literary authors also became increasingly common. Such collected editions, both of recent writers and long-dead ones, have continued to be produced ever since, and, though some of their functions may have shifted over the centuries, the overall ambition – of providing a definitive edition of an author's writings – has remained the same.

Yet there is obviously more to a collected edition than simple utility. Clearly, the production of such an edition is also a mark of prestige, indicating that the author in question was worthy of his writings being enshrined in this way. A case in point is that of Alexander Pope, whose lavishly produced *Works* appeared in 1717, thus (as with Jonson earlier) quite self-consciously using this means to establish his credentials.[6] Similarly, the juxtaposition of the first edition of Hooker's *Works* with the re-establishment of the Anglican church at the Restoration is far from coincidental, while, in the case of Wallis, the lavish three-volume edition of his writings published in the 1690s was produced at the expense of the Delegates of the newly established University Press, and was clearly intended to add not only to the lustre of the author but also to that of the university with which he had long been associated.[7] More recently, and perhaps particularly in the Unites States in modern times, large-scale collected editions of scholarly authors have become marks of prestige for academic institutions, supervised by illustrious editorial boards and working slowly and often with heavy subsidies towards the completion of lavish collections of the writings of the figure in question. The 'California' edition of John Dryden would be a case in point, or the Folger Library edition of Hooker or the 'Yale' edition of Samuel Johnson; on this side of the Atlantic, comparable initiatives include the 'Oxford Francis Bacon' and the 'Clarendon Edition' of the works of Thomas Hobbes.

What are the drawbacks of such editions? Obviously one is the practicality of producing them, particularly in the case of prolific authors. More were conceived than were realised even in the early modern period, as surviving prospectuses reveal.[8] In modern times, too, by no means all of them have ever achieved their goals. Indeed, with increasing printing costs, more may fall by the wayside in the future, even if electronic resources will perhaps come to the rescue. Perhaps more significant is a characteristic which represents the obverse of the value of such editions in offering a uniform system of reference. Thus they are prone to give an unduly homogeneous impression of an author's writings, ironing out differences of format which are obvious to those who see the originals in all their diffuseness, but which are less apparent when these are reduced to a uniform format. There is a danger of the reader rather losing sight of the original character of ephemeral works that are submerged in collected editions, and it is desirable to signal the characteristics in terms of format, typography and the like which a standard format necessarily effaces by including facsimiles of sample pages of the early editions of the books in question, and by giving detailed physical descriptions of them.

Certain such problems may be dealt with by the order in which works are placed in the edition, in that different kinds of writings can be presented separately, with more ephemeral works segregated from more substantial ones. In the case of the 'California' Dryden, for instance, the author's poems, plays and prose are presented in three separate series, with the poems occupying the first seven volumes of the series, the plays the next nine, and the collected prose starting at volume 17.[9] Yet this has its own potential dangers, encouraging a sense of segregation in the work of an author of the kind which arguably reached a climax in the treatment of Milton in the eighteenth and early nineteenth centuries, when his poetry was routinely collected separately from his political writings, thus encouraging a view of the author of *Paradise Lost* as an other-worldly and non-partisan figure, distinct from the author of *Areopagitica*.[10] Indeed, though the 'Columbia' edition of Milton's works, published between 1931 and 1938, sought to present his corpus as a whole, the separation has since been revived through the publication between 1953 and 1982 of a further edition of his *Complete Prose Works*.[11] Within this, on the other hand, the ordering is by date, and in general a chronological order is by far the commonest arrangement for a collected edition of an author's works. This is not only uncontroversial, but also illustrates the development of the author's interests and skills. Such editions as the Oxford Francis Bacon, for instance, follow such an essentially chronological ordering, as does *The Works of Robert Boyle*. There may be examples where this seems inappropriate, but a strong case would need to be made for a radically different arrangement.

There is also the question of 'completeness', which can itself become something of a problem in such collections. It is notorious that, in the early modern period, editions of this kind could be used as a method of self-censorship. In the case of Ben Jonson, for instance, he omitted from his *Workes* early writings, items that he evidently considered too trivial or too controversial to be reprinted, and works that he had written in collaboration with others.[12] Sometimes nothing can be done about this, because the production of an edition of a man's *Opera omnia* either during or shortly after his lifetime was accompanied by a clearing-up operation as far as his extant manuscripts were concerned, what was deemed worthy of it being incorporated in the *Works* and the rest destroyed.[13] In other cases, however, omitted material has survived, and here the impulse has been to attempt retrospectively to rectify such omissions and to make the corpus ever more complete. This raises questions as to just what materials are appropriate for inclusion in this way, and whether absolute completeness is attainable in any case. It has sometimes been felt that items that have had to be retrospectively retrieved in this way can detract from, rather than enhance, an author's *oeuvre*, though, if completeness really is the aim, this hardly seems a valid objection.[14] On the other hand, since such an edition could in principle include not only all an author's published writings, but also all his or her drafts and working papers, this potentially raises a further issue, of whether there is a point at which items cease to be 'works' – in the presumed sense of self-contained compositions intended for public consumption – at all.

As an example of where the line might be drawn on such matters, let me take the case of Robert Boyle. Despite advocacy from some of his supporters, no collected edition of Boyle's writings was produced during his lifetime apart from an unauthorised Latin collection of which he disapproved, and plans to produce such an edition in the aftermath of his death also failed to materialise. A collected edition was finally produced by the cleric and antiquary, Thomas Birch, in 1744, which not only included virtually all Boyle's published writings, but marked the start of an attempt to extend Boyle's published corpus by including material from his manuscripts, in this case a substantial unpublished section of his *Christian Virtuoso*, the preparation of which for the press was due largely to the efforts of Birch's collaborator, Henry Miles.[15] However, this still left thousands of pages of manuscripts, many of them directly related to Boyle's published writings, which formed part of an even larger archive with a much more miscellaneous content, and, in relation to the new edition published in 1999–2000, a strategy was needed as to what should appropriately form part of his *Works* and what should not. The policy adopted was that all material relating directly to Boyle's published works was tabulated, collated and compared with the extant printed version; significant variants were noted in the apparatus to the published text and, where appropriate, ancillary material was published as an annexe to the introductory material to the work to which it related. Then, the final two volumes of the edition made a more or less clean sweep of hitherto unpublished complete treatises by Boyle in the archive, or substantial fragments of them.[16] By contrast, the remaining more miscellaneous material seemed appropriate for a different kind of treatment which will be dealt with below.

The *Works of Boyle* was a printed edition, as almost all editions of authors' *Collected Works* have been hitherto, albeit sometimes supplemented by scanned versions which have made the writings in question searchable by electronic means. However, this is an area where electronic editions may offer fresh terms of reference, though they may do so partly by transmuting the notion of *Works* into something more inclusive. We will come to the concept of electronic 'archives' later in this chapter, but a compromise which may illustrate how certain aspects of the old functions of the collected edition can be combined with the greater flexibility provided by electronic media is provided by the planned Cambridge edition of Ben Jonson, which will appear both in electronic and printed forms. Its primary text will be a six-volume printed edition of Jonson's writings, replacing and updating the older edition of Herford and Simpson that has long held sway. Yet this will be linked to an electronic edition which will offer far more in the way of textual variants and contextual information 'that can rapidly be searched, collated and compared'.[17] It will be interesting to see this in operation, including the extent to which a digital format may obviate the need for some elements of print, and hence to observe its impact on the genre of *Collected Works* that has been dealt with here.

b: *Correspondence* and *Papers*

Sometimes, editions of the *Complete Works* of an author have also included a collected edition of his letters: cases in point include the standard editions of René Descartes or Christiaan Huygens. On the other hand, an equally common editorial genre has been of a person's *Correspondence*, by which is usually understood as complete a collection as is feasible of the letters to and from an individual, most frequently arranged in chronological order. Yet, as with the genre of *Complete Works*, the idea of a *Correspondence* in this sense is less straightforward than it may seem at first sight, and it is worth saying a little about it here.

The idea of collecting together the letters of an individual and publishing them goes back to the early modern period itself, inspired by the collections of letters of figures like Cicero and Pliny that had come down from classical antiquity. The genre was popular among Renaissance humanists, and it reached a climax in Erasmus, whose letters were known and emulated throughout Christendom: the printing press seems to have played a significant role in stimulating interest in such collections.[18] Similar compendia have come down to us from seventeenth- and eighteenth-century England. For instance, the posthumous collection, *Reliquiæ Wottonianæ* (1651), published by Izaak Walton to memorialise Sir Henry Wotton, included a series of his letters, while authors like Pope actually published collections of their own letters during their lifetime.[19] On the other hand, the aim of such publications was more to show off the literary skills of the author than to provide the kind of complete record to which modern *Correspondence* editions aspire, displaying a *belle lettrist* attitude which is now rare. Occasionally, a comparable rationale has been expressed more recently, as in Robert Halsband's 1958 essay on the subject, in which he suggested, in connection with the letters of Lady Mary Wortley Montagu, that only her own letters were appropriate for the text, those written by others to her being consigned to an appendix or quoted selectively in the notes, so as not to 'infect the book with a deadly tedium'.[20] The norm with modern editions, however, is to include letters to the individual whose correspondence is being edited as well as letters from him or her, and to make the collection as comprehensive as possible.

There may still be a role for selective editions insofar as these are intended to introduce readers to more complete editions that already exist: a case in point is Mark Goldie's selection from Esmond de Beer's complete edition of the *Correspondence* of John Locke, intended as a kind of appetiser to the real thing. On the other hand, unless such a resource also exists, such selections have distinct limitations for serious students, often reflecting a publisher's requirement to reduce a correspondence to the bulk deemed feasible for publication – a consideration which affects print editions but from which electronic ones are liable to be freed. What one hopes may be a late example of the drawbacks of print publication in such circumstances are illustrated by a work published in 1996 under the editorship of Andrea Rusnock and entitled *The Correspondence of James Jurin*. For this turns out not to be an edition of Jurin's correspondence as a whole, but a selection (it would more appropriately have been entitled *Selected Letters of James Jurin*), and in this case the result is deeply dissatisfying, leaving readers frustrated as to the criteria of selection deployed and curious to see the letters not included.[21] Indeed, such selections invariably have an unsatisfactory, provisional feeling to them, and, in a nineteenth-century context, it is symptomatic that the comparable selection of Michael Faraday's correspondence edited by L. Pearce Williams is now being superceded by a complete edition of *The Correspondence of Michael Faraday* edited by Frank James.[22]

Yet the idea of a 'complete' correspondence is a relatively recent one. Though the equivalent word in French has a longer history, in an English context the use of 'correspondence' in this sense was almost unknown before the late eighteenth century, and the ideal of a single 'correspondence' arranged in chronological order is more recent still. This may be illustrated by the case of the eighteenth-century connoisseur and writer, Horace Walpole, often seen as one of the great epistolary writers of his day. Various of Walpole's 'correspondences' with specific individuals were published in the last years of the eighteenth century and the early years of the nineteenth, but the emergence of the modern concept of an individual's 'correspondence' may be seen in the tendency of the editors of Walpole's letters from 1820 onwards to try to present them in a single chronological sequence. This was something of which one of them, Peter Cunningham, made a virtue in his 1857 edition of Walpole's letters, which prominently stated on its title-page that these were 'Now first chronologically arranged' (though, ironically, the claim was untrue, in that he had been preceded in this both by an anonymous editor of 1820 and by John Wright in 1840). The process was then completed by Mrs Paget Toynbee in her edition of Walpole's correspondence in the early years of this century.[23] Models like this have since been widely followed, and by far the bulk of editions of the 'correspondence' of major historical and literary figures published in the twentieth and twenty-first centuries have placed letters to and from the person on whom the collection is focused in a single, chronological sequence.

There have been exceptions to this, one of the most prominent, ironically, being Horace Walpole himself. In this particular case, the twentieth-century Yale edition of *The Correspondence of Horace Walpole* reverted to the more traditional arrangement of letters grouped by correspondent rather than ordered by date, following eighteenth-century precedents such as the original editions of Walpole's letters, or, earlier, Pope's collection of his letters, or the collection of Boyle's letters included by Thomas Birch in his edition of Boyle's *Works*.[24] An echo of this is to be found in cases where a correspondence between two men has been edited in its own right, to the exclusion of the remainder of either's epistolary output, as in Noel Malcolm's recent edition of the correspondence between John Pell and Sir Charles Cavendish.[25] In other cases, a thematic arrangement has been adopted, for instance with the correspondence of Sir Joseph Banks or that of G.W. Leibniz: in the latter case, letters on philosophy, politics, history and mathematics and natural philosophy have been edited separately.[26] On the other hand, such an arrangement often proves problematic, since it is almost inevitably arbitrary to a greater or lesser extent, in that few correspondents limited themselves to a single topic; indeed, by separating out the concerns of an individual, it is prone to obscure the way in which these were actually interconnected. It is also prone (like the arrangement by correspondent) to leave a miscellaneous residue which has to be swept up at the end. It is true that, with a printed edition of a particularly voluminous correspondent such as Leibniz, a non-thematic treatment would mean that a single volume would cover only a few months, but this is not in itself necessarily problematic.[27] In general, the chronological arrangement seems best, with the advantage not only of predictability but also of illustrating juxtapositions in a man or woman's concerns at any point in their life which other arrangements obscure.

There are minor, but perfectly superable, problems concerning a chronological arrangement. One is that parts of Europe used a different calendar from others for much of this period, due to the fact that the calendrical reform introduced by Pope Gregory XIII in 1582 was not adopted by Protestant countries like England until much later; this means that care has to be taken to ascertain which calendar a correspondent was using in dating a letter, and then to impose a double date on it in the form '14/24 September' according to which it would be allocated its correct place in the chronological sequence. In addition, careful allowance needs to be made for the related practice of beginning a year on 25 March (i.e. Lady Day, the start of the fiscal year in England until the introduction of the Gregorian calendar in 1752 led to that being changed to 5 April and the new year to 1 January). A letter that we would date '30 January 1643' would thus have been dated '30 January 1642', which can be dealt with by using the formula '1642/3'. A chronological arrangement also necessitates the dating of all or almost all letters, which is obviously a challenge, but not an insuperable one: in the case of *The Correspondence of Robert Boyle*, the number of undated letters was winnowed down from several dozen to a handful by painstaking study which had to be carried out in any case in connection with their annotation.[28] Indeed, in that instance, letters were identified solely by details of date, sender and recipient, which, in a chronological arrangement, makes it perfectly clear where a letter is to be found, though obviously this can be supplemented by volume and page reference to a printed edition. More commonly, however, editors have identified each letter with a number, which forms a less cumbersome (if less self-evident) form of identification. Traditionally, this led to the problem that, once the numbers had been allocated, additions to the sequence could only be made by adding supplementary numbers in the form '131a' (this is why the method was eschewed in the Boyle edition). On the other hand, this is a clear instance of the value of digitisation in projects of this kind, since each letter can be given a unique reference in an electronic catalogue, and the actual allocation of numbers can be postponed till all revisions have been completed.

A chronological arrangement emphasises the degree of artificiality involved in the idea of a 'correspondence' in the normally accepted sense. In particular, it bears no relation to archival survival. In contrast to a correspondence between two individuals, which may largely survive in one or two specific archives, this by definition brings together all letters to and from a specific individual, collected from whatever repositories they happen to be preserved in, which are often highly disparate. Archivally, it is thus a hybrid, in that in pursuit of completeness an editor will seek out letters wherever they survive: indeed, one of the most crucial and challenging tasks in preparing such an edition is the painstaking preparation of a complete calendar of the correspondence in whatever archive it is extant. On the other hand, this is unavoidable, since by definition an individual will have been in contact with a variety of others, each of whom is liable to have kept the letters that they received: the practice of returning letters to their author, as found in the eighteenth and nineteenth centuries, is rare before 1700.[29]

There is also a potential problem in that, by definition, a letter from Robert Hooke to Sir Isaac Newton belongs equally to two correspondences as defined in this way, that of Hooke and that of Newton, and this means that there could be a vast amount of overlap between different editions. Some editors have sought to avoid this by omitting or summarising letters that have recently been edited elsewhere.[30] But against this is the argument that as a group, the letters to and from an individual have a significance that is not reduced by the fact that some of them also fit into another, reciprocal ensemble; it is clearly also convenient to have all of the letters to and from an individual collected together in a single grouping. As more and more correspondences are edited, it may be possible to create a shared corpus comprising the letters exchanged between a large number of people, from which distinct ensembles of different individuals' 'correspondence' could be created, electronically or otherwise. Indeed, here, the possibilities of electronic media are particularly exciting. It is true that the prospect of such interchangeability raises acutely the need for standardisation of data format which we will address in later chapters. In addition, unless or until this covers virtually every repository of letters surviving from the period, it will remain dependent on the painstaking collection of the complete series of missives sent and received by different individuals. Nevertheless, there are exciting possibilities here, which it is hoped will begin to be realised over the next few years.

Even with the correspondence of an individual, electronic technology offers possibilities which are quite different from those of print. Thus if the documents are made available in digital form, there is no necessity to impose a single ordering on them, and users could instead be allowed to order the contents chronologically, thematically or by correspondent, according to their needs. Hence, some of the dilemmas referred to earlier would simply evaporate, though this will have to be accompanied by robust procedures for classifying letters which will entail a great deal of additional encoding of a kind which could be eschewed when the items were edited according to a fixed, pre-ordained sequence. (It will also make it crucial for every item to have a distinctive identifier within the correspondence series, which should be easy enough if – as suggested above – the calendar had been created by electronic means in the first place.)

If this conception of a man or woman's 'correspondence' seems clear enough, what should be its boundaries? Here, we encounter various complications. In part, this is due to the fact that the epistolary form has often been used for purposes other than simple letter-writing in the sense of the exchange of missives between private individuals. Many books of the period, for instance, take epistolary form, while books frequently open with more or less formal addresses set out in the form of a letter. Should these be included, as has been the case in some editions of an author's correspondence? A recent example of this is provided by the ongoing edition of *The Correspondence of John Wallis*, edited by Philip Beeley and Christoph Scriba, volume 1 of which includes a 67-page treatise addressed to Richard Baxter, which was clearly conceived as a book, together with various printed dedicatory letters, while a similar inclusiveness in relation to items of the latter type is to be found in the *Calendar* by Neil Keeble and Geoffrey Nuttall of the correspondence of Richard Baxter, the figure to whom Wallis' book was addressed. In the case of Baxter, matters were perhaps made easier by the fact that it was a calendar rather than an edition, but even then, the editors found it difficult to know where to draw the line: thus such epistles were 'thought to qualify when written informally in the first person with particular reference', but excluded if they were generally directed admonitions or apologies.[31] In fact, it might be questioned whether it is appropriate to include such materials at all, particularly since such dedications are often integral to printed books which might be worthy of editorial treatment in their own right.

In the case of *The Correspondence of Robert Boyle* such dilemmas were eased by the fact that this accompanied an edition of his *Works:* various items which had been assigned to Boyle's letters in a 'Tentative Index' of them made many years ago by Dr R.E.W. Maddison could therefore be omitted since they already appeared there, including the numerous works that Boyle himself presented as letters – not least his famous *New Experiments Physico-Mechanical Touching the Spring of the Air and its Effects* (1660) – together with certain literary compositions from his early years that took epistolary form.[32] Even had that not been the case, however, I would still argue for the exclusion of such items from a 'correspondence' as normally understood, and this also applies to items in epistolary form addressed to Boyle, such as dedicatory epistles in printed books, and even an entire volume, Gilbert Burnet's *Some Letters; containing an account of what seemed most remarkable in Switzerland, Italy &c* (1686), which were written up in book form before Boyle ever saw them, although ostensibly addressed to him.[33]

A further grey area is presented by the items which Douglas Chambers has dubbed 'essay-epistles' in relation to John Evelyn, who specialised in their production.[34] Here, we cannot always even be sure whether some of these were actually sent to the person to whom they were addressed, and the question of how a text survives is more important in this respect than some editors have realised, in that it cannot be presumed that a letter that survives only in the archive of its originator was ever sent; it is hence unclear whether it is to be seen as part of a *Correspondence* in the normally accepted sense at all. Indeed, some of these writings by Evelyn are really literary compositions which happen to take epistolary form, like some of the books which have already been referred to. Here, we return to the genre of letter collections, the popularity of which from the Renaissance onwards was noted at the start of this section, which are ill at ease with the conception of 'correspondence' underlying editions of the kind dealt with here, with their emphasis on private missives between identifiable individuals. Indeed, those who have studied such collections have warned against the dangers of modern editors treating letters from these compendia as authentic 'letters' and taking them out of context.[35]

This is exemplified by the 'correspondence' of Erasmus, of which the Oxford scholar, P.S. Allen, attempted to produce an edition according to the principles indicated here (i.e., a single sequence in chronological order), since it is now clear that this meant including a variety of items that were not 'letters' in the normally accepted sense at all, many of them either written or adapted to form part of letter collections.[36] In seventeenth-century England, a similar dilemma arises in relation to publications like the compilation entitled *Commercium epistolicum* which appeared in 1658, a printed work presenting various exchanges on mathematical issues in which John Wallis was involved. In the recent *Correspondence of John Wallis*, this is taken apart and reordered as part of Wallis' 'correspondence': but in many ways it might have been more appropriate to edit it as an artefact in its own right, akin (say) to a collection like the *Reliquiæ Wottonianæ*, which again bears an ambivalent relationship to the modern concept of a *Correspondence*.[37]

Some of these difficulties might be resolved by moving away from the concept of *Correspondence* to some more neutral formula like *Letters and Papers*, and in this connection it is appropriate to allude to a variation on the theme which has mainly flourished in the United States of America since the Second World War, namely of publishing documentary material relating to major figures in American history under the title of the *Papers* of the man in question, typically on a massive scale. This began with Julian Boyd's influential edition of *The Papers of Thomas Jefferson*, the first volume of which appeared in 1950 and which has now reached volume 31. Subsequent series, published under the auspices of the National Historical Publications Commission (renamed in 1974 the National Historical Publications and Records Commission), dealt with Benjamin Franklin and otherwise mainly with such nineteenth- and twentieth-century figures as Alexander Hamilton, John C. Calhoun or Woodrow Wilson. Basically, this genre extended the concept of a 'correspondence' as a chronological sequence of material relating to an individual to include a wider range of documents of biographical import, also placed in order of date.

There are various potential problems about this. One is of what gets included and what does not. Thus, pamphlets can be and are included in (for instance) *The Papers of Benjamin Franklin*, but a full-length book by the individual in question would be more problematic: in Franklin's case, the editors were spared this dilemma by the fact that his most substantial work, *Experiments and Observations on Electricity* (1751–3), was based on letters.[38] Equally problematic is the question of just how wide a range of documents is considered worthy of verbatim inclusion. It is revealing that, in the Franklin case, the editorial policy had to be made more selective as the work progressed, with more items being summarised rather than quoted in full.[39] A further complication is that not all papers or drafts are easy to date, in contrast to a letter, to which a precise date of dispatch can usually be given. Partly for this reason, and partly because of the need to summarise a range of material that was thematically rather than chronologically linked, the initial plan in the case of *The Papers of Thomas Jefferson* was to have a separate, thematic section accompanying the chronological series. Then, the method was adopted of departing from the normal chronological sequence and presenting related documents together in a 'file folder': however this has since been abandoned as being too dependent on the personal proclivities of different editors, and whether the idea of a separate annexe will be revived remains to be seen.[40]

A limited analogy to this genre in relation to early modern England is to be found in the tendency to include in some editions of an author's correspondence, for instance those of Flamsteed and Newton, ancillary materials considered to be helpful to the reader. In the case of Newton, these comprised 'shorter memoranda illustrating the life of Newton, particularly minor and hitherto unpublished manuscripts of Newton', including 'documents that are not strictly letters, yet are closely related to them', and even 'extracts from contemporary letters referring to Newton'.[41] On the other hand, though obviously well-intended as a means of providing a compendium of relevant information for those interested in the great man, the rationale of this policy seems dubious. Such inclusions are often rather random and partial in nature, offering a selection from documents which would more appropriately be systematically published elsewhere: thus some of the texts included have since been re-edited in the context of Newton's mathematical writings,[42] while, in the case of the memoranda concerning Newton by David Gregory, what is really needed is a proper edition of these in their own right, rather than piecemeal publication in a setting like this.[43] The moral is that it is best for the *Correspondence* to be limited to that, and for researchers to be referred to other publications for ancillary material.

Perhaps the closest equivalent to series like the *Papers of Jefferson* in an early modern English context is C.H. Josten's *Elias Ashmole* (1966), a very miscellaneous compilation of material relating to the life of that famous antiquarian and occultist which is arranged in chronological order, with letters interspersed by dated memoranda, often derived from horoscopes (though the horoscopes themselves are omitted). Yet this is arguably an example to be avoided, reading more like the arsenal of working notes of a biographer than a compilation appropriate for publication in its own right; in effect, volumes 2–4 of the set simply provide the documentation for the 'Life of Ashmole' in volume 1.[44] A further problem with Josten's book is that, though primarily based on the autobiographical notes by Ashmole to be found in Bodleian MS Ashmole 1136, the effect of interpolating into the text of this a wide range of ancillary material from disparate sources is that the compilation fails to do justice to this principal source in its own right: from this point of view, the edition of the manuscript produced in the early eighteenth century and subsequently republished by R.T. Gunther is more helpful, though falling far short of modern editorial standards. In this case, electronic publication might have made it possible for such disparate material to be more effectively handled than is the case with print, in that an edition of MS Ashmole 1136 could have been hyperlinked to supplementary material which could be consulted or ignored at will. But problems of selection would still have arisen, and, in this as in comparable cases, technological ingenuity would be no substitute for clear thinking as to just what it was, and what it was not, appropriate for inclusion.

A variant on the theme of 'Papers' is provided by the case of Isaac Newton, an extensive series of volumes of whose *Mathematical Papers* has been published by D.T. Whiteside, followed by the first volume of his *Optical Papers*, edited by Alan Shapiro. Whereas Whiteside's edition is arranged in chronological order, the papers being dated according to various criteria, including the editor's expertise in dating specimens of his handwriting, the first volume of Shapiro's departs from this, in that it is devoted to Newton's optical lectures of 1670–2: the editor defends this on the grounds that this is the great man's first physical treatise, and deserving of attention for that reason, even though this means that material dating from the 1660s has been postponed to a subsequent volume.[45] A project to accompany these by further series of Newton's theological and alchemical papers in printed form that was planned in the 1980s failed to materialise, but in 2001 the Newton Project was launched, aiming to make available in searchable, electronic form all manuscript material relating to the great man, 'an exhaustive rather than merely a comprehensive collection of papers'.[46] Here, there is exciting potential to recreate by electronic means a deposit which no longer survives, in that, though Newton's papers remained largely intact until the nineteenth century, when the 'scientific' material was removed from his descendents' family home and deposited at the University of Cambridge, the residue suffered a disastrous diaspora when sold by auction at Sotheby's in 1936.[47] A microfilm edition of much of this material was issued by Chadwick-Healey in 1991 as Newton's *Manuscripts and Papers*, but the plans of the Newton Project are much more ambitious. It has already produced a complete calendar of his manuscripts, and on the basis of this it plans over the next few years to provide digitised transcriptions of all his manuscripts, linked both to optically scanned images and to a full apparatus.[48] The ultimate goal is to provide an interface enabling readers to navigate electronically between all of the different parts of the Newtonian corpus, including the material published in the print editions already referred to as well as the digitised manuscript material that is now beginning to come online, perhaps along with annotations to books in his library and even relevant secondary sources. Though it is as yet too early to judge its ultimate success, this ambitious project is undoubtedly appropriate to perhaps the most celebrated English intellectual of all time.

c: Archives

In its conception, such an enterprise bears some resemblance to the 'Rossetti Archive' devoted to the remains of the Victorian artist and poet, Dante Gabriel Rossetti, that Jerome McGann has constructed at the University of Virginia.[49] As such, however, it will be a 'virtual' archive, transcending the limitations of any specific repository, and it is of course one of the great strengths of electronic media to make this possible. Yet, since the plan is to bring together all manuscript material relating to Newton, the rationale of the Newton Project is akin to that of the *Correspondence* or *Papers* of an individual, which transcend individual archives in pursuit of relevant material, rather than to that of 'archives' as normally understood, in other words the actual repositories in which these materials are housed.

To what extent, on the other hand, might a real archive be a suitable subject for an edition? This question has been raised by one of the pioneering exercises in digitisation in an early modern context, the Hartlib Papers Project, inaugurated in 1987. The aim of this was to produce a digitised text of Hartlib Papers, the archive of the seventeenth-century intelligencer, Samuel Hartlib, which was rediscovered in 1933 and has been on deposit at the University of Sheffield since 1962. As we saw in the Introduction, this was one of the first enterprises of its kind, and one only has to read the Project's early newsletters to get a sense of how pioneering it was when it began. As the inaugural newsletter of November 1989 explained: 'the

Project team works directly on computer, using the most up-to-date developments in information technology. As well as publishing sections of the collection in conventional form, it is planned that the entire edition will be made available to scholars both "on-line" through national and international computer networks, and in the form of an interactive optical disc for use with microcomputers'.[50] In the event, the resource was issued in the form of two CD-ROMs in 1995, while a second, revised edition came out in 2002. From the outset, its great virtue was that it was fully searchable, in that all the documents in the archive were transcribed and hence word searches could be made in the corpus thus created. As we saw in the Introduction, this limitless searchability is one of the main advantages of electronic texts. The Hartlib Papers also had a full set of images attached to the transcribed texts, so that users could examine these to check the transcript or to see a document's format, the images being connected to the transcribed texts by 'links' which could be electronically activated. In effect, therefore, the CD-ROMs replicated the entire content of the archive, providing a complete, transcribed version which offers an amazing treasure trove of raw material for those mining it.

Yet it is raw to the extent of being barely edited: indeed, it is perhaps to be seen more as a kind of electronic database than an edition at all. Each document is headed by a note giving its title, its author (where known), the identification of the scribe responsible for it, and (where appropriate) the whereabouts of other versions of the same text elsewhere in the archive. By simply copying out the archive in this way, less help was given to its potential users than might have been the case if the enterprise had been more like a traditional edition – in other words, if more attention had been given to collating and prioritising between duplicate versions, tracing sources and identifying material: this would in fact have reduced the amount of transcription needed, since instead of multiple copies being transcribed, one could have been prioritised and the variants in other versions noted. A corollary of this is that less was done to explore the nature of the deposit than might have been the case, in terms of the patterns of scribal activity to which it bears witness, which might have been the subject of an extensive commentary which would itself have thrown light on the individual components of the collection. It might also be felt that more could have been done in terms of editing and annotating the materials in the collection. On the other hand, it should be noted that, although the Hartlib Papers CD-ROM can be seen as an end product in its own right, in many ways the intention was for this to act as a resource inviting further exploitation, which has in fact begun to materialise in the form of separate editions of individual components of the archive in properly annotated form which the Hartlib Project has since produced – the letters of Sir Cheney Culpeper, for instance, or those of Jan Jonston.[51] On the other hand, it is perhaps revealing that, in this, the Project could be seen as having reverted to more traditional units of editorial attention.

Also significant is the story of the second edition of the Hartlib Papers, which sought to extend the corpus to which the original edition was devoted to include 'Hartlibian' materials surviving in other repositories. The rationale of this can be found in various papers by those responsible for the project, echoed by the brief introductory notes that accompanied the CD-ROM, in which the archive was presented as a kind of extended correspondence, linked in content and purpose by the philanthropic and pansophic goals to which Hartlib and his friends aspired.[52] Hence, the aspiration was to locate the 'hidden half' or 'scribal shadow' of the Hartlib archive, as Mark Greengrass put it, thus representing an impulse towards a kind of 'virtual' completion of the archive by digital means.[53] In many respects, however, the result has proved somewhat disappointing. What were included were often scribal copies of letters that were distributed to Hartlib's correspondents, such as Boyle, which were discrete items intended for such distribution, and which form an integral part of the collections in which they are preserved. Quite apart from the practical point that it did not prove possible to treat this material in the same way as the main archive, in that facsimiles of the originals were not included, there is a broader problem as to just what the boundaries of this larger 'archive' ought to be, made all the more transparent by the fact that, even within a single repository like the British Library, some material that might have seemed relevant was included while some was not.[54]

In fact, as this illustrates, 'virtual' archives require a clear rationale to be effective. On the other hand, the aspiration to 'complete' the archive in this way represented an implicit admission of the artificiality of the actual archive as the unit forming the subject of editorial attention. An alternative, exemplified by the treatment that has been applied to another archive, the Boyle Papers at the Royal Society, is to be comprehensive only in basic description and much more selective in exploitation. In this case, much effort was put into producing and refining a calendar of the archive, giving a brief description of every document, noting when they overlapped with other documents either within the archive or outside it, in such instances collating the different versions and recording variants, and only then moving on to selective publication. This cataloguing work was initially combined with the issue of a complete microfilm of the archive, and it is interesting that editors once hailed microfilm as the source of a revolution in editing in a manner somewhat comparable to more recent claims concerning digitisation.[55] In this case, it is certainly true that the publication of a complete microfilm gave widespread access to the material in facsimile, thus allowing editorial decisions to be checked; more recently, sets of digitised images of the core volumes of the archive have been made available online in conjunction with an online version of the calendar.[56]

Exploitation, however, was more selective, for various reasons. One was the realisation that, large as the archive still is, it is far from complete: surviving inventories of its content made in the eighteenth century reveal serious losses since Boyle's time, reinforcing the element of randomness about what survives.[57] In addition, this is a very disparate body of material, ranging from the manuscripts texts relating to Boyle's published works that have already been referred to, through transcripts of published books by other authors and other such miscellaneous items, to such gems as Boyle's workdiaries. The various components were dealt with in different ways. First, the substantial part of the archive which overlaps with Boyle's published writings was dealt with in the manner described earlier in this chapter, by tabulation and collation, and by the complete publication only of sections of Boyle's books that failed to be printed and of the hitherto unpublished treatises which appear in the final two volumes of his *Works*. With transcriptions of published books by others, it seemed more useful to collate the transcript with the original, noting any omissions or other features, than to copy the whole thing out, while some more miscellaneous material was simply described. The result of dealing with a very substantial proportion of the archive in this way was to enable attention to be focused on what was arguably the most significant parts of its content, namely such items as the workdiaries, in a way that would have been impossible if effort had been devoted to transcribing it from end to end.

The workdiaries are, indeed, worth describing briefly, since this is a coherent body of material which had to be extracted from virtually the entire archive, so widely had its components been scattered during the vicissitudes which the collection has suffered since Boyle's death. Yet it is a true 'edition', in that its components have been placed in a chronological sequence deduced by careful scrutiny; each is accompanied by careful introductory notes; and an apparatus is provided in the form of guides to those whose names appear in the text, to unfamiliar place-names, and to the writings by Boyle that are cited either in the workdiaries themselves or in his endorsements to them, all available through hypertext links. It also has a complete set of facsimiles linked to the text, and deploys electronic means to enable users to move between different versions of the text.[58] Arguably, a significant way forward in electronic editing is through focusing on manageable components within archives like this, and exploiting them intensively through the use of hypertext links to ancillary resources: an analogy is provided by the edition of Galileo's *Notes on Motion* which is currently in preparation by the Biblioteca Nazionale Centrale and the Istituto e Museo di Storia della Scienza in Florence and the Max Planck Institute for the History of Science in Berlin.[59]

As for archives which would be appropriate for exploitation in a similar manner, there are clear analogies to the case of Boyle, not least among figures who accumulated large quantities of manuscript material that was not of their own composition and where complete transcription may be comparably inappropriate. A case in point would be the holdings of an antiquarian collector like Elias Ashmole, C.H. Josten's somewhat mixed success in relation to which has already been noted. Of course, such treatment would need to be applied in a highly systematic way, with each item being carefully scrutinised: what appear simply to be transcriptions might prove to be the only record of lost originals, for instance, while even copies may provide evidence of the process of transmission which would be worth recording. In addition, such an approach has its potential pitfalls if it means that an archive is 'mined' for a misleadingly small part of its content.[60] But it is surely part of the editor's role to make such decisions, and to get them right. The key point is that an archive is rarely the kind of assemblage of material that is suited to publication in its entirety.

The issue of just what is viable also arises in relation to more voluminous groups of records. The problem is particularly acute with administrative records, which have in any case (properly, in my view) traditionally been dealt with predominantly by calendaring rather than complete publication, as in such venerable series as the *Calendar of State Papers*, the *Calendar of Treasury Books* or the 240 volumes of reports and calendars, in eighty-one series, produced by the Royal Commission on Historical Manuscripts between 1869 and 2004.[61] A similar approach has been taken with local records; a recent example is 'The Portsmouth Papers', of the rationale of which its editor, Paul Harvey, has given an account. In this case, an interesting innovation was attempted in the form of publishing a sample in full – a single year, or a specimen of a class, for instance of letter books – to give a flavour of a set of documents which were otherwise dealt with in standard, abbreviated form so as to make feasible the publication of large quantities of data in a manageable format.[62] Electronic publishing has here already begun to open up a wider range of possibilities not least due to the sheer flexibility of the genre, meaning, for instance, that what started as a calendar can gradually be extended into a full edition by adding transcriptions, as has been the case with the Wellington Papers.[63] Moreover, it is perfectly possible for users to contribute to this, thus helping to deal with the inevitable limitation of calendars in often failing to provide the very information that specific users may require, or of being slightly misleading in their summary of a document – though of course such calendars have in any case tended to become more inclusive over the years, reflecting changing views as to what was deemed interesting.[64] Either way, electronic publishing may offer the option of disseminating in full documents that it has hitherto seemed prohibitively expensive to deal with other than in calendared form. The implications of this remain to be seen, but the potential of the new technology in this area is clearly immense.

5
Presenting Texts (1) Printed

In this chapter we come to the heart of the editorial task, namely the actual presentation of the text that is being edited. It could be argued that, in creating an edition, an editor is trying to do three things at once. He or she is trying to reconstruct the intentions of the author whose text is being presented. She or he is, or should be, trying to do justice to the text's history. And he or she is attempting to provide a text that will be useful to potential readers, or offering materials that should enable users to adapt a text to their own requirements or to construct a new version of their own (this arises particularly in relation to electronic editions). These may sound straightforward goals, but all are complicated, as we will illustrate by looking at the issues involved, the decisions that need to be made, and the considerations that need to be taken into account in doing so.

On the whole, it seems best to deal separately with material reproduced from printed and manuscript originals since different procedures apply to each, though there are elements of overlap between them, particularly in relation to the survival of manuscript versions of texts that were printed (which will be dealt with in relation to printed texts). In many cases – here as elsewhere – electronic media offer solutions which transcend the potential of print, and I will devote extensive attention to these. But I will discuss printed as well as electronic solutions at length, since editions in printed form are currently being actively conceived and executed, while, although texts encoded in SGML may have the ability to supersede problems associated with print, those who have produced texts in this format have sometimes expressed ambitions to publish them in printed form as well as electronically, using the same markup. If they do so, they will have to confront many of the issues that have long arisen in relation to printed formats.

The first issue that needs to be addressed is authorial intention, which has been the subject of extensive discussion. The editor has a responsibility to try to reconstruct the aims of the author of a text, a task made more complex by the need to do justice both to its evolution in the author's hands and to its subsequent transmission to posterity. At the most basic level, there is a duty – essentially an ethical, rather than an aesthetic, duty, as James McLaverty has argued – to do our best to convey through the edition what we understand to be the author's meaning (assuming that we can divine this), rather than to invest him or her with a meaning that is in effect a retrospective invention.[1] That, after all, is what a reader looks to an edition for. Indeed, this sense of duty to the author may have implications for the kind of edition that is attempted: this obviously needs to be complex enough to catch the nuances of the original, but need not be more complex than that.

The issue of how authorial intention was best captured was at the heart of the tradition of literary editing associated with authors like Greg, McKerrow and Bowers that was surveyed in the Introduction: this was characterised by a search for principles according to which editorial decisions could and should be made, thus (it was hoped) leading to an enforceable set of standards on which users could depend. The goal was the reconstruction of a text as close to the author's intentions as was feasible, and the idea was that, through painstaking analysis, it would be possible to restore a text to its original or perfect state from the intrusions of intermediaries. It was equally accepted that the author him or herself might only slowly have brought this artefact to perfection after initial, less aesthetically successful attempts that he or she had discarded. Hence, it was taken for granted that it was both possible and desirable to establish the 'final' intention of the author, and to present the text in that form. Yet, at the same time a decision also had to be made about the activity of successive compositors who might have introduced trivial changes in resetting a book: these were to be erased as lacking in authority and hence distancing the text from the form in which the author 'left' it. Slightly crudely expressed, this was the essence of the theory of copy text as divulged by W.W. Greg, developed by Fredson Bowers and accredited by the CEAA: 'substantive' changes to later editions of a work were accepted as authorial and included in the edited text, whereas changes to accidentals were presumed likely to be the work of compositors and thus lacking in authority, and were therefore rejected.[2]

In principle, this was highly commendable, but in practice it led to problems, and in any case this tradition has come under sustained assault during the past two decades, reflected in conference proceedings such as that dramatically entitled 'Crisis in Editing' held in Toronto in 1988, and leading to editorial work like that for the recent *Oxford Shakespeare*, and to such syntheses as Peter Shillingsburg's, now in its third edition.[3] Indeed, it seems as if a new orthodoxy is now developing, which rightly asserts the extent to which the history of a text is inextricable from its documentary manifestations. It has questioned the idealistic, not to say Platonic, presumption central to much classic bibliography which made a distinction between the 'work', as a kind of ideal type in the mind of the author, and the 'text' or 'document' as the corrupt version or versions of it that have come down to us.[4] Authors like D.F. McKenzie have stressed the significance of actual manifestations of a printed work, rather than some hypothetical original lying behind them, and even the idea that there is an ultimate, single version which we can reconstruct has come under challenge. Thus the question has been posed of whether the author's 'final' intentions should necessarily override all previous ones, in that the author may have revised the work for different purposes at different times, and his or her rationale in earlier versions could have been quite as legitimate as that in the latest one. With plays by Shakespeare such as *Romeo and Juliet* or *King Lear*, some scholars have repudiated the idea that it is either necessary or desirable to conflate the distinct textual witnesses that we have into a single, composite artefact, as against presenting the two separately.[5] As a result, we may have to become as used to discrete versions of Shakespeare's plays as opera-goers have become accustomed to different versions of *Tannhäuser* or *Don Carlos*.

Neither do such considerations apply only to the literary canon. In a broader early modern context, similar issues arise in relation to works which remained in demand over many years and were subjected to a process of accretion by their authors, such as Edward Stillingfleet's *Origines Sacræ* (originally published in 1662), John Evelyn's *Sylva* (originally published in 1664) or Joseph Glanvill's demonological treatise, ultimately entitled *Saducismus Triumphatus* in its posthumous, 1681 version, but going back to differently titled texts of the 1660s. In such cases, the work as first published often has a freshness which later accretions tended to obscure, and one might well feel that there is something to be said for editing the original version rather than basing the edition on the last version with which the author was associated, albeit reverting to earlier versions for accidentals.

Indeed, insofar as the Greg–Bowers formula is followed, the result is in some ways a strange hybrid, whatever its rationale. To take an example, Robin Robbins' edition of Sir Thomas Browne's *Pseudodoxia Epidemica* follows the original edition of 1646 for all passages that were reprinted unchanged in all subsequent editions, but for material added to the second, third and sixth editions of 1650, 1658 and 1672 respectively, the text is incorporated from the earliest edition in which it appeared. In the editor's words: 'It is hoped that by judicious eclecticism this text, though such a one as was never seen by Browne, nor ever appeared before, approaches more closely, not necessarily his original manuscript (presumably irrecoverable, and in any case expected to undergo some standardization and clarification by the printer), but his considered intentions.'[6] How satisfactory this is may be left to the reader to judge. The alternative, as presented, for instance, by the Clarendon Press edition of Robert Burton's *Anatomy of Melancholy*, is to select a single, later version in which the author was involved, and to base the edition predominantly on that.[7]

A further issue which is problematic is what to do in cases where we not only have one or more printed editions to choose from, but also an authorial manuscript. For instance, in the case of book 5 of Richard Hooker's *Laws of Ecclesiastical Policy*, we have both a manuscript extensively corrected by the author and a slightly different, printed copy, which the author evidently approved, and in the correction of which he apparently also played a part.[8] In this instance, the editor of the recent Folger edition, W. Speed Hill, has argued that Hooker's most intensive attention was directed to the manuscript text rather than the printed one: for this reason, he based his text on the former rather than the latter. On the other hand, even in a rare case like this where both a manuscript and the printed version *do* survive, it is worth invoking a further consideration of a more historical nature which might have led to a reversal of the policy adopted in this instance. This is that, in choosing between the two versions of a text, we may want to give prominence to the one which was presented to the world as the work of the author, regardless of who was responsible for all the details of its presentation: thus we might actually want to prioritise the printed version for this reason, which is obviously not exclusive of giving a full record of variants between it and the manuscript, and commenting on their significance. In other cases, on the other hand, the matter is primarily academic, since, if no manuscript version of a text survives, we have no alternative to the printed version, and it would be as artificial to go through this trying to remove what we suspect of being compositorial embellishments as it would be to arbitrarily impose these on an uncomposited manuscript. As we saw in discussing such matters in Chapter 3, the resolution of such issues clearly needs to be dealt with case by case.

Turning to practicalities, therefore, what should the putative editor of a printed text do? It is obviously the duty of the editor to be aware of all versions of the work, both manuscript and printed, all of which should be tabulated and recorded. In the case of printed versions, it is necessary to compare all different editions which have any claim to authority, including those in Latin and other languages as well as English in cases where authorised translations of a work were made. Normally, all this should result in the choice of one version as a copy text. Whatever version is selected, it is axiomatic that all significant variants in other versions will be recorded, 'significant' implying differences in meaning as against differences of accidentals such as spelling, capitalisation and italicisation which there is reason to believe are solely the work of a compositor. In addition, as we saw in Chapter 3, the knowledge that we now have of printing practices in the period means that collation is necessary to detect press variants, including resetting and corrections made while printing was in progress. For this, the examination of multiple copies of the same edition is required, though just how far this is taken is a matter of discretion. In the case of the First Folio of Shakespeare, over fifty copies were examined, though this was made easier by the slightly obsessive behaviour of Henry Clay Folger in bringing together nearly eighty copies of the same book in one library.[9] In other cases, it has been suggested as a counsel of perfection that as many as thirty copies of the most authoritative edition should be collated in cases where stop-press corrections are suspected.[10] In other cases, on the other hand, where sample collation indicate that no such alterations were made, a more superficial examination may suffice. At the very least, a sample of copies should always be examined, since if exclusive reliance is placed on a single copy, it could turn out to be incomplete or defective.[11]

In cases where a manuscript text survives of all or part of the text, careful consideration needs to be given to this in preparing the edition, whether or not it is used as the copy text as in the case of Hooker. If (as is often the case) the printed text is clearly revised in relation to the manuscript version and hence preferable as the copy text, the manuscript should nevertheless be fully collated and significant variants noted, though some discretion may be appropriate as to just how many trivial rewordings and the like are recorded. Here, a factor to be considered is the completeness of the survival of the manuscript version(s), and discretion sometimes needs to be exercised. For instance, in the case of the writings of Boyle, it became apparent from scrutiny of his archive that the survival of manuscript texts of his published writings, though extensive, was almost wholly random: in many cases, just a few pages survived here and there of any individual work. Moreover it was clear that in most cases these were not the printer's copy, but were separated from the printed edition by a further intermediate stage. In view of this randomness, it did not seem appropriate systematically to record minor rewording of passages where drafts happened to survive, as against more substantial differences.[12]

To illustrate what has been said so far, let us take some examples to show the range of complexity which a text may present, and hence indicate the kind of work that an editor might expect to do in preparation for an edition of it. For this, two works related to texts published in Appendices 1 and 4 seem as appropriate as any, namely Boyle's *Experimenta et Observationes Physicæ* (1691) and Hobbes' *Leviathan* (1651). The former shares with many of Boyle's books the fact that extensive manuscript material survives, which, in his *Works*, it seemed appropriate to tabulate and collate with the printed text along the lines indicated in the previous paragraph. On the other hand, the printed text is very straightforward. It was published in a single edition in the last year of Boyle's life. The only reprints of it have been in collected editions of Boyle. An examination of three copies of the first edition revealed no evidence of stop-press corrections or other complications. Hence, as a printed book, this is about as simple as one could get.[13]

With Hobbes' *Leviathan*, on the other hand, things are much more complicated. To start with, there are three editions of the work all bearing the date 1651, one of which is probably the true first edition, and at least one of the others a later reprint (though where they were produced and when remains controversial). The 'true' first edition (known as the *head* after a type ornament on its title-page) had a complicated production history: it was printed at more than one press, and the proof corrections were entered onto the sheets at different stages during the printing process. However, in this case, a number of copies of the book were produced on large paper for presentation by the author, and, as might be expected, these have a fuller set of corrections than copies on standard-sized paper, including pasted-in cancels in two places. Hence in his edition of the book, Richard Tuck based his text on a large-paper copy.[14] In addition, a manuscript copy of the book survives in a scribal hand with corrections by Hobbes, which may have been presented to Charles II; this has various readings which differ from the printed text, and the mutual relationship between the two therefore needs careful scrutiny, which Noel Malcolm will be carrying out for the edition of the work for the Clarendon Hobbes (Tuck used some of these, but, since he was not producing a full critical edition, he did not make a systematic record). Lastly, there is a Latin edition of the work which often differs significantly from the English one. This was first published in 1668, and it is usually presumed that, though revealing of how Hobbes' thought developed – as also of the version of his ideas which reached an international audience – it is less 'authentic' than the original English edition. On the other hand, one editor of the work, François Tricaud, has championed the argument that it might derive from a version of the work preceding the first edition, thus adding to its interest. Two editions, by Tricaud in French and by Edwin Curley in English, have noted selected variants in this text, though again a complete collation is not yet available.[15] This illustrates the kind of complexity which a single text can present.

How, then, should the text and the ancillary information that is deemed relevant be presented? I presume that, in an edition, the text will normally be rekeyed, either manually or by scanning a previous edition and working from that (recent improvements in scanning technology mean that it is becoming increasingly feasible to scan early modern printed texts as well as modern ones; indeed Early English Books Online already provides searchable texts of many books, though the quality of these is variable). In general, this is preferable to a facsimile reprint which photographically reproduces the work's original format. This is partly because it provides much more flexibility for searching and encoding; it also enables the apparatus to be keyed directly to the text, all or part of it being placed on the page in juxtaposition with the text. Editors have occasionally experimented with the use of facsimile of the original printed text in a printed, critical edition: a case in point is the edition of Newton's *Principia* by Alexandre Koyré and I. Bernard Cohen, where a photocopy was presumably cut up with scissors and pasted together with the relevant apparatus, with a random quantity of each of the original pages appearing on each of the new ones.[16] But this is somewhat artificial in appearance, and it does not seem a good model to follow.

In an electronic edition a facsimile could be used to provide the text that is annotated, with hypertext links being made directly to coordinates on an image. On the other hand, the relative expansiveness of electronic editions makes it perfectly feasible for both a facsimile and a rekeyed text to be offered in parallel. A slightly bizarre example of this is provided by the CD-ROM of Robert Hooke's *Micrographia*, issued in 1998, which displays a facsimile of the first edition to the reader, but which can be searched, evidently because a complete digitised version is also included to which the reader does not have direct access and which therefore cannot be downloaded.[17] For editorial purposes, the keyed text should normally take priority. Indeed, in many instances, the provision of a facsimile might seem rather superfluous, not least in view of the extent to which Early English Books Online already offer digitised facsimiles, except that these are sometimes reproduced from rather ancient microfilms and their quality often leaves something to be desired.[18]

In addition to the obvious advantage of searchability, resetting also allows the copy text to be emended as appropriate. The issue of such emendation is a difficult one, since silent emendation can seriously compromise the authority of an edition.[19] Obviously, the copy text should be followed exactly unless it seems clear that it is erroneous in ways that cannot have been intended. On the other hand, certain of the most trivial such errors can be corrected silently: for instance, if a letter is printed upside down (unless this itself yields a coherent word, in which case the matter might merit a note). In addition, it seems right to emend the copy text if an alteration is specified in a list of errata issued as part of the original edition. In such cases, it is a good strategy to combine such silent correction of the errors that they list in the text with the inclusion of the errata list in its own right at the point at which it appears in the original, so that readers have a record of what was contained in it (and of the original reading which was corrected). In addition, where an author makes it clear that the content of a book was incorrectly ordered in the original edition, it is proper to reorder it in line with his intentions, of course clearly recording what has been done in the apparatus.

In cases where either the sense of the passage or the testimony of other versions suggests that a word has been omitted or misread by a compositor, it seems perfectly reasonable to emend the copy text, which need not be so slavishly followed as to negate the author's probable intentions: however, here it is crucial for the altered word to be clearly marked and the actual reading of the copy text recorded in the apparatus. With Latin and other ancient languages, it has commonly been the practice silently to correct errors, though here too it would be perfectly possible to record any such changes that seem controversial.[20] If there is any doubt about the intended reading, it is better to print the text as it appears, and to clarify the fact that what has been reproduced is what appears in the exemplar by annotation or by the sparing use of '[sic]'. (This suggestion takes it for granted that square brackets will be used for such editorial interventions in the text, on which see the discussion in Appendix 2.)

In terms of global changes that can appropriately be made to the text to avoid undue obfuscation without losing any essential aspect of the author's meaning, it is worth noting certain prescriptions that have been made for dramatic and other literary texts of the Elizabethan and Jacobean periods. The retention of the long 's', found in Herford and Simpson's edition of Ben Jonson, for instance, has long been abandoned, and in various other respects editors of the Jacobean drama have made minor adjustments to their texts of 'typographical conventions that are not meaning-bearing' so as to make their editions more user-friendly, such as altering consonantal 'i' to 'j' and 'u' to 'v', the latter a change that is also made in the Folger Library Hooker and in the Clarendon Press edition of Burton's *Anatomy of Melancholy*.[21] Other obsolete letter forms which are best abandoned include the double 's' dipthong, while this is even more the case with Greek letters, where early modern typesetters used a variety of ligatures that are unfamiliar to a modern reader.[22] Of course, if it is felt in any case that such matters *are* meaning-bearing, then there might be reason for taking a different line. In general, however, as Anthony Hammond and Doreen DelVecchio (the textual editors) nicely put it in their edition of John Webster, the objective is 'to present the reader with what he or she needs in a text, namely the "signal" (in information-theory terms), and to eliminate that which is purely "noise"'.[23] This seems an admirable editorial objective.

What else can properly be ignored? It does not seem appropriate to record words hyphenated at line-breaks, except in the occasional places where it is problematic whether the hyphen is simply the result of a line-break or would have appeared even if the word(s) had been in the middle of a line. Catchwords should also be ignored unless anomalous: these were a purely mechanical part of the original typesetting process, simply confirming the fact that a page break occurred at that point in a particular setting of type which it is pointless to record in a reset or digitised version. On the other hand, the original pagination should normally be recorded, thus enabling users to match citations of the edition with those of the original. For this, a system should be used which involves as unobtrusive a mark as possible in the text – a slash or a solidus – keyed to a record of the pagination, which can appear either in the margin or in the running head in a printed edition, while comparable solutions are available in electronic formats. On the other hand, if the use of material from more than one edition makes it hard to present this information in a straightforward way, the record may be best consigned to the apparatus.

Notes included by the author in the original edition should be preserved as such, but in a printed format it is perfectly appropriate to reflect normal modern as against early modern practice by printing these as footnotes rather than as shoulder notes. It may also help the reader to move the symbol in the text to which the note is keyed to the place where a modern reader would expect to find it, though this is optional, since it may seem an unwarranted intrusion into the integrity of the copy text. Within these notes, square brackets can be used to denote editorial elucidation of the original (again subject to the above proviso about the use of square brackets).

In the case of title-pages, facsimile has sometimes been used in an edition that is otherwise reset, as in the Pickering & Chatto edition of Aphra Behn.[24] However, this is not a very satisfactory practice. The most important reason for this is that material reproduced in facsimile in this context, especially if it is in half-tone, is prone not to be 'read' as part of the text, as against being seen as an illustration to it. In addition, quotations in foreign languages, especially Greek, are often hard to read, and fresh typesetting assists the reader here as in the text as a whole. However, there is something to be said for a format that retains some features of the original, it being up to the discretion of the editors how far they go in attempting to produce a type-facsimile of the original. For instance, in Howard Warrender's edition of the English text of Hobbes' *De cive*, an exact typefascimile was provided, including long s's, rules, original imprint, and the like.[25] In the Boyle edition, on the other hand, the original layout was echoed, but all in Roman type, without the use of italic, black letter, etc. It was also decided not to reproduce the original imprint, which was instead replaced simply by the year of publication: after all, each component of the Boyle edition was published by Pickering & Chatto in 1999–2000, not by Richard Davis or Moses Pitt or whoever's name appeared on the original title-page. Instead, this information was consigned to a note on the verso of the title-page.

This formed part of a general attempt to impose uniformity on the corpus that was presented in the edition, which had originally been published over a long period by a very disparate range of printers, and this is a legitimate goal in a collected edition. Thus a system of levels of heading was devised and imposed on the edition as a whole, with a standard amount of 'drop' for sections of books, chapters, and parts of chapters. This obviously depended on trying to work out which aspects of the original format of the works were significant, and which were simply contingent on the differing house-styles of the various printers to whom Boyle consigned his work in the course of his career: we hope that, in trying to enforce an appropriate degree of homogeneity, we did not obscure any features of individual works that were genuinely noteworthy. It is perhaps worth noting here that, in this, we were using a kind of 'markup', as also deployed in SGML, and almost all the remarks made so far in this chapter are equally applicable whether the end product is printed or published in electronic form, the only substantive difference being the way in which notes and other apparatus are presented. (It is, of course, worth noting that SGML and XML encoding can be processed to produce a range of outputs, including print as well as different screen interfaces, hence reinforcing this element of interconnection between different media.)

In the case of illustrations, the best policy is to reproduce engraved plates in the form of a high-quality facsimile, whether photographic or digital: it is surprising how often editors and publishers who should know better try to get away with using photocopies or print-outs from microfilm, which produce versions of inadequate quality. Diagrams in the text, on the other hand, usually reproduced at the time from woodblocks, often survive reproduction through such media perfectly satisfactorily. Alternatively, however, they may be redrawn so as to ensure the author's intention in them is conveyed: a case in point is Newton's diagrams, which have often been garbled by earlier printers.[26]

Lastly, how should differences between variant versions of a text be recorded? Often, where the differences between the copy text and either a manuscript original or another printed text are not great, it is more helpful to present one version annotated with a note of the differences in the other than to present the two separately. An example of this is provided by Robert Boyle's earliest published writing, his 'Invitation to a Free and Generous Communication of Secrets and Receits in Physick'. This was published in a volume put out by Samuel Hartlib in 1655, from the printed text of which it was republished by Margaret Rowbottom in 1950. Subsequently, another Boyle scholar, R.E.W. Maddison, found the original manuscript of the work, and in 1961 he published a separate transcription of this. The manuscript version is similar to but not quite identical with the published work, yet (so far as I can discover) no one ever bothered to compare the two until a complete collation was carried out for *The Works of Robert Boyle*. As a result, it was not only possible to note all the minor differences between the two, but in a few cases to introduce emendations into the printed text where there were obvious typos.[27] Another instance of such collation of variant versions is provided by the text in the *Works of Boyle* of his 'Articles of Inquiries touching *Mines*', published in *Philosophical Transactions* in 1666. Again, a manuscript text of part of the piece survives, while there is also a reprint in a collection of such 'articles of inquiry' put out by a bookseller in 1692, which was fathered on Boyle, though almost certainly without authority. Again, the differences were such that it was quite feasible to record all the variants in footnotes for the benefit of any interested readers, thus saving them the trouble of doing a collation themselves, which separate publication of all three versions would have necessitated.[28]

Greater problems are presented with authors who heavily revised their texts. As we have seen, though the norm in modern scholarly editing is to follow the first edition, incorporating substantive additions and alterations from later ones, and indicating by annotation where this has been done, the result is to produce a composite text which is often hard to disentangle, not least due to the telegraphic nature of the notes in which this information is typically recorded. In the case of Burton's *Anatomy*, as we have seen, the edited text was based on the final edition with which the author was involved, which is more comprehensive than its predecessors, and the same is true of the 1985 edition of Bacon's *Essays* produced by Michael Kiernan, which combines an edition of the final, 1625 version with an apparatus giving a complete record of all the differences between this and the earlier editions of the work. On the other hand, as critics have pointed out, it is very difficult to visualise from this what the *Essays* were actually like in the rather spare form in which they originally appeared in 1597 or the intermediate version of 1612.[29] Some editors have helpfully appended a separate version of the 1597 text, but this contributes only rudimentarily to illustrating the evolution of the work, and the closest that anyone has yet come to a solution to the problem was Edward Arber in 1871, whose edition set out the different versions side by side in parallel columns.[30] A similar state of affairs exists with Locke's *Essay concerning Human Understanding*, to the second edition of which Locke made significant additions which he solicitously had printed out on sheets of paper ready to be cut into slips and pasted into the copies of those who had bought the version originally published to supplement the text. Indeed, to view extant copies of the thirty-one pages of material that Locke had printed in this way is one of the more bizarre experiences of seventeenth-century intellectual history.[31] Yet although Peter Nidditch's classic edition of the *Essay* records the stages of accretion through its apparatus, it is again only partially successful in making it possible to visualise how the text actually evolved.

But such problems, seemingly intractable in printed formats, may well be soluble through the use of electronic technology, not least in cases where the original, briefer versions of such works have a distinctive character which later versions lack, and which is very hard to reconstruct even through the most painstaking apparatus to a revised text. Thus one could visualise an electronic edition of Bacon's *Essays* in which one could move back and forth by hypertext from the 1597 version of each essay to that of 1612 or that of 1625, and to recombine these along with title-page and front matter to recreate the entire edition of which they formed part in electronic form. In the case of Locke's *Essay*, the additions that were separately issued could be accessed piecemeal, and the text of which they form part made available either with them or without them. Much the same could be done for other texts as well, representing a real breakthrough and once again vindicating the role of electronic media in this field. Indeed, just to illustrate how this might be achieved, insofar as this can be replicated in a printed format, a specimen from the Bacon text marked up in such a way is shown in Appendix 3.

In this case, as will be seen, though the process was largely one of accretion from one version to another, it was not wholly so, since revisions and omissions occasionally took place, as is there illustrated, and it is not hard to see how an electronic version could represent these in an integrated way. In other cases, on the other hand, the differences between different versions can become so great that it may be best simply to present the different versions separately. A case in point comprises the manuscript versions of the *Essay* which Locke compiled prior to publication, since in this case Peter Nidditch decided to treat them as separate entities and started to prepare them for publication in the Clarendon edition of Locke, a task which is being completed by John Rogers and Paul Schuurman.[32] A comparable state of affairs exists with Bacon's *Historia densi & rari*, which exists in two versions which have been printed separately by their editor, or with Alexander Pope's *The Dunciad*, where the Twickenham edition simply prints both versions one after the other.[33] A further example of revision changing a work to the extent of making it almost unrecognisable is provided by Samuel Richardson's *Pamela* (1740). Whereas the editions of this work produced during Richardson's lifetime introduced only minor changes to the text of the first, the edition published posthumously in 1801 was not only completely rewritten, but its entire tone was altered. Again, a good case could be made for a separate edition of the two versions.[34] Here, the challenge to electronic media is all the greater. Obviously it would be possible for these texts simply to be made available separately online, as in a printed version, leaving the reader to compare them for him or herself (though in either case a full commentary explaining their mutual relationship is essential). On the other hand, though more labour-intensive, it would be more helpful for such connections as exist between the texts to be indicated by hyperlinks.

Both in cases like these, and in instances where the variants between different versions are smaller in scale, electronic media make it possible for such a huge amount of data to be presented to the reader that judgement is needed as to just where such data collection should stop, and how the results are best presented. Potentially, the deployment of electronic media could lead to the abnegation of the editorial role altogether, since the simultaneous presentation of multiple texts could mean that all versions of a work could be available at once, with every reader being left to construct his or her own text of a work, thus transforming the experience of using an edition. The nearest that any edition has yet come to this is the electronic edition of Chaucer's *Canterbury Tales* which was referred to in the Introduction, in which fifty-eight versions of the text are being made available in linked, digitised form.[35] This may be appropriate in the case of certain much-studied literary texts, where textual analysis requires complete texts of all variants – though even here there may be a limit to the number which it is helpful to make available in this way, since there is a danger of obtuseness in piling up different versions when the whole point of the study of stemmata that has long underlain the study of works like *The Canterbury Tales* is to prioritise some at the expense of others.[36] But the majority of editions are designed to be read rather than analysed in this way, and it is not clear that in these cases editions should be produced that are aimed primarily to serve the needs of textual analysis. Here, there is much to be said for the performance of laborious, one-off tasks such as the collation of different versions and the recording of variants between them, and for the exercise of editorial judgement in evaluating the results. Indeed, though the use of electronic media may make it possible to display more of the materials on which editorial decisions were made than would have been the case when print was used, it is worth bearing in mind that most readers positively prefer to defer to the editor in making an informed choice on such matters.

Indeed, though electronic editions clearly have immense potential to surpass what printed editions have traditionally done, it is crucial that this is seen a a challenge as well as an opportunity, and that the requirements of the specific edition are exactly matched, rather than accepting some off-the-peg solution which may not be suitable to the task in hand. The hierarchical nature of SGML/XML means that the choice of encoding strategy has a major effect on the final edition, the objectives of which need to be carefully considered before a decision is made as to what form of encoding is appropriate. Many features of the TEI guidelines that are often employed in editions were designed for the purposes of textual analysis, and their adoption may preclude the provision of other facilities in an edition which might be equally worthwhile, such as identifying different components of a book or other document. Indeed, careful thought is needed to ensure that electronic media help the reader, rather than make things more difficult. An electronic edition is like an iceberg, with far more data potentially available than is actually visible on the screen, and this is at the same time a great opportunity and a temptation to overdo things. When so many possibilities exist, there is a danger of technological considerations of what can be done taking priority over intellectual considerations of what is actually desirable or necessary in any particular case. What we need are electronic editions that capitalise on electronic technology without being overwhelmed by it. We thus return to the issues that we have been considering throughout this chapter: whether working in electronic or printed media, the editor is effecting a constant negotiation between author and reader, and at every stage in this process thoughtful and well-informed decisions are required as to what is appropriate as well as what is feasible.

6
Presenting Texts (2) Manuscripts

Turning now to manuscripts, there may well be comparable issues concerning copy text to those involving printed editions, particularly in the case of correspondence where more than one copy survives, and, especially with the letters of figures famous at the time, like Bacon, these can become highly complex in terms of the patterns of copying and recopying that may need to be explored.[1] As with printed texts, a full collation of significant variants is in order in all such cases. With letters, the logic of the concept of a *Correspondence* edition, as discussed in Chapter 4, dictates that the appropriate text to form the basis of the edition is that actually received by the person to whom it was sent, if this can be located. On the other hand, if other versions – for instance, that retained by its sender – survive, the differences between these and the copy text should be fully recorded in the apparatus. A figure who was much prone to rewrite the versions of his letters that he retained was John Evelyn, so his correspondence presents particular problems from this point of view.[2] Indeed, though Evelyn's changes were usually fairly minor, the differences between the two versions may sometimes be so marked that both versions of the text need to be given.[3]

In the case of non-epistolary texts surviving in manuscript, again a single version is if possible to be selected, and all variants in other versions recorded, preferably by establishing a line of descent from an authorial original to various, derivative versions by painstaking analysis. Matters are more complicated in the case of authors who constantly reworked a text, leaving multiple versions which raise acute issues of intentionality: a case in point is provided by some of Isaac Newton's theological manuscripts.[4] As with printed texts, a judgement has to be made in such cases as to the point at which it becomes impossible or inappropriate to present variants in the apparatus to a single text, as against presenting multiple versions with a commentary indicating their mutual relationship. The more complicated the evolution and transmission that a text has been through, the more of a challenge it is to understand it, and the greater the need for judgement and ingenuity – intellectual and technological – as to how best to present it to the reader.

In transcribing texts, particularly where we have the actual autograph of a composition, great care is needed in ensuring that all textual clues are noted, for instance evidence of different phases of composition as revealed by changes of ink or the like, or any clues as to the point at which deletions were made or underlinings or other markings added – in other words, whether they were integral to the composition of the text or retrospective. It might well be desirable to differentiate between these in the way in which the two are denoted in the edition. Though it is good practice actually to execute transcriptions from photographic or other copies, thus reducing wear on the original, it is imperative that the initial transcription so made is then collated with the original manuscript so that full justice is done to features in it that may not be clear in a reproduction. For instance, material written in pencil as against ink might not be visible on a copy at all. More generally, the physical composition of a manuscript may be revealing, for example whether the leaves on which a continuous text is written are conjugate or not. Indeed, for a true understanding of manuscripts it is absolutely essential to handle them rather than to rely on facsimiles.

Turning now to the question of how texts should be presented, here somewhat different issues arise from those concerning printed texts, where, as we saw in the last chapter, most editors nowadays expect to reproduce the text exactly as it appears in its exemplar with only minor modifications – for instance, as to where notes are placed, or how certain letter forms like the long 's' are treated. Though the same ambition applies in the case of manuscripts, its implementation is more complicated, in that these are frequently works in progress, incorporating within them signs of composition in the form of insertions and deletions, and also displaying the characteristic writing tricks to speed composition which were discussed in Chapter 2. The way in which they should be presented has been the subject of some controversy.

In particular, a key issue is whether we can differentiate between texts that were meant for publication and ones which were not. Are memoranda, drafts of works, notebooks, or letters essentially 'private' documents, intended only for the consumption of those who wrote them or their intimate friends, and, if so, should we try to do justice to this in editing them, in contrast to clearly 'public' documents set in type or otherwise widely distributed? A distinction between 'public', 'confidential' and 'private' has been made in relation to nineteenth- and twentieth-century texts by Donald Reiman, and, in an early modern setting, it is clear that some figures were deeply distrustful of print, preferring to keep some of their most important writings in manuscript form: Isaac Newton is a case in point, and John Aubrey seems to have taken a similar view, as Kate Bennett has pointed out.[5] Can we respect this sense of the 'private' sphere in a textual sense? In a nineteenth-century context, the Center for Scholarly Editions argued that we should, advocating a different form of edition for such documents than for published ones, including 'a record of canceled and inserted words and passages incorporated into the main text', and this has recently been echoed in an early modern context by Noel Malcolm.[6]

However, this raises some serious problems. One is whether manuscripts are quintessentially more private than printed texts and appropriate for different editorial treatment for this reason (particularly when the act of publishing them on the part of a modern editor has the effect of placing them in the public sphere even if they had not been there before). Some manuscript letters were clearly intended for wide dissemination: indeed, as Frances Willmoth has made clear in relation to John Flamsteed, there was almost a sense that, once out of the author's hands, a letter was a public possession which could be distributed and copied at will.[7] It is also worth pointing out that the fact that something is in manuscript does not automatically make it private, since, as we saw in Chapter 2, 'scribal publication' was extensively deployed in the early modern period to give circulation to manuscript texts through copying on an almost industrial scale.[8] Noel Malcolm has himself distinguished between 'a personal letter' and 'a poem by Milton or a treatise by Newton' from this point of view, arguing that the former is 'more private' than the latter.[9] Yet it is hard to see how one could be consistent in making such a distinction between different kinds of manuscript material, rather than treating the genre as a whole as homogeneous. Indeed, though it is clearly desirable for an editor or reader to be aware of potential differences in the audience for which manuscripts were intended, it is difficult to make hard and fast rules for their differential presentation, let alone to implement them systematically.

Some have argued that such 'private' texts transcribed from manuscript sources should be presented in a kind of type-facsimile, which strives to replicate in printed form the exact appearance of the original, attempting to do justice to features of handwritten texts which differ from printed ones such as the use of contractions, and with deletions and insertions reproduced as they occur in the original, thus giving within the text itself a sense of the process of composition that occurred.

However, I have reservations about the desirability of attempting to produce such an inclusive text. At the outset, it is worth pointing out that those particularly interested in a writer's methods of composition always have the alternative of recourse to a photographic or digital reproduction. Such consultation is preferable to even the most elaborate type-facsimile, which can never show absolutely all the details that an alert student would pick up from the original. This may be illustrated by what is the most elaborate attempt at such a type-facsimile that I have ever seen, that produced by Brian Southam in his edition of Jane Austen's juvenile play, *Sir Charles Grandison*. For, painstaking as this is, it fails to replicate all features of the original – not only different handwritings and letter forms, but also ink blots, different methods of striking through words, or exact details of layout, for which only a pictorial facsimile suffices.[10] The chief thing which a type-facsimile *can* do is to distinguish words in pen or pencil, or in different hands, but even this might be better achieved by a commentary on a photographic or digital reproduction.

In addition, it seems to me that there are significant intellectual arguments against presenting manuscripts in the form of a quasi-facsimile, in relation both to the letter forms used in manuscript composition, and to the author's treatment of the text through deletion and the like. Let us therefore look at these issues in turn, dealing first with letter forms and standard manuscript contractions and abbreviations. The usages in question are as follows. One is the use of the tilde to denote that 'n' or 'm' should be duplicated; related to this is the use of '-con' with (or without) a tilde to denote '-tion' (by the late seventeenth century, this may be worth recording as a symptom of relative conservatism in the hand in which appears, as it is in the Flamsteed correspondence, though whether it is worth reproducing, as is there the case, is less clear).[11] Then, there is the use of ligatures to denote words or parts of words, such as 'pro', 'per' and '-que'. Lastly, there is the use of superscript letters to abbreviate a word, as with 'w' with superscripted 'ch' for 'which', or the related use of a 'y' (in other words, the residual usage derived from the Anglo-Saxon thorn) together with a superscript 'e' to denote 'the'. As far as letter forms are concerned, we have (as in printed texts) the long 's' and the 'ss' diphthong, and the use of 'ff' for 'F'. The question is, should an attempt be made to replicate such manuscript forms in print?

The attempt to do so has a long history, beginning with eighteenth-century antiquaries like Abraham Farley, who tried in his edition of Domesday Book, published in 1783, to devise a form of type which would replicate typographically the contractions and other features of early manuscripts: this was developed into the so-called 'record type' used in the editions brought out by the Record Commissioners in the early nineteenth century.[12] Similar efforts to replicate manuscript usage have continued ever since, and if anything there has been a flourishing of a kind of superscript fetishism in transcriptions of seventeenth-century manuscripts in recent years, perhaps encouraged by the relative ease of inserting superscripts in such popular word-processing packages as Word. This undoubtedly adds to the quaintness of the appearance of texts, and some may feel that in this way they are adding 'authenticity': one American student of Locke wrote that to expand such contractions was to 'destroy their peculiar seventeenth-century flavor'.[13] But is this true?

In my view, all of these contractions should be expanded, for various reasons. First, the case for expanding them can be made by reference to the distinction between handwriting and print discussed in Chapter 3. As we saw there, the essential difference between manuscripts and print is not between private and public texts, but rather a technological one relating to forms of encodement, in that printing translates a text into mechanised letter forms, with attendant implications about how letters are shown and how they are combined into words. In my view, the only way to retain the distinctive qualities of manuscript in an edition is by facsimile, since only thus are the actual letter forms, and the interconnection between different letters characteristic of a handwritten text, preserved. As soon as the text is transcribed into mechanised letterforms – in other words, as soon as it is typed or word-processed – it has passed through the manuscript–print threshold, and it is therefore inappropriate to replicate the contractions used by early modern authors as writing tricks to increase their speed of composition. It is a delusion to think that a word-processed text is more similar to a manuscript one (and hence more in keeping with the proclivities of a man like Newton) than a printed one. The implication is that it is an equal delusion to think that the preservation of characteristic manuscript forms in a word-processed format is appropriate.

To this may be added other considerations, notably the convenience of the reader, and the need not to impose on him or her unnecessary 'noise' which has no significance and is potentially misleading. One issue is of meaning and pronunciation. Since we all know that 'y^e' was read and pronounced as 'the', it seems needlessly pedantic – even if it were proper – to transcribe it as it appears in the manuscript. Scholars may all know that the 'y' in such abbreviations is a substitute for the thorn and that 'y^e' should be read as 'the': but students and others who encounter this usage for the first time read it out as 'ye', as in 'ye olde', and are thus misled. Similarly, with abbreviations like 'M^{tie}': no one would ever have read it out like that, as against automatically expanding it to 'Majestie', so why should we not do the same when transferring it to print? There is a real danger of obfuscating a text unnecessarily, and at the very least scholars should be aware that they are making a choice in the way they present manuscript texts in this respect, and that there are very strong arguments – both intellectual and pragmatic – for expanding contractions. It is worth noting that editors of eighteenth-century correspondence have almost universally implemented the policy that I am advocating here, and it is far from clear why sixteenth- and seventeenth-century texts should gratuitously be made more difficult in this manner.[14]

If contractions are expanded in this way, the fact that this policy has been implemented should obviously be clearly stated in the apparatus. If desired, those who are squeamish about the loss of any evidence about the original may also wish to record it piecemeal, by placing the expanded component in italics (for instance, the second 'm' inserted as indicated by a tilde). On the other hand, this can seem almost as pedantic as printing the abbreviation itself: a particularly bizarre example that I have come across is to retain the thorn and denote the expansion by italics, so that, rather than 'that', 'y^t' comes out as '*yat*'.[15] (It is perhaps worth adding that the greatest solecism of all is to present 'y^e' as 'ye' with no superscript, since this removes the contraction without putting anything in its place.[16]) In the case of abbreviations like that for '-que', it is worth noting that it is not always clear how many of the letters involved the contraction is supposed to denote. Hence, silent expansion is in general preferable.

In the case of letter-forms which have changed since the seventeenth century, the following may be recommended. As with printed texts, the long 's' and the 'ss' diphthong should be silently modernised. With other letter-forms, I would suggest modernising them in line with the form that they would have taken if presented in print in the seventeenth century. Thus 'ff' should be rendered 'F', for instance. More of a problem is presented by 'i' and 'j' and 'u' and 'v', since, as noted in Chapter 3, these were the subject of evolution within the early modern period. For late seventeenth-century texts, when printing practice was more similar to what it is today than had been the case earlier, I would advocate that they be regularised in manuscript transcriptions so that 'i' and 'u' are always used for vowels and the 'j' and 'v' for consonants.[17] As we saw in the last chapter, even the editors of many printed texts from the Shakespearean period advocate the adoption of modern usage in relation to these letters, and there is a danger that, by retaining them in their original form, a text is given an unnecessarily archaic look. However, not all agree that this is appropriate – particularly in relation to sixteenth-century writings – and here a degree of latitude seems appropriate; there has also been disagreement as to what is appropriate in Latin texts, though a policy comparable to that advocated here has been widely adopted.[18]

This is an area where slightly different possibilities have been opened up by the use of electronic media. In particular, the use of SGML encoding makes it possible for the editor to have his or her cake and eat it, in the sense that the manuscript usage can be recorded as it is and a global instruction issued to effect the conversion that I have here suggested should be made silently. I am neutral about this: if the editor sees a value in preserving the abbreviated forms for the record, even though they will not appear in the outputted text, they are welcome to do so, but I would not bother. It is true that in this way we are catering for the very occasional reader whose philological interests leads him or her to be interested in the usage of the thorn in this period, but the crucial thing is that the default mode should suppress this information, so that the needs of the one reader in a thousand who wants this information should not be imposed on the other 99.9%. On the other hand, insofar as such encoding would enable readers to exercise their own discretion, there is one instance in which I am in favour of it, and this concerns the usage of the ampersand, either on its own for 'and' or in the formula '&c' to denote 'etcetera'. On the whole, I feel that it is better to retain the use of the ampersand than to replace it, since modern readers are perfectly familiar with the usage. But other editors have systematically modernised it, and here electronic media would allow a free choice to be made.

Moving now to the treatment of alterations, particularly deletions and insertions, in an edition of a manuscript text, again there are issues of principle at stake. In this case, it is essentially a question of what we are trying to do, and how this is best achieved. Thus it could be argued that, as editors, we are supposed to be producing an edition, reproducing as best we can the end product at which the author was aiming through the process of alteration. When the author crossed out words and replaced them, his or her aim was to produce a new text, in which the substituted words appear and from which the deleted ones are removed. Hence, as editors, it is surely this revised text that we should be presenting: if we are trying to do justice to the author's intention for the text, it is surely inappropriate to leave in it – even in struck-through form – material that he or she intended to remove from it. It is important to note that no information is suppressed in this way, since this is not exclusive of recording the changes in annotations keyed to the text, which the reader can study and thereby understand the process that produced this final version. Indeed, it is worth noting that this method has certain advantages over methods which reproduce deletions as part of the text, since it makes it easier to indicate whether an inserted word replaces a deleted one by being inserted above the line or whether it follows it; it is also easier to explain how a word was altered in composition. In addition, complex processes of revision, involving alteration or replacement as against straight deletion, are often very cumbersome to denote through notations to the text itself, and it is frequently clearer to explain the process by which the text took shape in words in a separate apparatus. It is perhaps worth adding that, with texts showing a very heavy pattern of deletion, even some editors who normally try to include everything in the text simply have to give up.[19]

All this, of course, takes it for granted that it is appropriate to see the revisions as piecemeal changes which are best represented in this way. It is worth reiterating here what was stated at the start of this chapter, namely that in cases where the original and final versions are so different as to effectively constitute different versions, they are best presented separately, and it is worth noting that a composite transcript probably impedes rather than aids their comprehension as such. Here, though slightly outside our period, it is salutary to consider the way in which the *Cornell Wordsworth* has presented separate texts of various of Wordsworth's early versions of poems that he later heavily revised, and an early modern equivalent of this would be equally appropriate.[20]

To return, however, to compositions which – albeit revised – appear to represent single texts, I would make a plea that if, in spite of all that has been said so far, the decision is made to record deletions within the text, the deleted material is denoted in a manner that distinguishes it clearly from non-deleted text. For this, almost any form of bracket is liable to be confusing, and strike-through (now widely available through word-processing packages) seems by far the best option, though even this can lead to ambiguities (e.g., a struck-through 'e' can easily be confused with an 'o'). However, I would argue that any such presentation is inappropriate, detracting from the intelligibility of the text and making comprehension of the author's final version difficult and sometimes impossible. In my view, those who produce such texts seem not to have properly thought through the needs of their users, since, if they really wanted to enable readers to understand how the text emerged, the publication of a narrative of the changes accompanied by a facsimile would be a more appropriate strategy than an attempt to reproduce the appearance of the manuscript in type. The rationale given here echoes that set out in my 1995 article on editing seventeenth-century manuscripts, and I was interested subsequently to discover that a comparable strategy had been independently evolved by Peter Nidditch for his edition of Locke's drafts of his *Essay concerning Human Understanding*. His telling exposition of how his method evolved from the early phases onwards is worth quoting at length, and is included here as Appendix 5. What is most notable is its stress on Nidditch's consultation with users of the preliminary versions of his edition, and I consider that those who reject such methods, particularly in order to present a more fussily pedantic text, need to ask themselves whether they have given their readers' needs as careful consideration as Nidditch did.

Of course, as so often, electronic media here offer possibilities that differ from those of print. In print, when a composite text can easily be achieved, it may seem rather pedantic (and wasteful of space) to present two parallel versions on facing pages, one showing the final version of the text, the other a version with all the changes present – as J.E. McGuire and Martin Tamny did, for instance, in their edition of Newton's Trinity notebook.[21] But this is much more feasible – indeed, appropriate – electronically, where space is not a problem and where two version can be simultaneously available, either on parallel screens, or through hypertext links. Whereas in a printed edition, the deletions can only be presented in one manner, either as part of the text, or removed from it and recorded in notes, an electronic version can use hypertext to link together a diplomatic version with all the deletions and alterations recorded in full and an edited one, in which the deleted words are removed but a mark is retained on which users can click to switch to the diplomatic version of the text at the appropriate point. As an alternative, or in addition to this, electronic media can replicate footnotes by using mouseover notes to act as a commentary on the text, particularly at points where the emendations are complex.[22] In many ways, this already seems an ideal compromise, though further refinements in the relevant technology will no doubt be made. Indeed, by extension, a package could be devised that oscillated between even more versions, so that the individual reader could tailor a text to do away with specific features of a transcription which he or she found tiresome (for instance, the retention of superscript letters), while keeping others. But, of course, all this is totally dependent on consulting the text on a computer screen. Hence, insofar as editorial projects aspire to produce printed versions of texts as well as electronic ones, the problem will recur and the arguments which have been rehearsed here about how manuscripts are best presented will have to be revisited.

What should be made clear is that, although a text produced in the manner that I have advocated above – with contractions and abbreviations expanded, and with deletions removed from the text to the notes – is an 'edited' text, it is in no sense a modernised one. Indeed, I should perhaps note here that, whereas in the original electronic edition of Boyle's workdiaries launched in 2001, we used the term 'normalised' to describe the version of the text in which the encoded material was suppressed, this may have given an impression of editorial license which was not intended, and the current edition prefers the more neutral 'edited'. In such texts, whether presented on the printed page with notes or on the screen with mouseovers, everything that appears in the original is retained, but editorial judgement has (properly) been deployed in deciding how and where it should be presented. In this sense, it seems to me that to invoke a separate – implicitly superior – category for 'transcriptions', in effect type-facsimiles as against critical editions, is not helpful. To advocate an inclusive text with the rider that 'one can read the final text simply by skipping all the bracketed material' avoids the entire issue of intelligibility on which the discussion here has been focused.[23]

By comparison, the treatment of additions is relatively straightforward, in that it is axiomatic that they should stay in the text and the question is only whether and how they should be denoted. Some editors have silently ignored the fact that certain words are added: indeed, I have to admit that this is what I did in the earliest editions that I produced. But I have since seen the error of my ways, since the physical evidence of insertion often provides important information about the history of a text which it is important to preserve. Hence, how is the fact that words have been inserted to be shown? One possibility is physically to replicate the interlineations, as Heather Wolfe does in her edition of Lady Falkland's *Life and Letters*, but this has the defect of being cumbersome and more in the nature of a facsimile than an edition; it should be added that the use of superscript makes the words printed thus seem less significant than the surrounding text, while (as with her use of strikethrough for deletions), it also looks rather ugly and out of keeping with the typographical elegance that her edition otherwise displays.[24] As an alternative, it is possible to annotate the word to the effect that it is inserted, but this greatly adds to the size of the apparatus. Instead, a form of marking within the text seems preferable.

Some have used insertion signs for this (^), which have the drawback that they are the same at the start and finish of an insertion, which could cause confusion in a passage which displayed multiple interpolations. Other have used half square brackets, which lack that problem, but normally have to be inputted as special character sets during word-processing. The Boyle editions used arrow-heads, effectively insertion marks turned on their side to denote the start and finish of an insertion. The only snag about this is that they can be mistaken for angle brackets, thereby causing confusion, since other editors have used angle brackets for totally different purposes, in some cases for deleted words.[25] (Matters are further complicated by the fact that angle brackets are integral to SGML encoding, denoting the codes that become invisible when the markup is activated, hence providing a further disincentive to use such characters for other purposes.) Where substantial passages are added, or additions are in a different hand from the original, more ingenuity may be required. In the Hartlib Papers, editorial additions by Hartlib were denoted with an 'H', but an alternative would be to deploy contrasting typefaces to denote material in different hands.[26] This can be achieved in print, but in the context of electronic editing the implementation of a well-designed interface should be able to produce more elegant solutions, for instance through the use of colour-coding – though even this raises issues to do with colour-blindness which a responsible editor will have to take into account. Here as elsewhere, however, the virtue of SGML is that, if all additions are consistently coded, users can potentially choose for themselves exactly how they are denoted.

Turning to other aspects of manuscript transcription, it is axiomatic that the transcript should be literal, preserving the original spelling, capitalisation and punctuation. Only in exceptional circumstances should this rule be deviated from. For instance, in the case of capitalisation, if it is unclear whether a word is capitalised or not, the editor might wish to use his or her discretion in preferring upper or lower case in accordance with normal modern usage. Alternatively, however, and particularly if the problem is frequent in the case of a specific hand, a study could be made of the practice of the author in such matters, and his or her normal style adopted as a rule. Either way, it is proper to add a note of what has been done in such cases.

As for punctuation, here problems are potentially presented by various factors discussed in Chapter 3, notably the degree of evolution that occurred during the early modern period, and the extent to which some authors may actually have expected a typesetter to add punctuation to their texts. Some authors were undoubtedly erratic in this respect, including far fewer punctuation marks than a contemporary typesetter would have done, and this can sometimes present problems of intelligibility to a modern reader. To some extent, a *laissez-faire* policy may be appropriate in this regard. Thus the editors of *The Correspondence of John Flamsteed* took the view that erratic punctuation was best left much as it was, 'since it seems inappropriate to clarify what may not have been clear to the original reader'.[27] They did, however, use extra spacing to mark the end of sentences, which works quite well, and in other circumstances it may be appropriate for extra punctuation to be added editorially, preferably marked by square brackets or whatever other notation is used for editorial supply (see Appendix 2). (In an extreme case, if all the punctuation in a passage or text is editorial, meaning that the number of square brackets would be irritatingly obtrusive, it might be possible simply to add an overall note to the effect that all punctuation is editorial.) A specific difficulty is presented by the difference between early modern and modern usage as to the use of a capital letter after a full-stop: as noted in Chapter 3, though mandatory today, this was not so established in the seventeenth century, when the 'semi-period' was a recognised form of punctuation, and it is probably best left as such, though the alternative would be editorially to alter the full-stop to a colon.

With symbols, various possibilities are open. One possibility, typography permitting, is to reproduce them. Thus the standard symbols for the planets are relatively easily available. Matters get more complicated with the much wider range of symbols used for chemicals and for quantities, and here the alternative is to transliterate the symbol within editorial square brackets. (In SGML, it would be possible to denote each symbol as an entity, which could be interpreted in a standard way, either instead of, or in conjunction with, the transliteration.) Further complications are presented by recipes and the symbols and abbreviated formulae that they often contain, since contemporaries may themselves often only have been familiar with the formulae (as with certain acronyms in common use today) and it is not certain that they would have known what the correct expanded form was. In a specific, technical context like this, the answer may be to leave the text in unexpanded form, and to include a separate translation in the apparatus.

Material that is illegible or damaged should be denoted by ellipses (. . .). It is helpful to the reader to try to give some indication of the approximate number of words or letters that are affected, which can be done by having a set of ellipses for each word-length, or, within a word, a single point for each illegible letter. Alternatively, the approximate length of the illegible or damaged passage could be explained in an adjacent note, which may be preferable where it is several lines long, or if the damage is patchy, meaning that legible and illegible words are interspersed over a quite a lengthy passage. Uncertain readings should be followed by an editorial query (in square brackets if these are being used for editorial supply).

In most other respects, manuscript texts should be treated in a manner similar to printed ones. Thus in reproducing such portions of a manuscript as its title-page, or the address on the cover of a letter, it may be appropriate to reproduce the original lineation and (in the case of a title) to use type sizes that give a flavour of the original. Elsewhere, line breaks and catchwords do not seem worth recording unless they are problematic in some way. With page breaks, these should be recorded either in a manner comparable to that for printed texts – by having a solidus in the text with a note of the foliation in the margin or running head – or by inserting the folio references in the text itself: the latter method was preferred in the Boyle editions, where foliation of manuscripts was sometimes erratic and potentially confusing, while in particularly complex cases it may be necessary to record it in a note. It is essential, however, that the foliation is recorded in some way so that users can collate the edited text with the original manuscript if they wish. Ideally, the foliation should be shown in the form 'fol. 17r' and 'fol. 17v'. In the past, and particularly when scholars made more use of handwriting, in which 'r' and 'v' were easily confused, it was commonly suggested that the 'r' was superfluous and that a folio number without 'v' could be presumed to be a recto;[28] but it is better practice to use 'fol. 17' only to refer to the whole leaf, i.e., including both sides. In other cases, a more complex foliation may be required, particularly in order to provide separate references for the components of a multi-leaf section archivally denoted as a single unit: here, some formula like '46(1)v' may be appropriate to denote the verso of the first leaf of item 46.

Though the foliation should be recorded, however, it is not desirable to present each page of a manuscript separately. Though some editions, such as that of the Hartlib Papers, have done so, evidently in order better to 'fit' the transcripts to the images with which they were juxtaposed, this practice smacks of a facsimile rather than an edition. In a continuous manuscript text, as in a printed one, page breaks are almost incidental, and to reify them by inserting a line break or a heading between each page breaks up the flow of the text in an inappropriate manner. Only in documents where the components on different pages are intended to be discrete should they be broken up in this way. In fact, so long as page breaks are consistently entered, these can be linked to images as easily in a continuous text as in a discontinuous one, though if in an electronic edition with images it is felt desirable for the image and transcription to match, it would be quite possible to provide two texts, one divided up in this way and the other a continuous one for editorial purposes.

Overall, the aim is to produce an edition which does justice to the content of the manuscript, paying attention to its actual appearance but not fetishising this. On the other hand, special treatment may be required in the case of manuscripts prepared for circulation along the lines indicated in Chapter 2, and here we may take as an example John Aubrey. One experiment which has been tried in relation to Aubrey's manuscripts is of using a mixture of facsimile and transcription: this occurred in the edition of his *Monumenta Britannica* by John Fowles and Rodney Legg, but it proved unsatisfactory and should not be repeated (the fact that one of the most crucial components of the work, Part IV, was omitted completely means that a new edition is required in any case).[29] A much more sophisticated project that is currently in progress is Kate Bennett's edition of *Brief Lives*, the manuscript of which not only has a distinctive format to which it seems appropriate to try to do justice in some way, but which also bears the marks of the process of revision and emendation to which the work was subjected during the many years when it was in progress. Here, as elsewhere, there is a danger that something that comes too close to a type-facsimile may prove a hybrid, a curiosity worthy of Aubrey himself, but almost as different from his precious manuscripts as a more rigorously edited version would be. Indeed, it is revealing that Dr Bennett herself admits the extent to which she has moved away from her early, idealistic strategies for replicating every detail of the appearance of Aubrey's manuscripts as her plans have developed.[30] Indeed, this may well be an instance where electronic media will provide opportunities beyond those of traditional printed forms, particularly in terms of making available facsimiles of Aubrey's original manuscripts in conjunction with transcriptions of them: this could enable the edited version to move away from type-facsimile in ways that enhance the reader's understanding of the text, while at the same time remaining linked to reproductions of Aubrey's manuscript pages in a manner that will constantly remind the reader of his original. Even an unusual case like this one thus reinforces the overall message that undue fidelity to the actual appearance of the original manuscript may actually obscure an author's meaning rather than helping to clarify it.

7
Modernised Texts

It seems worth dealing here with a rather different kind of edition from those that have been considered hitherto, namely of 'modernised texts', editions in which features of early modern texts which are deemed distracting to modern readers, such as original spelling, italicisation, capitalisation and punctuation, are removed so as to make the texts more approachable. The aim is to remove much of the strangeness of an early modern text, thereby making it accessible to twenty-first-century readers who might be alienated by the unfamiliar conventions of writings of that period, evidently with an eye particularly to the student market. Since such editions raise some significant issues relating to the audience for editions of the kind with which this book has so far been concerned – not least of whether such modernisation is compatible with seriousness in an edition, or, indeed, whether it is necessary at all – it seems appropriate to devote a brief chapter at this point to the issues involved.

Though such texts may seem a predominantly recent phenomenon, in fact, they could be seen as having a long pedigree, albeit a less self-conscious one: most eighteenth-century editors of sixteenth- or seventeenth-century texts left their compositors to set the texts in the typographical style of their period. Consciously exact reprints of early texts of the kind to which this book has hitherto been devoted were initially an essentially antiquarian enterprise. It was only in the twentieth century, with the increasing provision of editions seeking exactly to reproduce the spelling and other features of the original which have been dealt with in previous chapters, that a parallel genre has grown up of modernised texts aimed at students and general readers. This includes such series as the Longman Annotated English Poets, which has been in existence since 1965, or two more recent Cambridge series, of 'Texts in the History of Political Thought' and 'Texts in the History of Philosophy'. What can be said about these in the context of this book?

The objective is undoubtedly an admirable one, not least in terms of increasing the availability and accessibility of the texts in question, and it certainly raises the issue of just how accessible editions of the kind that have been referred to so far in this book actually are. As we have seen, the acme of editing is the full, diplomatic, critical edition, often with a Latin text as well as an English one and a full record of all textual variants, including authorial second thoughts as well as alternative readings in contemporary editions. The result is bound to be complex, particularly if much of this information is placed adjacent to the text on the page, with the apparatus keyed to the text by note references or line numbers. Editions of manuscripts are, if anything, potentially more complex still. Indeed, it was an edition of such a text – admittedly a nineteenth-century rather than an early modern one, in the form of the journals of Ralph Waldo Emerson sponsored by the Center for Editions of American Authors – which inspired Lewis Mumford's memorable reaction to the first volume when it appeared in a review in the *New York Review of Books* as 'Emerson behind barbed wire'. Mumford likened the editorial intrusiveness characteristic of such editions to the constant overhead presence of a helicopter.[1] The subsequent intervention in the debate by Edmund Wilson raised even more acutely the issue of what kind of texts were needed, in that he seems to have aspired to something much more in the nature of a 'reading edition' of the authors on whom the CEAA were lavishing such attention through their critical editions. Herbert Davis once remarked in a similar connection that, if asked, many eighteenth-century authors would probably have preferred their work to be available in a modernised text than in the laboriously edited versions which many scholars spend years perfecting, since they would thus be more widely read and understood.[2]

In fact, the two may not be mutually exclusive. In fairness to the CEAA, it should be pointed out that that body itself took for granted that there might be more than one potential readership for its editions of the major literary works of the authors who were edited under its auspices, advocating that a plain text be presented which could be reprinted for student use in isolation from the elaborate description of variant readings and the like which accompanied it in the 'official' edition.[3] Though this led some critics to question whether this meant that the elaborate apparatus was dispensable altogether,[4] it surely reflected a commendable awareness that scholarly editions and student texts could properly co-exist. As Davis' example of modernised texts of eighteenth-century authors indicates, a hyper-critical text may not be appropriate for all readers, and this surely needs to be taken into account in planning editions. Indeed, at least some of those who have produced formidably complex editions of major texts have taken it for granted that their books, aimed at scholars seriously interested in the author in question, need to be supplemented for a general readership by more popular editions.

Let us take an example. Francis Bacon's *Novum organum* is available as volume 11 of the Oxford Francis Bacon, *The Instauratio magna, Part II*, immaculately edited by Graham Rees with Maria Wakely. The entire text is set out both in Latin and in English translation on facing pages with textual variants noted at the foot of the page over a total of 485 pages: this is preceded by 110 pages of introductory material dealing comprehensively with the history of the work and its complex publishing history, and followed by an elaborate commentary and two technical appendices occupying a further 127 pages. It is obviously indispensable to anyone with a serious interest in the work, but, equally, it retails at a price which means that it is to be found almost wholly in university libraries. On the other hand, those responsible for this edition would naturally expect that other, more accessible versions of the *Novum organum* will also appear, aimed at a less specialist audience, and such editions will in future be able to draw on the erudition of the version in the Oxford Francis Bacon, disseminating its new findings about the history of the book as appropriate. In the meantime, a specimen of such a more popular edition is already available in the form of the version of the work produced for the 'Cambridge Texts in the History of Philosophy' by Lisa Jardine and Michael Silverthorne. This and other texts in the same series (which include works by Robert Boyle, René Descartes and others) indicate the kind of characteristics that such editions typically have.[5] Thus the Cambridge edition of the *New Organon* presents only an English text of the work, dispensing with the Latin original. It is also much more succinctly introduced and annotated, reflecting the perceived needs of its intended audience. Overall, the text of the work occupies 238 pages and the introductory material 35. The result is that it can sell at an eighth of the price of the definitive text, and is hence within the purchasing power even of students.

Other volumes in the series are of texts which started life in English rather than Latin. Here the elements of automatic modernisation which a translation can bring with it do not arise, and we encounter the typical characteristics of texts published in such series aimed at students, in that spelling, italicisation, capitalisation and punctuation are self-consciously modernised so as to make the texts more accessible. One point worth making about such modernisation is that it is hard work, as I can report from my experience in producing the text of Boyle's *Free Enquiry into the Vulgarly Received Notion of Nature* for the 'Cambridge Texts in the History of Philosophy'. I and my co-editor, Edward B. Davis, found the task of modernisation, especially of punctuation, a surprisingly difficult one: we spent much time going through the text agonising over the punctuation and ensuring that the imposition of a modern sentence structure had not obscured Boyle's meaning.[6] Indeed, in my case, this led me to wonder whether it was worth the trouble at all, not least since, for those who have no difficulty understanding the original and who positively relish the nuances that such facets of an early modern text give it, a 'smoothed out' text like this is much inferior to one in which such features have been retained.

The issue of what to do with punctuation is, in fact, a particularly problematic one, and views differ as to how best to resolve it. The difficulty of modernising punctuation satisfactorily has been noted by Edwin Curley in the introduction to his modernised text of Hobbes' *Leviathan*, where he noted when commenting on the alterations that he made how, in his experience, 'for students the seventeenth-century punctuation is an even greater barrier to understanding than is the seventeenth-century spelling'.[7] Others, on the other hand, have taken the view that the original punctuation should be retained even when spelling is modernised, on the grounds that it is connected to the sense – 'an organic part of the grammatical system'.[8]

This is a quotation from the preface to John Carey and Alastair Fowler's edition of Milton's poems in the Longman Annotated English Poets, and the problems raised by modernisation have been pointed out by Phillip Harth in a thoughtful review of the edition of Dryden in that series.[9] Here, matters are all the more acute because this is a series which has pretensions to present a text which, though modernised, otherwise carries as elaborate an apparatus as a more traditional edition, hence offering a serious contribution to scholarship. The combination, as Harth points out, goes back to the founder of the series, F.W. Bateson, who believed passionately that in this way an early modern text could retain the contemporaneity of its appeal in a way that unmodernised editions made difficult. Yet, as Harth points out, inescapable dilemmas are presented by such an approach, which go to the heart of the meaning of the text. For instance, in the context of early modern poetry, where personifications are widely invoked, should these be capitalised or not? Some editors have ruthlessly removed all capitals, which is a policy which is at least simple and easy to implement. Paul Hammond, on the other hand, editor of the Longman Dryden, tries to effect a compromise, which is only partially satisfactory. There is a similar problem with italics. Clearly much of the italic which was used by early modern printers could be seen as superfluous by a modern reader. But italic is still used for emphasis, and, where it is clear that that is the purpose for which it was being deployed in an early modern setting, it is appropriate that it is there retained. Again, a modernising policy, if systematically applied, is liable to obscure aspects of the meaning of the original, whereas the alternative of a sensitive policy of compromise, as implemented by Hammond – with some such features retained but others removed – is open to the charge that it is a slightly unsatisfactory halfway house.

In fact, when allowance is made for the fact that, in the context of a serious student text like this, no one would consider taking modernisation so far as to alter the vocabulary of the author – which in my experience is as likely to be a hurdle to twenty-first century readers as punctuation styles – it might well lead one to question whether, in such a setting, modernisation serves much purpose at all. That is not to say that there may not be contexts where it is inevitable, for instance in relation to texts intended for schools (though, for school use, even a text modernised to the extent discussed here is unlikely to be satisfactory, and an element of paraphrase may well be needed). But for texts of the seriousness that we are here considering – comprising not anthologies of brief extracts, but unabridged editions of complex texts from the period – it could be argued that the advantages of modernisation are not as clear as they might at first seem. Here, there are interesting echoes of the attack by G. Thomas Tanselle on the tradition of 'documentary editing' noted in the Introduction, because one of his objections was to the policy of partial modernisation which was rife in the editions that he considered, the rationale of which was evidently exactly that found in editions of the kind that are being discussed here – namely that unmodernised language erected an unnecessary barrier between readers and the texts to which they required access. As he pointed out, this was based on untested and often rather patronising presumptions about what readers could understand and what they wanted, and it displayed a failure to understand the extent to which the very features of a text which modernisation removed might form part of its meaning.[10]

Indeed, it is interesting to note that those responsible for the Longman Annotated English Poets have over the years become more flexible in their policy in this respect. The general editors of the series acknowledge that 'modernization has presented difficulties, which have been resolved pragmatically, trying to reach a balance between sensitivity to the text in question and attention to the needs of a modern reader', and insisting that 'the requirements of a particular author take precedence over principle'.[11] Similarly, with the Cambridge Texts in the History of Political Thought, although the overall policy remains one of modernisation, certain volumes have been allowed to depart from this, including Richard Tuck's edition of Hobbes' *Leviathan* cited in Chapter 5.[12]

This is revealing in itself, and it is also germane to a further problem which takes us back to some of the issues raised in earlier chapters, which is as follows. That there should be both learned and popular editions of authors like Bacon or the major seventeenth-century poets stands to reason, and the same may also be true of Newton's *Principia* and his *Opticks*. But is this going to be possible for all texts? What about the writings of nonentities whose writings nevertheless seem worthy of dissemination in edited form, such as Samuel Jeake of Rye, or William Hobbs of Weymouth?[13] This applies even to a better-known author like Boyle: it seems unlikely that there will ever be sufficient demand to justify parallel editions, both in fully-edited and in modernised form, of more than a small part of his voluminous corpus, whereas there is significant demand from scholars and other readers for an edition that is reasonably accessible. It is partly for this reason that I would advocate texts which, while not being modernised, in that spelling, punctuation, capitalisation and italicisation are retained exactly as in the original, are nevertheless presented in as intelligible a manner as possible, freed from pedantic attempts to replicate manuscript usage, and with variants and authorial alterations denoted in the form which is least likely to distract the reader. Here, one might quote the rationale for omitting superscripts, contractions and the like of the scholars who produced the definitive edition of *The Diary of Samuel Pepys*, namely that, however much the retention of such features might delight a tiny minority, 'For all other readers, even the most scholarly, it would make reading the diary like walking on stones.'[14]

The result, it is to be hoped, is to produce editions which are readable and complex at the same time, taking for granted readers who are serious enough to be able to read a seventeenth-century text without it being modernised for them, but respecting the kind of irritation expressed by Lewis Mumford at editorial over-obtrusiveness. It is interesting that, in the context of his edition of Beaumont and Fletcher, Fredson Bowers himself advocated limiting the apparatus to a text, so as to avoid distracting readers.[15] The ideal is surely to minimise the extent to which unreasonable demands are made on the user, without depriving him or her of any substantive information about the history of the text to which he or she may require access. The vogue for modernisation may well have been based on a miscalculation as to how this was best achieved.

8
The Apparatus

The apparatus is one of the most crucial parts of an edition, codifying and encapsulating for the reader's benefit all the research that the editor has done to make sense of the text at both a general and a specific level. Indeed, in many ways this is where editors are at their most important. Of this information, some is best presented as an introduction, for the reader to consult in order to make sense of the text as a whole prior to embarking on it, while some is more appropriately consigned to footnotes or a commentary, to be consulted in relation to specific individual passages. Lastly, reference material for use in relation to the text as a whole may be best placed at the end of the book – or at the end of each volume in the case of multi-volume editions – while certain forms of technical information may be appropriately presented as appendices. All these categories can, of course, be equally easily presented electronically by the use of hypertext. Here, each type of editorial matter will be dealt with separately, giving consideration to the coverage that is proper and hence what readers might expect in each case.

a. Front Matter

First, the general introductory material. This is crucial, and it should explain as much as possible about the rationale of the edition and its sources. The following components should be seen as mandatory, since any reader would feel a legitimate sense of grievance at their absence. First, there is a need for a detailed history of the composition of the work and, where appropriate, its publication. This is fundamental for any proper understanding of the work, and the user should habitually turn to this prior to studying the text itself. More certainty about exactly when a work was composed may be possible in certain cases than others; sometimes, so few scraps of information may be available that every one of them is crucial, whereas in other cases there may be plentiful data, which can be succinctly summarised. Either way, an adequate account of such matters is indispensable. Secondly, the introduction must itemise in full the sources on which the edition is based. In the case of texts with complicated stemmata, their mutual relationship needs to be set out in full here, as does the rationale of the choice of text presented (or texts, in cases where more than one text is included); if appropriate, this should be keyed to the detailed information about variants appearing in different versions that will appear piecemeal in the notes or commentary. It may also be appropriate to give information about versions (e.g., later editions) which throw light on the subsequent history of the work.

In the case of a correspondence, information about the actual archival sources deployed is helpful, making sense of the differential survival of letters and hence of the physiognomy of the extant correspondence as a whole; it is also useful for the history of previous publication to be outlined. An example of an edition in which details of its archival basis are regrettably eschewed is that of John Flamsteed's correspondence, though I have attempted to indicate the ways in which this omission might be rectified in a review essay, in which I outlined the degree of serendipity in the survival of certain key manuscripts which are there heavily deployed and the need for this to be taken into account in interpreting the material that *is* extant.[1] This is the kind of information which is crucial, whereas it might be felt that a commoner component of the introduction to many correspondence editions, in the form of a rather bland summary of the content of each of its volumes, serves no particular purpose which could not be achieved by a contents list and an index.

As for editions of an author's writings, whether of an individual work or of the author's *Works* as a whole, the introductory material needs to have a certain amount of general information about the author and about the work(s) being edited. If the introduction is to the *Works*, the coverage will need to extend to his or her corpus as a whole and its component parts. How extensive this part of the apparatus should be is a matter of opinion, and, as with so many issues addressed in this book, the decisions reached will vary somewhat from author to author. Particularly with writers who are the subject of intense scholarly interest, it seems most crucial for the introduction to contain information needed to understand the content of the edition, rather than information about the writer more generally. In other words, the kind of topics that are appropriate concern authors' method of writing, the overall evolution of their *oeuvre*, their relations with publishers, the subsequent fate of their writings, and the like: these are the topics covered in the 'General Introduction' to *The Works of Robert Boyle*. Not only is this the kind of information which is most appropriate to this setting; it is also quite likely that the account given can be a nearly definitive one. When it comes to the evaluation of current thinking about the author and his or her work, and the analysis of the ideas expressed in the book being edited – along with the sources deployed, issues of later influence and the like – my own view is that such matters are best dealt with elsewhere, as their treatment is almost bound to 'date' much more quickly than material relating more specifically to the history of the work. Thus, although the edition of the *New Organon* in the Oxford Francis Bacon devotes 79 of its 110 pages of introductory material to such an account of the work's intellectual significance, the editor has himself admitted elsewhere that such introductions 'will, in the nature of things, be superseded relatively quickly by new scholarship and innovative methods in intellectual history' – in contrast to the longevity which he rightly expects for the text itself – and I personally would publish such evaluative studies separately.[2] On the other hand it goes without saying that this is the place to set out the editorial methods used as fully as possible, including the decisions that have been made as to how to present manuscript and printed texts, and the nature of the apparatus that is provided.

With individual works – whether presented in their own right or forming part of a collection – it is also worth emphasising the need to make readers aware of aspects of the format of the original that by definition cannot be reproduced in a reset form. This applies both to things like format and typeface, both of which could, if desired, be replicated by the use of selective facsimiles, and also to things that cannot, such as the quality of the paper used, if this seems significant. Indeed, this sense of the physicality of the original may in some ways be more important to readers' appreciation of the work than some of the minutiae of accidentals and the like by which scholarly editing has traditionally been preoccupied. It is worth reflecting here on the element of paradox in the editor's role, in that in a collected edition, in particular, he or she strives to present a standardised text for the benefit of the reader; yet the reader legitimately feels entitled to full information as to what it has been standardised from. The apparatus may well be the best place to achieve this.

If this type of introductory material deals with what might be called background, equally crucial is an apparatus giving all the information that is required for understanding each section of the text or texts being edited. In the case of correspondence, for instance, each letter should be accompanied by full details of the manuscript or printed exemplar on which the text is based. Ideally, this should include information about its handwriting, format (including 'significant space'[3]), endorsements and the like, and possibly also watermarks, postmarks and seals, though one or more of these is often overlooked. Information should also be given as to the grounds on which an undated letter has been allocated its place in a dated sequence, or where an identity is postulated for an unidentified recipient. This information should be presented in standardised form: indeed, such standardisation will make easier the intercalation of different correspondences that was referred to as a desideratum in Chapter 4.

b. End Matter/Appendices

The general apparatus may also include such aids as a glossary and a biographical guide. These can be very useful in minimising the extent to which it is necessary to intrude on the text with annotation. With a glossary, in particular, there is liable to be so wide a range of expertise among readers that it is better to let them look up words that puzzle them than to mark all words that appear in the glossary within the text, which is liable to be obtrusive (This may be more appropriate in an electronic edition than a printed one, where every such word could be encoded, though care would still need to be taken over how this was interpreted, since excessive hyperlinking can itself be irritating.) In relation to a glossary, it is perhaps worth mentioning that at least some words that are not in everyday usage can be taken for granted, how many depending on the level of readership predicted for the edition. One helpful rule of thumb is to presume that readers ought to be familiar with all words that appear in a work such as *The Concise Oxford English Dictionary*, or, if they are not, can be expected to consult a relatively accessible work of this kind. How fully the glossary is referenced is again a matter of discretion: some editors give references for all the information they include; a more succinct alternative is to note in the heading what works have been chiefly deployed; but the alternative is simply to present the data without reference, except in specific cases where a word is very unusual.

A biographical guide can also be useful and editors have made provision for this in various ways. Some have included in it all biographical information on those who appear in the edition, usually in a fairly brief form; just how much documentation is given varies from edition to edition, but it is usually fairly telegraphic.[4] This has the advantage (as with the glossary) of reducing intrusiveness in the text. The disadvantage is that there is relatively little correlation between the amount of information given about someone and either the extent to which they appear in the text or the exact context in which they do so. The alternative, adopted in *The Correspondence of Robert Boyle,* is to restrict the biographical notes to those who appear repeatedly – between four and ten such people per volume – and to give a slightly fuller account of them, accompanied by bibliographical references which act as a guide to further reading on the individual in question. All other persons are there dealt with, not in the biographical notes, but in a brief footnote at the first point in each volume at which they appear, with a cross-reference back to them at each subsequent point. However, this system has the disadvantage that it requires much insertion of cross-references at proof stage, which may be why some editors prefer not to use it, instead sometimes repeating the information each time the person in question appears, which can be a little tiresome to the reader. An even more elaborate variant on the theme of biographical notes is to be found in Noel Malcolm's edition of *The Correspondence of Thomas Hobbes,* which devotes 143 pages in its second volume to lengthy biographies of its chief protagonists, some of them comprising the fullest extant life of the person in question.[5] It is doubtful if this would be feasible for a more voluminous correspondence than Hobbes', and in any case it might be felt that the provision of such elaborate notes is erring on the side of over-inclusiveness, going beyond what is really appropriate to an edition.

As for appendices of a more technical kind, this might well be the appropriate place to give detailed information about aspects of the edition which editorial scrutiny has brought to light but which is too voluminous to include at the appropriate point in the introduction. In fact, such appendices can become valuable reference tools in their own right. A case in point is the appendix which appears in volume 6 of the Oxford Francis Bacon dealing with Bacon's compositional methods and the extent to which he relied on his amanuenses to improve the spelling, capitalisation and punctuation of his writings.[6] More common, however, is the use of appendices to record textual variants of which a full record would have overburdened the notes to the texts in question, as in the case of Howard Warrender's edition of Hobbes' *De cive* or Nigel Smith's of the poems of Marvell.[7]

c. Annotation

Turning to the apparatus relating to specific passages, the nature of this will be affected by two things. One is the type of text that is being annotated, since readers may expect a different kind of notes in an edition of a literary work from those that would seem appropriate to a diary.

Secondly, the content of the notes will obviously be affected by what has appeared in such general sections of the apparatus as have already been described. Thus, if all individuals are identified in the biographical notes, there will be no need for biographical data in footnotes. But, in general, what these notes should do is to provide the background information that is essential to understand the passage to which they relate. In the case of correspondence, diaries, and related sources, there will be a myriad of persons, places and events crying out for annotation in this way. In general, succinctness is a virtue in such matters, and it is as easy to over-annotate a text as to under-annotate it. For instance, it might be felt that, valuable as is Esmond de Beer's edition of John Evelyn's diary, it is prone to over-annotate the text, and particularly to over-reference it: it is not clear that a reference to a secondary source is needed when Evelyn mentions the Colosseum.[8] The editor should also not be afraid to note ignorance where a reference has proved untraceable: simply to ignore it might imply that it had been overlooked. Indeed, judgement is required not only in how much information to provide but also in how many references to include. It might be felt that there are certain 'obvious' sources that readers will expect the editors to have consulted and which therefore do not need to be cited, such as *The Dictionary of National Biography*, or, now, *The Oxford Dictionary of National Biography*. (To avoid any possible misunderstanding or confusion, not least as to which of these has been used, a list of such sources can be given in the general apparatus.) On the other hand, it is helpful to give references for more recondite information, the source of which might otherwise leave readers puzzled. This is one of the ways in which the editor can share with the reader the research that has gone into the production of the edition, which undoubtedly enhances its value.

As for where the note references are placed, I consider that in printed texts it is best to place them at a natural break in the sense of the text, such as a full-stop or semi-colon, rather than attaching them to the actual name or word annotated. Indeed, often such information is appropriately grouped together at the end of a sentence or paragraph. There are two reasons for this. One is that references in mid-sentence interrupt the reader and distract him or her from understanding the sense of the passage in question. In addition, there is often some commonalty to the people or events referred to in a passage, which makes it appropriate to introduce them all together. However, this recommendation applies primarily to printed texts, and is not applicable to electronic ones. Here, links are activated by clicking on or passing the mouse over hyperlinked words, and it is therefore more appropriate for the annotation to be directly keyed to the name or word to which it refers (indeed, it is actually difficult, and sometimes potentially confusing, to postpone it to a punctuation mark).

With more self-conscious authorial compositions, such as literary or philosophical texts, quite different styles of annotation may be appropriate. In contrast to the full annotation of the above kind that Noel Malcolm provided for Hobbes' correspondence, for instance, Howard Warrender, in editing *De cive* for the Clarendon Hobbes, was much more austere, limiting himself to textual matters, and to parallels with other writings by Hobbes. The edition of *The Works of Robert Boyle* is fairly lightly – if, one hopes, adequately – annotated, the intention being (in the perceptive words of one reviewer of the work) 'to provide the wherewithal to other scholars to investigate as they find best'.[9] With the Oxford Bacon, on the other hand, the complex textual variants that exist are dealt with in an elaborate apparatus which also offers a profuse commentary on Bacon's text, adducing parallel passages in other works, suggesting sources, and the like; indeed, it is so profuse that it is placed at the end of the book rather than on the page, where it might almost swamp the text. A similar profusion is often in evidence in annotations to literary works such as poems, which may be justified by the sheer denseness of the composition in question. A case in point is Nigel Smith's text of 'To His Coy Mistress' in his edition of *The Poems of Andrew Marvell* in the Longman Annotated English Poets, which has only a few lines of text at the top of each page, followed by a mass of learned annotation which not only gives textual variants but also provides a commentary on Marvell's sources and allusions and seeks to survey critical responses to the poem.[10] In this instance the treatment seems legitimate (and it is in fact exceptional even within the edition). But, as so often in matters of this kind, it is a matter of judgement just how far things are taken, since in theory the amount of data that could be included is almost limitless. My personal view – though it is based more on 'informational' texts than creative compositions – is that the notes are best restricted to information necessary to make sense of a text rather than providing a complete commentary on its content, or attempting to interpret it: I believe that this is best left to ancillary studies published separately.

As already noted, with a printed text, a decision has to be made as to whether notes should go at the bottom of the page or at the end of the book, with different decisions being reached on such matters according to publishing constraints and the sheer bulk of the material. In addition, where there are separate series of textual and editorial notes, it has sometimes seemed appropriate to place one series in one of these positions and the other in the other (though the Bacon and Boyle editions take diametrically opposed positions as to which goes where). Needless to say, here, as so often, an electronic edition resolves some of the dilemmas which editors of printed editions face. Whereas in printed texts, invidious choices have to be made as to whether the notes should appear on the page or not, the use of hypertext links means that any such information can be instantly accessed, regardless of its bulk. Yet, as so often, as careful consideration is required in relation to an electronic edition as to a printed one, since the apparatus can otherwise become cumbersome and inappropriate. Indeed, I would argue that the need for concision and relevance – my cardinal rules for appropriate annotation – are here more than ever crucial, because the sheer ease of providing links to embedded information increases the temptation to overannotate. Once again, electronic editions at the same time present great opportunities, but also ancillary dangers.

c. Translations

Another key component of the apparatus comprises translations. In an age when an increasing number of scholars are monolingual, it is desirable for translations to be provided of all texts in languages other than English. Whereas Esmond de Beer in his edition of *The Correspondence of John Locke* took it for granted that educated readers would be able to read French, though not Latin, Greek or Dutch,[11] even that regrettably no longer seems to be the case, and texts in French should be translated as well as those in all other languages than English. The objective of the translation should be to give a lucid, reasonably elegant rendering of the original. An attempt at a pastiche of early modern style should not be attempted, and instead a limpid and unobtrusive version in modern prose should be the goal. On the other hand, as far as vocabulary is concerned, it is desirable for the translator to soak him or herself in the language of the author whose work is being translated, or in other vernacular writings from the period on the topics that the texts in question deal with. A striking illustration of how effective this can be may be given from my own experience when working on Boyle with a highly adept Latin translator, David Money. The final two volumes of *The Works of Boyle* include a number of works by Boyle which, although almost certainly originally written in English, survive only in Latin translations, and we therefore presented the extant Latin with an accompanying English version. In a handful of cases, fragments of the original English text survived, which we were able to insert at the relevant points in the translated version. In one instance, such a fragment came to light only after the passage in question had been translated, and I was delighted to find that the translation almost exactly matched the original.[12]

There are sometimes difficulties with the translation of specialist and technical terms, where it is better to attempt to use contemporary words rather than modern equivalents. Some may be best left in Latin: for instance, as Graham Rees has put it in his commentary on his translation of Bacon's natural philosophical writings, '*nitric acid* may be the same substance as *aqua fortis* but it is a term belonging to a conceptual framework of which Bacon had no inkling'.[13] In other cases, literalism may be in order, and inelegance may have to be preferred to elegance in order to try to keep as close as possible to an author's meaning and to avoid invoking inappropriate modern overtones. On the other hand, this can be taken too far: as Brian Vickers has observed concerning the Oxford Francis Bacon, the result is sometimes to leave the reader reaching for a lengthy dictionary to find words which, though still in current usage, are so rare as to puzzle a reader, as with 'densations' or 'introception'.[14] Similarly, the title of the recently rediscovered 'Abecedarium novum naturæ' is there rendered as 'A New Abecedarium of Nature', when 'A New Alphabet of Nature' would surely have been much clearer for most readers without doing any harm to the sense.[15]

With vernacular languages of the period, some of the same issues arise, in that technical terms are liable to require particular attention. The same is true of such items as proverbs, colloquialisms and formulae, where a literal translation may be less appropriate than an attempt to find an English equivalent. For instance, in French letters one may find the formula, 'Je me vous recommend', which could be literally translated into English as 'I commend myself to you'. However, this arguably sounds rather stilted and it might be better replaced by some such wording as 'I greet you'. There are potentially also problems for the translator in the form of dialects, or of writers who were only partially literate (of course, with Latin, too, there may be problems with writers whose command of the language was less than perfect). In addition, there are issues relating to sentence structure that arise in any language, for instance of deciding to whom pronouns refer. On the other hand, in general fewer problems are presented in giving an appropriate modern rendering of early modern vernacular languages than is the case with Latin.

As for the manner in which the translation is set out, this is another case where in an electronic version a range of options is available, for instance of using hypertext links to allow versions in two languages to be open concurrently and scrolled through in parallel with one another.

For printed editions, there are various possibilities. The least satisfactory, though by no means the least common, is for the translation to follow on after the text in the original language:[16] this makes it extremely difficult for the two versions to be studied in conjunction with one another. It is much better to juxtapose them, most commonly by printing them on facing pages. The only drawback about this is the differential amount of space taken by the same text in different languages, English being notably less succinct than Latin, though this can be compensated for to some extent by the placing of footnotes. A more elegant solution – pioneered by de Beer in the Locke correspondence and since followed by the Boyle editions – is to print the original text and the translation one above the other on the same page. Since the two texts have to open and close on the same pages, if they are distributed in proportion to one another on each of the intervening ones this automatically evens out their length, with only a small number of words having to be moved backwards and forwards in proof to make them exactly match one another. It transpired with the Boyle edition that a typesetter with no Latin could achieve this with only a little final tinkering by a Latinist. The result is a pleasing one, and it has since been replicated in other editions.[17] Indeed, it is a testimony to the value of good book design even in the age of the computer.

9
Indexing/Searching

Indexing is one of the skills that has long been associated with editing. Indeed, in the past, certain editors almost made it their *raison d'être:* Esmond de Beer spent three whole years compiling the index to *The Diary of John Evelyn*, which occupies nearly the whole of volume 6 of his edition of that work, and which illustrates some of the intellectual functions that a full and carefully organised index can serve.[1] In a case like this, it could be argued that de Beer lays out the entire structure of Evelyn's life and milieu, and to a more limited extent other indexers may feel that they have achieved something similar. This therefore raises issues as to how an index may illustrate deep structures in an edited text of the kind which hypertext might aspire to reveal, and we will return to the connection between indexing and electronic media later in this chapter. It also illustrates – contrary to what some might presume – that an index has a role going beyond the functions of a mere word search, though here again the mutual relationship between these phenomena requires elucidation.

Let us start, however, by dealing with some rather more basic points about an index as traditionally conceived, in other words as the final component of a printed book, compiled – usually at speed – when the book is in proof. The most important point to be made is that the needs of the reader are paramount. Unless an index is useful to someone approaching the book looking for the kind of guidance that an index can be expected to offer, it might as well not be there at all. This will obviously have an effect on the topics that are included as index headings, as we will see in a moment, but initially it has a more immediate and basic implication. The expectation of any user of any index is that it is reliable in the sense that it is complete – that every instance of a name or place that appears in the book is indexed. This is crucial in that, if it turns out that instances have been missed, confidence in the index will collapse, and it might as well not have been made in the first place. Hence completeness is paramount, and accuracy hardly less so: an incorrect key stroke that alters a page number means that the correct reference is lost for ever.

A basic index would simply be a complete list of all references to each person, place or topic mentioned in a book. But obviously such an index would be a very crude tool, since this could result in a list of hundreds or even thousands of undifferentiated entries, as would be the case if, for instance, all reference to 'Evelyn, John' in the de Beer edition were brought together with no subdivision. Hence, indexing almost invariably involves subdivision in pursuit of more manageable and helpful units. At just what point subdivision is required to avoid 'that bane of indexes – the unbroken run of numerals', in the words of another indexer to a seventeenth-century diary, Robert Latham, is to some extent a matter of opinion.[2] This may depend on the size of the work, since a run of twenty such instances may be more acceptable in a large index than in a small one. But there has to be a cutting-off point, and it is doubtful if it can be very much higher than twenty and may often be lower.

How, then, should entries be subdivided? Here again, we return to the criterion of the convenience of the reader, in conjunction with the constraints of the subject-matter of the book. The subdivisions should be clear, meaningful and useable, while, ideally, they should also not be excessively numerous. There are various methods of deciding what the most appropriate subdivisions should be. For a topic which has some twenty or thirty entries, it may be easiest simply to sort them manually when the index is in draft, choosing a set of sub-headings that neatly divide the references up into meaningful groups. However, for larger groups, it may be desirable to decide on a structure before indexing commences, perhaps by reading the entire text with this in mind and devising a structure on that basis, according to which entries are sub-classified as they are made. This is particularly the case with the figure who is at the heart of an entire edition, as with the diary of Evelyn, or the correspondence of Boyle. It must have been by such means that de Beer came up with his elaborate structure for the entry on Evelyn in his index, and this was certainly how the index to the Boyle correspondence was organised. The alternative is to add a kind of sub-heading to each entry as it is recorded, in the form 'Boyle, and great plague', or 'Boyle, theft of his writings'. This approach was adopted in indexing *The Works of Robert Boyle*, but, as that index illustrates, this tends to produce an excessive number of one-off entries, hence reducing – though not negating – its advantages over an unsorted set of entries, unless a further stage of editorial interference occurs in which cognate entries are brought together (as was to some extent implemented in that edition at the editorial stage).

In the case where a single figure is at the heart of a work (which is quite common in connection with editions, which are frequently focused on one person, be it the writer of the diary or the author of a collected works), there is something to be said for defining topics 'away' from the central figure where possible. For instance this would lead to entries like 'Oxford, Boyle at', or 'Avery, William, and Boyle's *General History of Air*', with references being placed under the heading in question rather than under Boyle. This could be combined with a cross-reference in the Boyle entry indicating that this has been done, and a further general point that is worth making is that cross-references are a useful tool for combining economy and clarity with comprehensiveness. Indeed, it is generally better for an index to have too many than too few cross-references.

In fact, as most scholars who have made an index will be aware, many entries can be indexed in a number of different ways, between which a choice has to be made, in which the needs of the user should again be paramount. Almost by definition, not everything can be indexed under every conceivable heading to which it might be relevant (in fact, indexes which attempt to do this can be slightly irritating to use, leading the reader back over and over again to the same references by different routes). Though cross-referencing can go some way towards providing the best of both worlds, there is an element of arbitrariness in the process, an attempt to second guess the needs of potential users which may or may not be successful in all cases. Hence all sorts of decisions will have to be made as to the heading under which index entries are most effectively placed, in which judgement is required as in all other facets of the editorial task.

The above remarks apply particularly to index entries relating to individuals and places. Subject entries present further problems, largely because of the disparity between modern and early modern terminology, and here the editor needs to be more alert than ever to the need to balance the content of the text against the needs of the reader, though again cross-referencing can be used to maximise the extent to which users find entries even if they do not encounter them in the place where they first expected them. Thus an entry on 'engineering' might bring together all references to bridges, canals, drainage, paving and water-supply, while one on 'horticulture' might link grafting, nurseries, orchards, roses and vines. Alternatively, if this led to too bulky an entry, parts of it could be freestanding, but with cross-references to and from the main heading. Either way, the editor will have to do some intellectual work in terms of 'translating' concepts into terms under which his or her modern reader would expect to search for them. In addition, the editor will have to decide whether some subjects or concepts are too general or vague to be worth indexing at all, in that it is unlikely that any user will ever want a list of instances where they occur, for instance generalised references to 'God' in a work which is not a theological treatise. Again, judgement will be required on such matters.

Of course, as throughout this book, this is another area where electronic media offer novel tools which need to be assessed alongside more traditional methods, partly because of the extent to which they can be deployed in making the traditional tasks of indexing easier, and partly because they offer new possibilities in accessing and organising data which may even make some of the functions of a traditional index superfluous. One can almost visualise Dr de Beer going about his indexing task, equipped with thousands of slips of paper which had to be filled out and then sorted by hand, the whole series being stored in a succession of shoe boxes prior to being collated, edited and typed out as copy for the typesetter who produced the final text of the index. Even scholars not particularly geared to the use of electronic media will have discovered that these can be used to short-circuit some of these processes. Thus, even if the text to be indexed is in hard copy and is manually indexed by transcribing all the entries to be indexed from the pages on the book on which they appear, the file created can be an electronic one which can be automatically sorted through the use of appropriate software.

Matters are transformed when the text to be indexed is itself in electronic form. Though it is perhaps worth noting here that my experience of existing proprietary indexing packages is that they are prone to be over-elaborate and disappointing, geared to the indexing of much briefer documents than a monograph, let alone a multi-volume edition, the more basic uses of electronic technology are manifold. The great advantage of texts in electronic form is that they can be systematically searched, either for words, parts of words, or groups of words. To start with, it is axiomatic that searching such a text reduces the chance of accidentally missing an entry which so easily occurs with a manual search. In addition, searches can be made for combinations of words, which is usually done by a 'Boolean' search, using the logical operators 'AND', 'OR' or 'NOT' in conjunction with the words in question. As any user of search engines on the Internet will be aware, it is possible to use such searches to limit the correlations that are retrieved to significant rather than insignificant ones. Hence, such a search could be used to replicate some of the sub-categories that might appear within an individual entry in a traditional index. More significantly, work can actually be done in the course of designing and executing an edition or database to assist the user in searching. Indeed, whereas (as already noted) in print editions the indexing process typically occurs right at the end of the production process, when the book is in proof, with electronic editions it is desirable to consider what indexing facilities will be needed at the start of the project. The amount of support for indexing that is included in the encoding scheme and the consistency with which it is applied can make a significant difference both to the quality of the index and ease with which it may be generated.

One possibility would be to encode all proper names, which would prevent a search for the natural philosopher, Boyle, producing a string of references to boiling water. In addition, means can be found to deal with another potential problem which can mislead the wary in relation to the early modern period, namely the variety of spellings used, even of the surname of a single individual. Hence, in the case of 'Boyle', the aim would be to include such spellings as 'Boyl', 'Boil', possibly even – in the case of his contact, the Stratford physician, John Ward – 'Boghil', evidently an eccentric back-formation from the title of Boyle's illustrious sibling, Lord Broghill.[3] In a traditional index, these spelling variants would be 'read through' almost instinctively (though the overall index entry might read 'Boyle (Boghil, Boil, Boyl), Robert', as a means of indicating the entries that it juxtaposed), whereas encoding could be used to identify and link together all spellings of a word, perhaps by providing search strings which bring up alternative spellings. (The alternative to this would be to allow the user to include in the search terms a wildcard (i.e., a string of characters with an asterisk at the end, which brings up all variants on the stem), but this is unsatisfactory as it depends on users knowing what variants are likely.) In addition, just as an alert indexer using manual methods will pick up a reference to an individual even if they are not specified by name, tagging could be extended to include all such instances in an electronic edition.

Another area where the old and new technology can work together is in connection with the kind of massive entry which is normally subdivided in a printed index, since, as has already been noted, such undifferentiated lists are the bane of indexers and are normally subdivided. Though such subdivision may add to the overall clarity and usability of the index, it by definition entails the deconstruction of the overall list from which it originated, to which readers are therefore denied access. Since there may be a minority of readers who actually want to work their way through an undifferentiated list and whose needs are not served by the subdivided one, in an electronic version – where space is not at the same premium as is the case with a printed book – it would be perfectly easy to allow readers access both to a complete list of entries and to a sorted one at the same time. By the same token, it would also be possible to provide further, optional subdivisions which went beyond the initial level of sorting that was presented to the reader, if this seemed appropriate.

An electronic index could also provide a solution for a vexing problem in a traditional index, namely how to deal with conjectural as against definite identifications. To take an example from *The Correspondence of Robert Boyle*, where a footnote sought to identify a chemist at the Bourdelot academy as possibly Monsieur Lizardiere:[4] here, a traditional index is hard put to register the element of uncertainty recorded in the relevant footnote, but it would be quite feasible in an electronic index systematically to differentiate conjectural identifications from actual ones in the manner in which they were denoted (e.g., by some form of highlighting).

What needs to be clarified in the relationship between electronic tools and more established techniques is that word searches, even of quite a sophisticated kind, have not superseded traditional indexing. Of course, after users have scrutinised the index for information relevant to their inquiry, they can then carry out further searches of their own on an electronic text to check that further, ancillary information is not lurking there, although not indexed under the heading in question. On the other hand, it could be argued that the traditional equivalent to the word search was less the index than the concordance, as prepared for the Bible and for major literary texts, which listed words in an undifferentiated way. For concepts, personal names, placenames and the like, the word search is a rather crude tool, since, unless the searcher has a very specific quarry in mind, there is a danger of his or her being overwhelmed by the amount of data that comes to light by such means. Here, an index of a more traditional kind can be invaluable not only in bringing together material that a word search would miss, but also in helping to process and structure entries along the lines already indicated in this chapter, typically subdividing what would otherwise be an almost unmanageable mass of data which the user would otherwise have to sort from scratch for him or herself.

On the other hand, word searching is only the most basic of the kind of searching that electronic media are capable of, particularly where hypertext is involved, and the potential of the use of digitisation to explore the structure of a text more fully – in a manner analogous to the methods employed in an index like de Beer's to Evelyn's *Diary* – are only just beginning to be explored. For this point of view, some pioneering work was done by the Hartlib Papers Project in connection with the original version of the Hartlib Papers in seeking a search mechanism which allowed each individual user to create his or her own 'topic' for searching in the archive, in addition to providing built-in topics like traditional subject entries, which linked together related concepts into groups likely to interest a researcher: for instance, 'agriculture' brought together all references not only to what might be described as 'husbandry' in an early modern context, but also to such topics as 'crops', 'fodder', 'fruit', 'land use', 'livestock' and 'vegetables', while 'church government' brought up 'Calvinism', 'consistory', 'Independency', 'Presbyterianism' and 'toleration'.[5] In the second edition, this system (which was admittedly little used) was abandoned, but there has more recently been much activity in related areas which goes far beyond what was attempted in the Hartlib case. This has particularly focused around the so-called 'semantic web', as pioneered by Tim Berners-Lee and others, which aims to encode data so that computers can not only display data but also understand and manipulate it – giving them 'access to structured collections of information and sets of inference rules that they can use to conduct automated reasoning'.[6] This will involve encoding data using the RDF (Resource Description Framework) and thesauri; the idea is that each concept will be allocated a URI (Uniform Resource Identifier), which will identify its properties and on the basis of which it can then be systematically linked, structured and analysed.

As yet, these development have made little impact on academic electronic editions, and some have expressed reservations as to whether they will be viable, due to doubts as to whether they are worth the huge amount of effort that would be involved in producing the formalised definitions and specifications that would be needed. However far these particular developments go, on the other hand, there seems little doubt that there is great potential here, and that electronic media will not only provide sophisticated analytical tools which have as yet only been dreamt of, but do so in user-friendly packages which will require no special expertise on the part of their users: indeed, it is possible that analysis of the semantic content of a document will routinely be able to provide at least parts of an index automatically. As so often in this book, it is safe to predict that advances in electronic technology will provide all sorts of fresh opportunities which should lead to a fruitful interchange of traditional and new skills.

Appendix 1: Alternative Methods of Transcribing a Seventeenth-century Manuscript

As a commentary on the discussion of how best to transcribe manuscripts in Chapter 6, this appendix juxtaposes various ways in which a manuscript can be presented in print in terms both of denoting deleted and added matter, and of reproducing contractions and abbreviations in the original. For this purpose, a single short text has been taken, which is reproduced here (Plate 1) and which has been subjected to five contrasting editorial treatments. This is a page from one of the notebooks kept by Robert Boyle in his later years, into which he dictated to amanuenses drafts for sections of his works. The passage in question, Royal Society MS 186, fol. 105v, is in the hand of Hugh Greg; it comprises a self-contained draft which was intended as a prefatory note to the second volume of Boyle's *Experimenta et Observationes Physicæ*, which was never published. Volume 1 of the work came out in 1691, but it had been planned for much longer, since its preamble takes the form of a letter to Henry Oldenburg, who died in 1677 (see Hunter and Davis, *Works of Boyle*, vol. 11, pp. 367ff.). The note states Boyle's intention to publish as part of vol. 2 of the work certain of the medical recipes that he had long accumulated, a collection of which did in fact see the light of day, first in a privately printed edition of 1688 entitled *Some Receipts of Medicines. For the most part Parable and Simple. Sent to a Friend in America*, and secondly in Boyle's *Medicinal Experiments* (1692–4 and subsequent editions). For an account of Boyle's various stratagems concerning this material, see Hunter, 'The Reluctant Philanthropist'.

The options available for transcribing such a document are as follows. One is to print the text inclusive of all insertions and deletions, indicating these by the use of brackets, or by showing deleted words with a line through them; editors who choose such a method also frequently try to replicate the contractions and abbreviations in the original to a greater or lesser extent (samples 1–3). Alternatively, it is possible to print a text in which contractions and abbreviations are expanded and the deleted material is removed from the text, being recorded either by a commentary keyed to the text by line, with the text itself left clear, or by the inclusion of note references at the places in the text at which the deletions occur. Additions may either be recorded in the separate commentary or be marked by brackets (samples 4–5). Here, the following methods of transcription have been deployed, each based on an extant edition (in each case, a key is provided to the symbols used):

(1) an attempted replication in an early modern context of the method used in CEAA/CSE editions of nineteenth-century American texts;
(2) a method of transcription similar to that used by McGuire and Tamny in their edition of Newton's *Certain Philosophical Questions*, with an accompanying modernised version;
(3) a replication of the method used by Noel Malcolm in *The Correspondence of Thomas Hobbes* and *John Pell and his Correspondence with Sir Charles Cavendish*;
(4) a clear text method, with the lines numbered for ease of reference to the accompanying notes, which refer to the text by line, as used (for instance) by Frederick Burkhardt et al. in their edition of *The Correspondence of Charles Darwin*;[1]
(5) a system similar to that used in Hunter, *Robert Boyle by Himself and his Friends*, and in Hunter et al., *Correspondence* and *Works* of Boyle.

Appendix 1   111

Sample 1: an attempted replication in an early modern context of the method used in CEAA/CSE editions of nineteenth-century American texts

[In margin: T[ranscri]b[e]d]

Being ⸤by philanthropy made⸥ unwilling y^t a considerable number of <Receipts & processes> <⸤Re?⸥ > Receipts & processes, y^t were either freely given me or procur'd by me from <profess'd Physicians, or other persons> ⸤divers Experienc'd Persons⸥ many if not most of them <known> Physicians or surgeons should be lost to the publick, I ⸤once⸥ thought fit to compyle them into one Body for which I <propounded> ⸤drew up⸥ a large preface ⸤to⸥ show y^t ⸤notwithstanding ⸤some⸥ objections which ⸤therein⸥ were answer'd ⸥such collections were <very> ⸤both⸥ allowable, & might be very use- | full. <Want?> But want of leisure oblidging me to lay asyde y^t worke ⸤at present ⸥, <& reserve it for a <freer> ⸤more⸥ seasonable tyme,> The opportunity y^t is presented me by ye publication of ye 2^d Tome of the *Experimenta & Observationes Physicæ* invites me to adde to the <other> Chapter of other Communicated Observations two or three <Decads> ⸤Chapters⸥ of Receipts & Processes ⸤relating to⸥ Medicin<all> ⸤e⸥ which may not only serve as a specimen of those contain'd in the <greater> ⸤larger⸥ collection, <&> ⸤but⸥ perhaps <be> ⸤may⸥ some of them ⸤be⸥ found <of notable> considerable <enough ⸤use⸥> enough to be usefull on y^{eir} own account.

[Endorsed in margin: 'h']

Key:
⸤⸥ Inserted < > Deleted | Hyphenated form at line-break.[2]

112 *Editing Early Modern Texts*

Sample 2: a method of transcription similar to that used by McGuire and Tamny in their edition of Newton's *Certain Philosophical Questions*, with an accompanying modernised version

[In margin: T[ranscri]b[e]d]

‖ Being by ⌞philanthropy made⌟ unwilling y^t a considerable number of ~~Receipts & processes~~ ⌞Re?⌟ Receipts & processes, y^t were either freely given me or procur'd by me from ~~profess'd Physicians, or other persons~~ ⌞divers Experienc'd Persons⌟ many if not most of them ~~known~~ Physitians or surgeons should be lost to the publick, I ⌞once⌟ thought fit to compyle them into one Body for which I ~~propounded~~ ⌞drew up⌟ a large preface ⌞to⌟ show y^t ⌞notwithstanding⌟ ⌞some⌟ objections which ⌞therein⌟ were answer'd⌟ such collections were ~~very~~ ⌞both⌟ allowable, & might be very usefull. ~~Want~~ (?) But want of leisure obligding me to lay asyde y^t worke ⌞at present⌟, ~~& reserve it for a freer⌟ ⌞more⌟ seasonable tyme~~, The opportunity y^t is presented me by ye publication of ye 2^d Tome of the *Experimenta & Observationes Physicæ* invites me to adde to the ~~other~~ Chapter of other Communicated Observations two or three ~~Decads~~ ⌞Chapters⌟ of Receipts & Processes ⌞relating to⌟ Medicinall ⌞e⌟ which may not only serve as a specimen of those contain'd in the ~~greater~~ ⌞larger⌟ collection, & ⌞but⌟ perhaps ~~be~~ ⌞may⌟ some of them ⌞be⌟ found considerable ~~enough of notable use~~ enough to be usefull on y^{eir} own account.

[Endorsed in margin: 'h']

Key:
⌞ ⌟ Inserted. —— Deleted. ‖ Lengthy passage deleted by author.

Modernised text

Being by philanthropy made unwilling that a considerable number of recipes and processes that were either freely given me, or procured by me from divers experienced persons, many if not most of them physicians or surgeons, should be lost to the public, I once thought fit to compile them into one body, for which I drew up a large preface to show that, notwithstanding some objections which therein were answered, such collections were both allowable and might be very useful. But want of leisure obliging me to lay aside that work at present, the opportunity that is presented me by the publication of the second tome of the *Experimenta et observationes physicae* [*Physical experiments and observations*] invites me to add to the chapter of other communicated observations two or three chapters of recipes and processes relating to medicine, which may not only serve as a specimen of those contained in the larger collection, but perhaps may some of them be found considerable enough to be useful on their own account.

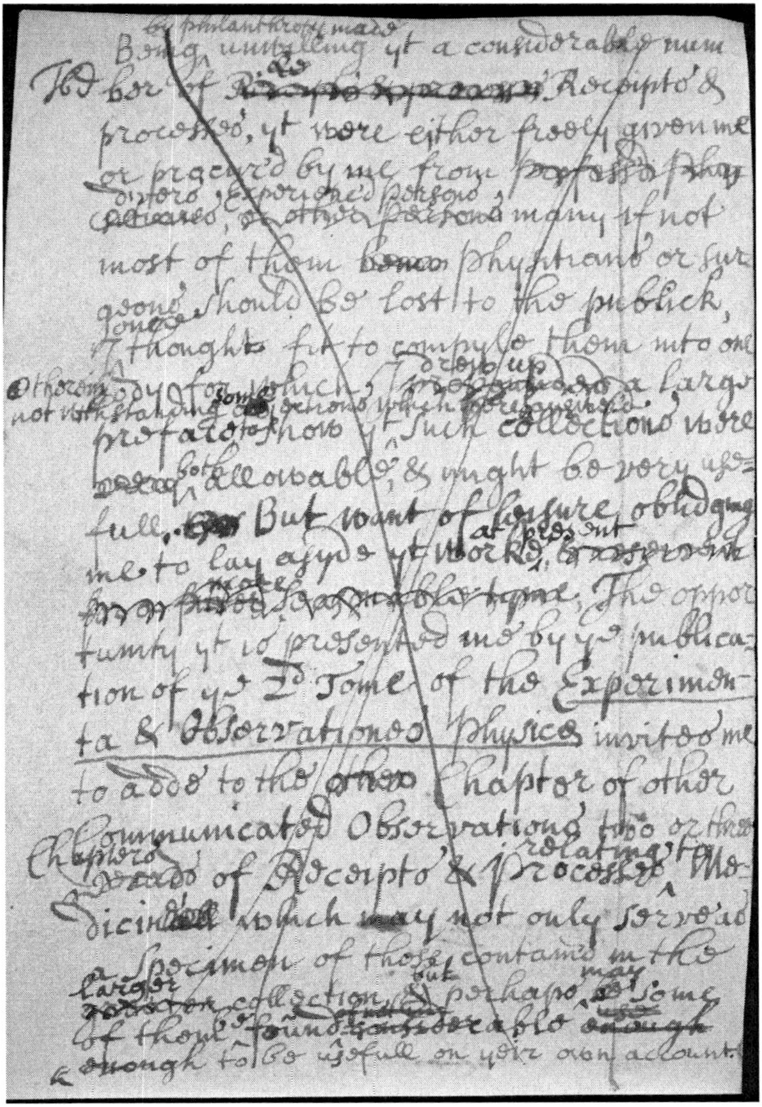

Plate 1: Royal Society MS 186, fol. 105v (dimensions of original: 155 mm × 100 mm)

114 Editing Early Modern Texts

Sample 3: a replication of the method used by Noel Malcolm in *The Correspondence of Thomas Hobbes* and *John Pell and his Correspondence with Sir Charles Cavendish*

[In margin: T[ranscri]b[e]d]

Being [>by philanthropy made] unwilling y^t a considerable number of [Receipts & processes *deleted* >Re? *deleted*] Receipts & processes, y^t were either freely given me or procur'd by me from [profess'd Physicians, or other persons *deleted* >divers Experienc'd Persons] many if not most of them [known *deleted*] Physitians or surgeons should be lost to the publick, I [>once] thought fit to compyle them into one Body for which I [propounded *deleted* >drew up] a large preface [>to] show y^t [>notwithstanding >some objections which >therein were answer'd] such collections were [very *deleted* >both] allowable, & might be very usefull. [Want? *deleted*] But want of leisure oblidging me to lay asyde y^t worke [>at present], [& reserve it for a [freer *deleted* >more] seasonable tyme, *deleted*] The opportunity y^t is presented me by ye publication of ye 2^d Tome of the *Experimenta & Observationes Physicae* invites me to adde to the [other *deleted*] Chapter of other Communicated Observations two or three [Decads *deleted* >Chapters] of Receipts & Processes [>relating to] Medicin[all *deleted* >e] which may not only serve as a specimen of those contain'd in the [greater *deleted* >larger] collection, [& *deleted* >but] perhaps [be *deleted* >may] some of them [>be] found considerable [enough *deleted*] [>of notable use *deleted*] enough to be usefull on y^{eir} own account.

[Endorsed in margin: 'h']

Key:
Deleted words shown in square brackets followed by *deleted*; insertions shown in square brackets preceded by >.

Sample 4: a clear text method, with the lines numbered for ease of reference to the accompanying notes, which refer to the text by line, as used (for instance) by Frederick Burkhardt et al. in their edition of *The Correspondence of Charles Darwin*.

1   Being by philanthropy made unwilling that a considerable number of
2   Receipts & processes, that were either freely given me or procur'd by me
3   from divers Experienc'd Persons many if not most of them Physitians
4   or surgeons should be lost to the publick, I once thought fit to compyle
5   them into one Body for which I drew up a large preface to show that
6   notwithstanding some objections which therein were answer'd such
7   collections were both allowable, & might be very usefull. But want of
8   leisure obligding me to lay asyde that worke at present, The opportunity
9   that is presented me by the publication of the 2nd Tome of the
10 *Experimenta & Observationes Physicæ* invites me to adde to the Chapter of
11 other Communicated Observations two or three Chapters of Receipts &
12 Processes relating to Medicine which may not only serve as a specimen
13 of those contain'd in the larger collection, but perhaps may some of
14 them be found considerable enough to be usefull on their own account.

Notes
Endorsed in lefthand margin opposite second line of text, *T[ranscri]b[e]d*, and the whole crossed through with two intersecting diagonal lines in ink. In addition, a pencil line runs from top to bottom of the page approximately 10 mm from the righthand edge. Marked *h* in the lower lefthand margin below the last line of text.
In lower margin, below the last line of the text, is the mark *h*.
l.1: *by philanthropy made* inserted; *of* followed by *Receipts & processes* deleted, above which is an indeterminate, deleted insertion: *Re?*
l.3: *divers Experienc'd Persons* inserted, replacing *profess'd Physicians, or other Persons* deleted; *them* followed by *known* deleted.
l.4: *once* inserted.
l.5: *drew up* inserted, replacing *propounded* deleted; *to* inserted.
l.6: *notwithstanding some objections which therein were answer'd* inserted, with *some* inserted within it, and with *therein* inserted in the margin, with a mark keying it to the text, where the equivalent mark overlaps with *were*.
l.7: *both* inserted, replacing *very* deleted; *use-* | *full* hyphenated at line-end; followed by *Want* [?] deleted.

Continued on p. 116

l.8: *at present* inserted, followed by & *reserve it for a more* [inserted, replacing *freer*] *seasonable tyme,* deleted.
l.10: *to the* followed by *other* deleted.
l.11: *Chapters* inserted, replacing *Decads* deleted.
l.12: *relating to* inserted; *Medicine* altered from *Medicinall*.
l.13: *larger* inserted, replacing *greater* deleted; *but* inserted, replacing & deleted; *may* inserted, replacing *be* deleted.
l.14: *be* inserted; *considerable* partially deleted and replaced by *of notable use*, but reinstated; followed by *enough* deleted, and then *enough* partially deleted, which has been retained for the sense. An alternative reading of this passage would be *perhaps may some of them be found able to be usefull* (with the *able* of *considerable* retained and the second *enough* deleted).

Sample 5: a system similar to that used in Hunter, *Robert Boyle by Himself and his Friends,* and in Hunter et al., *Correspondence* and *Works* of Boyle.

[1]Being ‹by philanthropy made› unwilling that a considerable number of[2] Receipts & processes, that were either freely given me or procur'd by me from ‹divers Experienc'd Persons›,[3] many if not most of them[4] Physicians or surgeons should be lost to the publick, I ‹once› thought fit to compyle them into one Body for which I ‹drew up›,[5] a large preface ‹to› show that ‹notwithstanding ‹some› objections which ‹therein›[6] were answer'd› such collections were ‹both›,[7] allowable, & might be very usefull.[8] But want of leisure oblidging me to lay asyde that worke ‹at present›,[9] The opportunity that is presented me by the publication of the 2nd Tome of the *Experimenta & Observationes Physicæ* invites me to adde to the[10] Chapter of other Communicated Observations two or three ‹Chapters›[11] of Receipts & Processes ‹relating to› Medicine[12] which may not only serve as a specimen of those contain'd in the ‹larger›[13] collection, ‹but› perhaps ‹may› some of them ‹be› found considerable[14] enough to be usefull on their own account.

Key:
‹ › Inserted

[1] Endorsed in lefthand margin *T[ranscri]b[e]d*, and the whole crossed through with two intersecting, diagonal lines in ink. In addition, a pencil line runs from top to bottom of the page approximately 10 mm from the righthand edge. Marked *h* in the lower lefthand margin below the last line of text.
[2] Followed by *Receipts & processes* deleted, above which is an indeterminate, deleted insertion: *Re* [?].
[3] Replacing *profess'd Physicians, or other persons* deleted.
[4] Followed by *known* deleted.
[5] Replacing *propounded* deleted.
[6] Inserted in margin, with mark keying to text, where the equivalent mark overlaps with *were*.
[7] Replacing *very* deleted.
[8] Hyphenated *use-* | *full* at line end. Followed by *Want* [?] deleted.
[9] Followed by *& reserve it for a* ‹*more*› [replacing *freer*] *seasonable tyme*, deleted.
[10] Followed by *other* deleted.
[11] Replacing *Decads* deleted.
[12] Altered from *Medicinall*.
[13] Replacing *greater* deleted. Two words later, *but* replaces *&* deleted, and two words after that, *may* replaces *be* deleted.
[14] Partially deleted and replaced by *of notable use*, but reinstated; followed by *enough* deleted. In addition, the second *enough* is partially deleted, but has been retained for the sense. An alternative reading of this passage would be *perhaps* ‹*may*› *some of them* ‹*be*› *found able to be usefull* (with the *able* of *considerable* retained and the second *enough* deleted).

Appendix 2: A Confusion of Brackets

As a corollary to the previous appendix, it is perhaps worth drawing attention to the diversity of existing editorial practice by juxtaposing the way in which brackets and symbols have been used in various textual editions. Figure 2 illustrates such usages, which takes as representative examples:

(1) The critical symbols which are standard in modern classical editing, as outlined in West, *Textual Criticism and Editorial Technique*, pp. 80–2, and Maas, *Textual Criticism*, p. 22.
(2) The sigla used by W.W. Greg in the Malone Society reprints and in his *Companion to Arber*, pp. vi–vii.
(3) The conventions used in the editions of the *Works* and *Correspondence of Robert Boyle*, for which I have been responsible.
(4) The symbols used in J.C. Higgins-Biddle's transcriptions from manuscripts in his edition of Locke's *Reasonableness of Christianity*: these are expounded on pp. xiii–xiv and 181.
(5) A further example of an edition of early modern texts, in this case Sylvia Brown's *Women's Writing in Stuart England*, where the editorial conventions are laid out on pp. xi–xii.
(6) The symbols used in the edition by W.H. Gilman and others of Emerson's *Journals* (see vol. 1, pp. xlix–l). For other editions using comparable conventions, see Kline, *Guide to Documentary Editing* (pp. 134–8 in the first edition, reprinted virtually unchanged in the second edition on pp. 148–52).

As will be seen, brackets have been deployed editorially in such a range of mutually contradictory ways that one might despair of any *lingua franca* ever being established. Indeed, this is almost exemplary of the kind of practical problems of editing to which this book is addressed, and at the very least it might be hoped that further proliferation of differing usages could have been avoided, though even this seems unlikely. In the case of angle brackets, for instance, the edition of *The Papers of Benjamin Franklin* has since volume 28 taken to using these to denote 'a resumé of a letter or document', thus adding yet another meaning to the tally noted here.[1] As observed in Chapter 6, in this case matters are further complicated by the widespread use of such brackets for purposes of encoding in SGML.

As for square brackets, as will be seen these have been used for almost diametrically opposite purposes – to indicate deletions in the original; to denote text lost through mutilation; or to denote editorial supply. For early modern texts matters are additionally complicated by the usage of such brackets by the authors themselves, which might suggest that some other notation should be used for editorial supply. On the other hand, since square brackets are widely used to indicate editorial intrusion in other scholarly contexts, my sense is that they should remain the principal signal of editorial interference for early modern texts: any alternative is less conventional and hence more likely to puzzle the reader. Yet this leaves the problem of how to differentiate authorial square brackets from editorial ones. In a nineteenth-century context, a method that has been used in the edition of the letters of Mark Twain is to denote authorial usage by a distinctive form of square bracket with 'handles' attached.[2] This option was considered in the Boyle editions, but in the end we decided it was simpler explicitly to identify authorial square brackets as such in footnotes where they occurred, since the occasions on which they are used are relatively rare, and readers might find an alternative form of notation confusing.

Hence, individual editors will have to make their own decisions on such matters, but they should do so in the light of full knowledge both of what is standard and what is possible. On the other hand, here as elsewhere, digitisation may be able to transcend traditional printed forms, in that editorial intervention can be indicated by other means, for instance by highlighting (this is perhaps foreshadowed by Higgins-Biddle's use of shading for authorial insertions). On the other hand, there is not much sign of a standard practice emerging in digitised texts, either, and the kind of divergence noted here looks almost ineradicable.

Figure 2: Contrasting editorial uses of brackets and other symbols

	1. Classical editing (from West, *Textual Criticism*, and Maas, *Textual Criticism*)	2. Greg, *Companion to Arber*, and Malone Society reprints	3. *Works and Correspondence* of Boyle	4. Higgins-Biddle, Locke's *Reasonableness*	5. Brown, *Women's Writing in Stuart England*	6. Emerson, *Journals* and other editions of 19th-century US texts
( )	Expansion of abbreviation	Authorial	Authorial	Authorial	Authorial	Authorial
< >	Conjectural addition	Mutilation in MS	[In form of arrowhead, ‹ ›] Authorial insertion	Editorial restoration of accidentally missing letter(s)		Deletion
[ ]	Supplement where text lost through damage	Deleted passage	Editorial insertion, unless identified as authorial	Prior level of manuscript deletion within deleted passage, which shown by strikethrough	Editorial insertion	Editorial insertion
[[ ]]	Scribal deletion			Deletion effected by superimposition of correction that follows		
{ }	Editorial deletion			Editorial deletion of letter(s) written in error	Material in margin	
ˆ	Scribal insertion	Interlineated words or passages		Second level of added material	Authorial insertion	
⌐ ¬ or ⌞ ⌟	Supplement to text from further copy					
…	[Under word] Uncertainly deciphered	Illegible or (with <) reading uncertain	Illegible or damaged material	[Under word] illegible or conjectured character		Unrecoverable matter, accompanied by ‖
*		Query	Authorial footnote			Authorial footnote
†	Irremediable corruption	Reading clear but apparently erroneous	Authorial footnote			
/		Virgule	Page or line break			Variant
Shading				Authorial insertion		
‹					Authorial insertion [used with half brackets	Insertion with author's symbol [as against insertion without, which denoted by ‹ ›]

Appendix 3: Separate and Combined Versions of a Revised Text – the 1597, 1612 and 1625 Versions of Francis Bacon's Essay 'Of Regiment of Health'

This sample is intended to show the potential of an electronic edition, not only to give various versions of a text that was revised by its author, but also to indicate at a glance in composite form exactly what was added or removed in each. Editors of Bacon's *Essays* have attempted to indicate the mutual relationship of their different versions in various ways. Michael Kiernan, like many modern editors, indicates these differences in footnotes (on pp. 100–2 of his book in the case of the essay reproduced here), but, as noted in Chapter 5, this is often extremely difficult to follow; it is even harder to utilise this to visualise a version of the text other than the final one.[1] A number of editors have printed the (admittedly very brief) 1597 version verbatim, from W.A. Wright in 1862 to Brian Vickers in 1999 (he also provides selections only from the 1612 edition).[2] An alternative, adopted by Edward Arber in 1871, was to set out the different versions in parallel columns, and this is replicated for three essays by John Pitcher in his 1985 edition.[3]

In an electronic edition, each of these versions could be separately available, but hypertext could be used to link them together and thus illustrate at a glance just what was added (or removed) and when. However, matters are complicated by the fact that, apart from substantive additions and deletions, there are also significant differences in accidentals between the different versions. Here, the composite text is that of 1625 with the main additions and deletions in each previous version marked on it: but readers may like to compare the separate 1597 and 1612 versions of the text with this, since both differ significantly in their accidentals from that of 1625, even though it seemed artificial to try to incorporate these differences into the composite text. Note that, though I have expanded two contractions marked by tildes in the 1597 text (and have followed my normal practice, in the case of words broken at the page break, of leaving the word entire and placing the page break after it), I have left 'u's serving as consonants and 'v's as vowels as in the original in the 1597 and 1612 versions so that readers can form their own opinion as to the desirability of regularising these (see above, pp. 65, 77–8).

(1) The text in *Essayes* (London: for Humfrey Hooper, 1597, fols. 8v–9: in l. 12 of this text, 'when' has been expanded from 'whē', and in l. 20, 'condition' from 'cōdition', the contraction in both cases clearly being dictated by the need to fit a line)

Of Regiment of health

There is a wisdome in this beyond the rules of Phisicke. A mans owne obseruation what he finds good of, and what he findes hurt of, is the best Physicke to preserue health. But it is a safer conclusion to say, This agreeth well with me, therefore I will continue it, then this I finde no offence, of this therefore I may vse it. For strength of nature in youth passeth ouer many excesses, which are owing a man till his age. ¶ Discerne of the comming on of yeares, and thinke not to doe the same things still. ¶ Beware of any suddain change in any great /9/ point of diet, and if necessitie inforce it, fit the rest to it. ¶ To be free minded, and chearefully disposed at howers of meate, and of sleepe, and of exercise, is the best precept of long lasting. ¶ If you flie Physicke in health altogether, it will be too strange to your body, when you shall neede it, if you make it too familiar, it will worke no extraordinarie effect when sicknesse commeth. ¶ Despise no new accident in the body, but aske opinion of it. ¶ In sickenesse respect health principally, and in health action. For those that put their bodies to indure in health, may in most sickenesses which are not very sharpe, be cured onelye with diet and tendring. ¶ Physitians are some of them so pleasing and conformable to the humours of the patient, as they presse not the true cure of the disease; and some other are so regular in proceeding according to Arte for the disease, as they respect not sufficiently the condition of the patient. Take one of a middle temper, or if it may not bee found in one man, compounded two of both sorts, & forget not to cal as wel the best aquainted with your body, as the best reputed of for his facultie.

(2) The text in *The Essaies of Sir Francis Bacon Knight* (London: John Beale, 1612, pp. 103–8)

17. Of Regiment of health.

There is a wisdome in this, beyond the rules of *Physicke*. A mans owne obseruation, what he findes good of, and what hee findes hurt of, is the best *Physicke* to preseue health. But it is a safer conclusion to say; this agreeth not well with mee, therefore I will not continue it; then /104/ this, I finde no offence of this, therefore I may vse it: for strength of nature in youth, passeth ouer many excesses, which are owing a man till his age. Discerne of the comming on of yeeres: and thinke not to doe the same things still. Certainly most lusty old men catch their death by that aduenture; For age will not be defied. Beware of sudden change in any great point of diet, and if necessitie enforce it, fit the rest to it. For it /105/ is a secret both in nature and state, that it is safer to change many things then one. To bee free minded and cherefullie disposed at houres of meat, and of sleep, and of exercise, is the best precept of long lasting. If you fly Phisicke in health altogether, it will bee too strange for your body, when you shall need it: if you make it too familiar, it will worke no extraordinarie effect, when sicknesse commeth. Despise no new accident in your /106/ body, but aske opinion of it. In sicknesse respect health principally, and in health action. For those that put their bodies to endure in health, may in most sicknesses, which are not very sharpe, be cured onely with diet and tendering. *Celsus* could neuer have spoken it as a Physitian had he not been a wise man withall: when he giueth it for one of the great precepts of health and lasting. That a man doe varie and interchange contraries, but with an /107/ inclination to the more benign* extreame; vse fasting and full eating, but rather full eating; watching and sleepe, but rather sleepe; sitting and exercise, but rather exercise, and the like. So shall nature be cherished and yet taught masteries. Physitians are some of them so pleasing & conformable to the humors of the Patient, as they presse not the true cure of the disease; and some other are so regular, in proceeding according to art for the disease, /108/ as they respect not sufficiently the condition of the Patient. Take one of a middle temper, or if it may not be found in one man, combine two of both sorts: and forget not to call aswell the best acquainted with your bodie, as the best reputed of, for his faculty.

---

*Altered in ink from *beinge* in ten out of fifteen copies of this edition: see Kiernan, *Bacon's Essayes*, pp. lxxx–lxxxi, 101.

(3) The text in *The Essayes or Counsels Civill and Morall of Francis Lord Verulam* (London: printed by John Haviland for Hanna Barret and Richard Whitaker, 1625, pp. 187–90)

Of Regiment of Health.
XXX

There is a wisdome in this, beyond the Rules of *Physicke*: A Man's owne Observation, what he findes Good of, and what he findes Hurt of, is the best *Physicke* to preserve Health. But it is a safer Conclusion to say; *This agreeth not well with me, therefore I will not continue it*; Then this; *I finde no offence of this, therefore I may use it*. For Strength of Nature in youth, passeth over many Excesses, which are owing a Man till his Age. Discerne of the comming on of Yeares, and thinke not, to doe the same Things still; For Age will not be Defied. Beware of sudden Change in any great point of Diet, and if necessity /188/ inforce it, fit the rest to it. For it is a Secret, both in Nature, and State; That it is safer to change Many Things, then one. Examine thy Customes, of Diet, Sleepe, Exercise, Apparell, and the like; And trie in any Thing, thou shalt judge hurtfull, to discontinue it by little and little; But so, as if thou doest finde any Inconvenience by the Change, thou come backe to it againe: For it is hard to distinguish, that which is generally held good, and wholesome, from that, which is good particularly, and fit for thine owne Body. To be free minded, and cheerefully disposed, at Houres of Meat, and of Sleep, and of Exercise, is one of the best Precepts of Long lasting. As for the Passions and Studies of the Minde; Avoid Envie; Anxious Feares; Anger fretting inwards; Subtill and knottie Inquisitions; Joyes, and Exhilarations in Excesse; Sadnesse not Communicated. Entertain Hopes; Mirth rather then Joy; Varietie of Delights, rather then Surfet of them; Wonder, and Admiration, and therefore Novelties; Studies /189/ that fill the Minde with Splendide and Illustrious Objects, as Histories, Fables, and Contemplations of Nature. If you flie Physicke in *Health* altogether, it will be too strange for your Body, when you shall need it. If you make it too familiar, it will worke no Extraordinary Effect, when Sicknesse commeth. I commend rather, some Diet, for certaine Seasons, then frequent Use of *Physicke*, Except it be growen into a Custome. For those Diets alter the Body more, and trouble it lesse. Despise no new Accident, in your Body, but aske Opinion of it. In *Sicknesse*, respect *Health* principally; And in *Health*, *Action*. For those that put their Bodies, to endure in *Health*, may in most *Sicknesses*, which are not very sharpe, be cured onely with Diet, and Tendering. *Celsus* could never have spoken it as a *Physician*, had he not been a Wise Man withall; when he giveth it, for one of the great precepts of Health and Lasting; That a Man doe vary, and enterchange Contraries; But with an Inclination to /190/ the more benigne Extreme: Use Fasting, and full Eating, but rather full Eating; Watching and Sleep, but rather Sleep; Sitting, and Exercise, but rather Exercise; and the like. So shall Nature be cherished, and yet taught Masteries. *Physicians* are some of them so pleasing, and conformable to the Humor of the Patient, as they presse not the true Cure of the Disease; And some other are so Regular, in proceeding according to Art, for the Disease, as they respect not sufficiently the Condition of the Patient. Take one of a Middle Temper; Or if it may not be found in one Man, combine two of either sort: And forget not to call, aswell the best acquainted with your Body, as the best reputed of for his Faculty.

(4) Composite text (see key for typographical identifiers)

Of Regiment of Health. XXX

There is a wisdome in this, beyond the Rules of *Physicke*: A Man's owne Observation, what he findes Good of, and what he findes Hurt of, is the best *Physicke* to preserve Health. But it is a safer Conclusion to say; *This agreeth not well with me, therefore I will not continue it*; Then this; *I finde no offence of this, therefore I may use it.* For Strength of Nature in youth, passeth over many Excesses, which are owing a Man till his Age. Discerne of the comming on of Yeares, and thinke not, to doe the same Things still; Certainly most lusty old men catch their death by that adventure; For Age will not be Defied. Beware of any sudden Change in any great point of Diet, and if necessity inforce it, fit the rest to it. For it is a Secret, both in Nature, and State; That it is safer to change Many Things, then one. Examine thy Customes, of Diet, Sleepe, Exercise, Apparell, and the like; And trie in any Thing, thou shalt judge hurtfull, to discontinue it by little and little; But so, as if thou doest finde any Inconvenience by the Change, thou come backe to it againe: For it is hard to distinguish, that which is generally held good, and wholesome, from that, which is good particularly, and fit for thine owne Body. To be free minded, and cheerefully disposed, at Houres of Meat, and of Sleep, and of Exercise, is one of the best Precepts of Long lasting. As for the Passions and Studies of the Minde; Avoid Envie; Anxious Feares; Anger fretting inwards;

Subtill and knottie Inquisitions; Joyes, and Exhilarations in Excesse; Sadnesse not Communicated. Entertain Hopes; Mirth rather then Joy; Varietie of Delights, rather then Surfet of them; Wonder, and Admiration, and therefore Novelties; Studies that fill the Minde with Splendide and Illustrious Objects, as Histories, Fables, and Contemplations of Nature. If you flie Physicke in *Health* altogether, it will be too strange for your Body, when you shall need it. If you make it too familiar, it will worke no Extraordinary Effect, when Sicknesse commeth. I commend rather, some Diet, for certaine Seasons, then frequent Use of *Physicke*, Except it be growen into a Custome. For those Diets alter the Body more, and trouble it lesse. Despise no new Accident, in your Body, but aske Opinion of it. In *Sicknesse*, respect *Health* principally; And in *Health*, *Action*. For those that put their Bodies, to endure in *Health*, may in most *Sicknesses*, which are not very sharpe, be cured onely with Diet, and Tendering. `Celsus` could never have spoken it as a `Physician`, had he not been a Wise Man withall; when he giveth it, for one of the great precepts of Health and Lasting; That a Man doe vary, and enterchange Contraries; But with an Inclination to the more benigne Extreme: Use Fasting, and full Eating, but rather full Eating; Watching and Sleep, but rather Sleep; Sitting, and Exercise, but rather Exercise; and the like. So shall Nature be cherished, and yet taught Masteries. *Physicians* are some of them so pleasing, and conformable to the Humor of the Patient, as they presse not the true Cure of the Disease; And some other are so Regular, in proceeding according to Art, for the Disease, as they respect not sufficiently the Condition of the Patient. Take one of a Middle Temper; Or if it may not be found in one Man, combine two of either sort: And forget not to call, aswell the best acquainted with your Body, as the best reputed of for his Faculty.

Key:
The Rules of *Physicke*: 1597 text retained in both 1612 and 1625 editions
any: discarded in 1612 edition
`Age will not be Deifed`: added to 1612 edition; retained in 1625
`Certainly most old men:` added to 1612 edition; discarded in 1625
Examine thy Customes: added to 1625 edition

Appendix 4: Unmodernised and Modernised Versions of the Last Section of Chapter 47 of Thomas Hobbes' *Leviathan* (London: for Andrew Crooke, 1651), pp. 385–7

This short extract has been chosen to illustrate the advantages and disadvantages of providing a modernised text of a seventeenth-century book. The modernised version is undoubtedly less archaic in spellings and less complicated in its punctuation. But it may be felt that the italicisation in the original forms part of its meaning, particularly in the emphasis that is given to the parallelism between the Catholic church and the kingdom of the fairies. There is obviously some latitude as to exactly how punctuation is modernised: here, dashes have been used to articulate complex sentences, whereas Edwin Curley in his modernised version of the same passage makes much more extensive use of brackets.[1] Others might prefer other options, including the insertion of extra sentence breaks, though this would in places necessitate rewording.

(1) Text as published

Comparison of the Papacy with the Kingdome of Fayries
[shoulder note on p. 385]

But after this Doctrine, *that the Church now Militant, is the Kingdome of God spoken of in the Old and New Testament,* was received in the World; the ambition, and canvasing for the Offices that belong thereunto, and especially for that great Office of being /386/ Christs Lieutenant, and the Pompe of them that obtained therein the principall Publique Charges, became by degrees so evident, that they lost the inward Reverence due to the Pastorall Function: in so much as the Wisest men, of them that had any power in the Civill State, needed nothing but the authority of their Princes, to deny them any further Obedience. For, from the time that the Bishop of Rome had gotten to be acknowledged for Bishop Universall, by pretence of Succession to St. Peter, their whole Hierarchy, or Kingdome of Darknesse, may be compared not unfitly to the *Kingdome of Fairies;* that is, to the old wives *Fables* in England, concerning *Ghosts* and *Spirits,* and the feats they play in the night. And if a man consider the originall of this great Ecclesiasticall Dominion, he will easily perceive, that the *Papacy,* is no other, than the *Ghost* of the deceased *Romane Empire,* sitting crowned upon the grave thereof: For so did the Papacy start up on a Sudden out of the Ruines of that Heathen Power.

The *Language* also, which they use, both in the Churches, and in their Publique Acts, being *Latine,* which is not commonly used by any Nation now in the world, what is it but the *Ghost* of the Old *Romane Language?*

The *Fairies* in what Nation soever they converse, have but one Universall King, which some Poets of ours call King *Oberon;* but the Scripture calls *Beelzebub,* Prince of *Dæmons.* The *Ecclesiastiques* likewise, in whose Dominions soever they be found, acknowledge but one Universall King, the *Pope.*

The *Ecclesiastiques* are *Spirituall* men, and *Ghostly* Fathers. The Fairies are *Spirits,* and *Ghosts. Fairies* and *Ghosts* inhabite Darknesse, Solitudes, and Graves. The *Ecclesiastiques* walke in Obscurity of Doctrine, in Monasteries, Churches, and Church-yards.

The *Ecclesiastiques* have their Cathedrall Churches; which, in what Towne soever they be erected, by vertue of Holy Water, and certain Charmes called Exorcismes, have the power to make those Townes, Cities, that is to say, Seats of Empire. The *Fairies* also have their enchanted Castles, and certain Gigantique Ghosts, that domineer over the Regions round about them.

The *Fairies* are not to be seized on; and brought to answer for the hurt they do. So also the *Ecclesiastiques* vanish away from the Tribunals of Civill Justice.

The *Ecclesiastiques* take from young men, the use of Reason, by certain Charms compounded of Metaphysiques, and Miracles, and Traditions, and Abused Scripture, whereby they are good for nothing else, but to execute what they command them. The *Fairies* likewise are said to take young Children out of their Cradles, and to change them into Naturall Fools, which Common people do therefore call *Elves,* and are apt to mischief.

In what Shop, or Operatory the Fairies make their Enchantment, the old Wives have not determined. But the Operatories of the *Clergy,* are well enough known to be the Universities, that received their Discipline from Authority Pontificiall. /387/

When the *Fairies* are displeased with any body, they are said to send their Elves, to pinch them. The *Ecclesiastiques,* when they are displeased with any

Civill State, make also their Elves, that is, Superstitious, Enchanted Subjects, to pinch their Princes, by preaching Sedition; or one Prince enchanted with promises, to pinch another.

The *Fairies* marry not; but there be amongst them *Incubi,* that have copulation with flesh and bloud. The *Priests* also marry not.

The *Ecclesiastiques* take the Cream of the Land, by Donations of ignorant men, that stand in aw of them, and by Tythes: So also it is in the Fable of *Fairies,* that they enter into the Dairies, and Feast upon the Cream, which they skim from the Milk.

What kind of Money is currant in the Kingdome of *Fairies,* is not recorded in the Story. But the *Ecclesiastiques* in their Receipts accept of the same Money that we doe; though when they are to make any Payment, it is in Canonizations, Indulgences, and Masses.

To this, and such like resemblances between the *Papacy,* and the Kingdome of *Fairies,* may be added this, that as the *Fairies* have no existence, but in the Fancies of ignorant people, rising from the Traditions of old Wives, or old Poets: so the Spirituall Power of the *Pope* (without the bounds of his own Civill Dominion) consisteth onely in the Fear that Seduced people stand in, of their Excommunications;* upon hearing of false Miracles, false Traditions, and false Interpretations of the Scripture.

It was not therefore a very difficult matter, for Henry 8. by his Exorcisme; nor for Qu. Elizabeth by hers, to cast them out. But who knows that this Spirit of Rome, now gone out, and walking by Missions through the dry places of China, Japan, and the Indies, that yeeld him little fruit, may not return, or rather an Assembly of Spirits worse than he, enter, and inhabite this clean swept house, and make the End thereof worse than the Beginning? For it is not the Romane Clergy onely, that pretends the Kingdome of God to be of this World, and thereby to have a Power therein, distinct from that of the Civill State. And this is all I had a designe to say, concerning the Doctrine of the POLITIQUES. Which when I have reviewed, I shall willingly expose it to the censure of my Countrey.

(2) Modernised text

Comparison of the papacy with the kingdom of fairies

But after this doctrine – that the church now militant is the kingdom of God spoken of in the Old and New Testament – was received in the world,

---

* MS has *Excommunication*. See Tuck, *Hobbes' Leviathan*, p. 482.

the ambition and canvassing for the offices that belong thereunto, and especially for that great office of being Christ's lieutenant and the pomp of them that obtained therein the principal public charges, became by degrees so evident that they lost the inward reverence due to the pastoral function in so much as the wisest men of them that had any power in the civil state needed nothing but the authority of their princes to deny them any further obedience.

For from the time that the bishop of Rome had gotten to be acknowledged for bishop universal by pretence of succession to St. Peter, their whole hierarchy or kingdom of darkness may be compared not unfitly to the kingdom of fairies, that is to the old wives' fables in England concerning ghosts and spirits and the feats they play in the night. And if a man consider the original of this great ecclesiastical dominion he will easily perceive that the papacy is no other than the ghost of the deceased Roman Empire sitting crowned upon the grave thereof. For so did the papacy start up on a sudden out of the ruins of that heathen power.

The language also which they use both in the churches and in their public acts being Latin, which is not commonly used by any nation now in the world, what is it but the ghost of the old Roman language?

The fairies in what nation soever they converse, have but one universal king which some poets of ours call King Oberon, but the scripture calls Beelzebub, prince of demons. The ecclesiastics likewise in whose dominions soever they be found acknowledge but one universal king, the pope.

The ecclesiastics are spiritual men and ghostly fathers. The fairies are spirits and ghosts. Fairies and ghosts inhabit darkness, solitudes and graves. The ecclesiastics walk in obscurity of doctrine in monasteries, churches and churchyards.

The ecclesiastics have their cathedral churches which in what town soever they be erected by virtue of holy water and certain charms called exorcisms have the power to make those towns cities, that is to say seats of empire. The fairies also have their enchanted castles and certain gigantic ghosts that domineer over the regions round about them.

The fairies are not to be seized on and brought to answer for the hurt they do. So also the ecclesiastics vanish away from the tribunals of civil justice.

The ecclesiastics take from young men the use of reason by certain charms compounded of metaphysics and miracles and traditions and abused scripture, whereby they are good for nothing else but to execute what they command them. The fairies likewise are said to take young children out of their cradles and to change them into natural fools which common people do therefore call elves and are apt to mischief.

In what shop or operatory the fairies make their enchantment the old wives have not determined. But the operatories of the clergy are well enough known to be the universities that received their discipline from authority pontifical.

When the fairies are displeased with anybody they are said to send their elves to pinch them. The ecclesiastics when they are displeased with any civil state make also their elves – that is superstitious, enchanted subjects – to pinch their princes by preaching sedition or one prince enchanted with promises to pinch another.

The fairies marry not but there be amongst them incubi that have copulation with flesh and blood. The priests also marry not.

The ecclesiastics take the cream of the land by donations of ignorant men that stand in awe of them and by tithes. So also it is in the fable of fairies that they enter into the dairies and feast upon the cream which they skim from the milk.

What kind of money is current in the kingdom of fairies is not recorded in the story. But the ecclesiastics in their receipts accept of the same money that we do, though when they are to make any payment it is in canonisations, indulgences and masses.

To this and such like resemblances between the papacy and the kingdom of fairies may be added this: that as the fairies have no existence but in the fancies of ignorant people rising from the traditions of old wives or old poets, so the spiritual power of the pope, without the bounds of his own civil dominion, consists only in the fear that seduced people stand in of their excommunications upon hearing of false miracles, false traditions and false interpretations of the scripture.

It was not therefore a very difficult matter for Henry VIII by his exorcism, nor for Queen Elizabeth by hers, to cast them out. But who knows that this spirit of Rome, now gone out and walking by missions through the dry places of China, Japan and the Indies that yield him little fruit, may not return – or rather an assembly of spirits worse than he enter and inhabit this clean swept house and make the end thereof worse than the beginning? For it is not the Roman clergy only that pretends the kingdom of God to be of this world and thereby to have a power therein distinct from that of the civil state.

And this is all I had a design to say concerning the doctrine of the politics, which when I have reviewed I shall willingly expose it to the censure of my country.

Appendix 5: Peter Nidditch's Description of the Evolution of his Editorial Method

As explained in Chapter 6, Peter Nidditch's account of the stages by which he reached his user-friendly method of presenting his transcriptions of Locke's manuscripts is highly revealing of his attempt to distinguish the significant from the insignificant, and his solicitude for the needs of users. It is quoted here from appendix 4 of vol. 1 of the edition of the *Drafts* for Locke's *Essay* that John Rogers brought out after Nidditch's death, pp. 294–5. Initially, this had appeared in the preprint of Nidditch's edition of Draft B published by the Philosophy Department of the University of Sheffield in 1982, pp. 11–13. It is perhaps worth noting here as further evidence of Nidditch's solicitude for his readers that his edition of Locke's *Essay* contains what is to my knowledge a virtually unique 'Appendix' to a scholarly edition (pp. 805–20), containing an 'Explanation of Bibliographical, Text-Critical and Typographical Terminology', in other words a kind of glossary, which has been drawn on for some of the entries in the glossary in this book. (Nidditch's solicitude for his readers was not shared by his publishers, who omitted the glossary – admittedly along with much of the apparatus to which it referred – from the 1979 paperback reprint of his edition.)

The text by Nidditch printed in Appendix 4 of vol. 1 of *Drafts for the 'Essay'* opens with a paragraph from his introduction to his preprint of Draft A of the *Essay*, published in 1980, in which he alluded to Zacharie Tourneur's editions of Pascal's *Pensées* (1938, 1942) as arousing his long-lasting interest 'in the palaeographical-cum-stratigraphical editing of a range of challenging seventeenth-century MSS', and to the models of notation in classical editing which he had followed but adapted. In the introduction to Draft B, he explained how he had transcribed the text and collated it with the printed *Essay*. He continued:

> At that initial stage the alterations in the MS were recorded in the appropriate places within the body of the transcription. The latter was intended to be a close representation of the MS. Accordingly, it retained, so far as I could manage to make it do so, the literal character and the lineation of the MS. Thus, e.g., consonantal 'u' and Locke's differently shaped 'd's, 'e's, and 's's were preserved, as were his abbreviations and his slips of the pen. Corrections of the latter and the other editorial interferences (especially the completion of uncompleted words in deletions) were confined to footnotes.
>
> Since then, I have repeatedly revised and retyped versions of the material. Changes of method have been made, in large or small measure, at each step, as a result partly of my own maturing editorial judgement and partly of my feeling the need to respond helpfully, and to make concessions to, certain Locke scholars and certain members of my potential readership of *Drafts*, whom I consulted and who expressed strong preferences or complaints. Lineation, and differentiation of the forms of the 'same' letter, were the first to go, as needlessly fussy; adopting 'v' and 'j' for consonantal 'u' and 'i', and expanding Locke's abbreviations, came next; finally, in the mid-1970s, after years of resistance on my part, I transferred to footnotes the registration of the MS's alterations from their incorporation within the transcription.
>
> What has emerged as required is a compromise between a version that is, as near as possible, a reproduction of the form and the forms of the original, and a version that suits a superficial reader's easiest convenience. The compromise consists of a palaeographical text with separate textual annotations, the textual representation being as plain, on-line, readable, and quotable as possible, while, as palaeographical, it retains basically the spelling and punctuation of the MS; the handling should, as diplomatic scholarship, not fall below the standards generally recognized by historical scholars in their editing of documents of Locke's period. I should emphasize, in addition, that the textual annotations should be readily apprehensible, in respect both of their MS content and of this content's character (as deletion, interlineation, etc.). Reactions to my edition of Draft A that have been notified to me by a considerable number of Lockian or seventeenth-/eighteenth-century scholars have confirmed my earlier sampling consultations, to the effect that I have struck a reasonable compromise and that my application of the methods I have come to use is up to scratch.

Notes

1 Introduction

1. See Grafton, *Joseph Scaliger*, passim. For the earlier phase, see Gaisser, *Catullus and his Renaissance Readers*, esp. ch. 1.
2. See Reynolds and Wilson, *Scribes and Scholars*; Kenny, *The Classical Text*; Pfeiffer, *History of Classical Scholarship*; Brink, *English Classical Scholarship*.
3. See esp. Metzger, *Text of the New Testament*; Pfeiffer, *Introduction to the Old Testament*.
4. See Maas, *Textual Criticism*; West, *Textual Criticism and Editorial Technique*; Reynolds and Wilson, *Scribes and Scholars*, ch. 6.
5. See esp. Greg, *Collected Papers*; McKerrow, *Prolegomena for the Oxford Shakespeare*; Wilson, *Shakespeare and the New Bibliography*.
6. See esp. Bowers, *Principles of Bibliographical Description*; id., *Bibliography and Textual Criticism*; id., *Textual and Literary Criticism*; id., *Essays in Bibliography*. For the work of his principal successor, see esp. Tanselle, *Textual Criticism and Scholarly Editing*; id., *Rationale of Textual Criticism*.
7. CEAA, *Statement of Editorial Principles and Procedures*; Boydston, 'Standards for Scholarly Editing'; 'Center for Scholarly Editions', esp. p. 583.
8. For these and other terms, see Glossary. Greg, 'Rationale of Copy-Text'; for discussion, see, for instance, Davis, 'The CEAA'; Tanselle, 'Editing without a Copy-Text'.
9. McGann, *Critique of Modern Textual Criticism*; McKenzie, 'Printers of the Mind'; id. 'Typography and Meaning'; id., *Bibliography and the Sociology of Texts*.
10. In addition to the works cited in n. 6, see esp. Shillingsburg, *Scholarly Editing in the Computer Age*, and Greetham, *Textual Scholarship*, which is useful if a little longwinded.
11. For instance, Greetham, *Theories of the Text*; Tanselle, 'Textual Criticism at the Millenium'. However, there are honourable exceptions, notably Gaskell, *From Writer to Reader*.
12. See 'Report on Editing Historical Documents' and 'Report on Editing Modern Historical Documents'.
13. Hunnisett, *Editing Records for Publication*; Harvey, *Editing Historical Records*.
14. Carter, *Historical Editing*; Kline, *Guide to Documentary Editing*. See also the relevant section of Handlin et al., *Harvard Guide*, pp. 88ff., for which the primary responsibility was that of S.E. Morison (cf. the revised edition by Freidel, pp. 21–36). More recently, see the anthology by Stevens and Burg, *Editing Historical Documents*.
15. Tanselle, 'Editing of Historical Documents'. See Kline, *Guide*, esp. pp. 17ff. for a synopsis of the debates that ensued.
16. For full citations, see the Bibliography, where editions appear under their editors but are cross-referenced under their authors.
17. For the workdiaries, see: www.livesandletters.ac.uk/wd. For texts published by the Robert Boyle Project, see: www.bbk.ac.uk/boyle.

18 E.g. Dainard, *Editing Correspondence*; Levere, *Editing Texts in the History of Science and Medicine*.
19 Hunter, 'How to Edit a Seventeenth-century Manuscript'.
20 Hunter and de Mowbray, 'The Editor in the Republic of Letters'; Hunter 'Whither Editing'; van Maanen et al., 'John Pell'. See also the proceedings of the conference on early modern scientific archives that I organised in 1996: Hunter, *Archives of the Scientific Revolution*.
21 See Gaskell, *New Introduction to Bibliography*, pp. 137–8.
22 See esp. McKitterick, *Print, Manuscript and the Search for Order*.
23 See Gaskell, *New Introduction*, passim. For a broader perspective on some of the issues dealt with in chapters 2 and 3, see Martin, *History and Power of Writing*.
24 See: www.shef.ac.uk/hri/projects/projectpages/hartlib.html.
25 See: sql.uleth.ca/dmorgwiki/index.php/CTP_(Canterbury_Tales_Project).
26 On the origins of SGML, see: www.sgmlsource.com/history.
27 See: www.tei-c.org.
28 McGann, 'Rationale of Hypertext', esp. pp. 41–2.
29 Kennedy, *The Internet*, p. 445.
30 See: www.perseus.tufts.edu.
31 I am indebted for this information to Jan Broadway, whose advice on such matters has been invaluable.
32 From this point of view, it is salutary to compare the different editions of Shillingsburg, *Scholarly Editing in the Computer Age*.
33 For examples, see McGann, *Radiant Textuality*; Shillingsburg, *Scholarly Editing*. For writings of a more technical character, see Hockey, *Electronic Texts in the Humanities*, and some of the essays in Sutherland, *Electronic Text*. In addition, a huge amount of such material is available on the web.
34 See: www.livesandletters.ac.uk/wd. The original edition is archived on the Boyle website, www.bbk.ac.uk/boyle.

2 Manuscripts

1 See Stallybrass et al., 'Hamlet's Tables'; Woodhuysen, 'Writing-Tables and Table Books'.
2 See, for instance, McKerrow, *Introduction to Bibliography*, pp. 252ff., and Wilson, *Shakespeare and the New Bibliography*, esp. ch. 4.
3 For a helpful discussion of many of the matters dealt with in this chapter, see Petti, *English Literary Hands*, Introduction. On the entire paraphernalia not only of pens but also of pen-cases, ink-wells, etc., see Finlay, *Western Writing Implements*.
4 See Finlay, *Western Writing Instruments*, ch. 10; Petroski, *The Pencil*, esp. pp. 41ff.
5 For helpful guides, see, in addition to Petti, *English Literary Hands*, Preston and Yeandle, *English Handwriting 1400–1650*.
6 This is true of various of Robert Boyle's amanuenses, including Robert Bacon and Hugh Greg: see Hunter et al., *The Boyle Papers*, ch. 1.
7 Whiteside, *Mathematical Papers*, esp. vol. 1, p. xi n. 2; Hall, 'Pitfalls in the Editing of Newton's Papers', esp. p. 409.
8 See Johnson and Jenkinson, *English Court Hand*, pp. xxii–xxxv.
9 For an example of a scholar puzzled by such marks, see Harwood, *Early Essays and Ethics of Boyle*, lxix.

10 Gaskell, *New Introduction to Bibliography*, p. 60; Heawood, 'Paper Used in England'; id., 'Further Notes'.
11 See esp. Briquet, *Les filigranes*; Gaudricault, *Filigranes*; Heawood, *Watermarks*.
12 Pebworth, 'Towards a Taxonomy of Watermarks'; Shapiro, 'Beyond the Dating Game'.
13 Chapman, 'An Inventory'.
14 Pollard, 'Notes on the Size of the Sheet', p. 117.
15 See Long, *Summary Catalogue*, esp. pp. xi–xii for formats; Hunter et al., *A Radical's Books*, app. 3; Hunter and Gregory, *An Astrological Diary*, passim.
16 See Frank, 'The John Ward Diaries'.
17 Chapman, 'An Inventory'.
18 For a listing, see Matthews, *British Diaries*. For a survey, see Bourcier, *Journaux privés*.
19 For a useful survey, see Beal, 'Notions in Garrison'. See also Sharpe, *Reading Revolutions*.
20 See, e.g., the studies in Hunter and Hutton, *Women, Science and Medicine*.
21 Woodhouysen, *Sidney and the Circulation of Manuscripts*, p. 15. See also Marotti, *Manuscript, Print and the English Renaissance Lyric*, and Hobbs, *Early Seventeenth-century Verse Miscellany Manuscripts*. For a useful survey with specific reference to women, see Ezell, *Patriarch's Wife*, pp. 64–83.
22 Woodhouysen, *Sidney and the Circulation of Manuscripts*, esp. Conclusion.
23 Hervey (ed.), Reyce, *Breviary of Suffolk*, p. 2. See also Broadway, *William Dugdale*, and Woolf, *Social Circulation of the Past*.
24 Kiernan, *Bacon's Essayes*, pp. xxiii–iv, lxxi–vii; Tuck, *Hobbes' Leviathan*, pp. li–vi.
25 See Love, *Culture and Commerce of Texts*, pp. 9ff. and passim. See also Beal, *In Praise of Scribes*.
26 Lord, *Poems on Affairs of State*, vol. 5, pp. 528–38.
27 McKenzie, 'Speech-Manuscript-Print', p. 94.
28 See the works cited in Chapter 1, n. 4. For seventeenth-century England, see esp. Love, *Culture and Commerce of Texts*, ch. 8.

3 The Role of Print

1 Febvre and Martin, *Coming of the Book*; Eisenstein, *Printing Press as an Agent of Change*; Hunter, 'Impact of Print'; Johns, *Nature of the Book*, esp. Intro.
2 Instances from Davies, 'Humanism in Script and Print', pp. 51, 54, juxtaposed in Rhodes and Sawday, *Renaissance Computer*, p. 4.
3 Pollard, 'Notes on the Size of the Sheet', p. 119.
4 See Johns, *Nature of the Book*, esp. Intro.
5 For instance, see Barnard and McKenzie, *Cambridge History of the Book*. For older surveys, e.g., Bennett, *English Books and Readers*. On Latin books, see Binns, *Intellectual Culture*.
6 Chesterfield, *Letters*, vol. 4, p. 112. For comments in a European context, see Martin, *History and Power of Writing*, pp. 310ff.
7 Pollard, 'Notes on the Size of the Sheet', pp. 122–4; McKenzie, 'Typography and Meaning', pp. 111–12.
8 MacKenzie, 'Printers of the Mind'; id., *Cambridge University Press*, esp. vol. 1. For introductory texts, see, in addition to Gaskell, *New Introduction to Bibliography*, McKerrow, *Introduction to Bibliography*; Steinberg, *Five Hundred Years of Printing*.

9   Wright, *Bacon's Essays*, pp. 350–3; McKitterick, *Print, Manuscript and the Search for Order*, pp. 121–2 and chs. 4–5, passim.
10 Gaskell, *New Introduction*, p. 162 (quoting Greg, *Companion to Arber*, pp. 43, 94–5).
11 McKerrow, *Introduction*, app. 4.
12 Moxon, *Mechanick Exercises*, p. 333.
13 Nash, 'Abandoning of the Long "s" '.
14 McKerrow, 'Some Notes', esp. p. 248, and *Introduction*, app. 3.
15 Salmon, 'Orthography and Punctuation', pp. 29–30, 40–1 and passim; McKerrow, *Introduction*, pp. 315–18.
16 Osselton, 'Spelling-Book Rules and the Capitalisation of Nouns'.
17 Salmon, 'Orthography and Punctuation', pp. 23ff., 38ff. and passim; Scragg, *History of English Spelling*, ch. 5. See also Febvre and Martin, *Coming of the Book*, pp. 323ff.
18 Thomas, 'Meaning of Literacy', pp. 99–100.
19 Smith, *Printer's Grammar*, pp. 12–14, 91, 220.
20 Moxon, *Mechanick Exercises*, p. 213 (and pp. 212–14 passim).
21 Barker, 'Typography and the Meaning of Words'; McKerrow, *Introduction*, pp. 88ff.
22 McKerrow, *Introduction*, pp. 85–6.
23 Ibid., pp. 73–84.
24 For a useful inventory of such survivals, with illustrations of examples, see Moore, *Primary Materials*. By an odd coincidence, none of the MSS she illustrates makes use of the thorn, but for a specimen that does, and where this – like other standard contractions – was expanded, see the MS of Pierre Allix's *Discourse concerning the Merit of Good Works* (1688), in Bodleian Library, MS Rawlinson D 730, fols. 103–5 (Moore, p. 25).
25 See Thorpe, *Principles of Textual Criticism*, ch. 5, esp. pp. 141ff.
26 Rees, *Philosophical Studies c. 1611–19*, appendix 2, pp. 460–6.
27 Edward Tyson to Robert Plot, 5 Feb. 1683, in Gunther, *Early Science in Oxford*, vol. 12, p. 9. See also Harth, 'Text of Dryden's Poetry', pp. 229–31.
28 Thorpe, *Principles*, p. 144; Nidditch, *Essay concerning Human Understanding*, pp. xxxix–xl, xlix–liii; Laslett, *Locke's Two Treatises*, pp. 7–10.
29 Hill, 'English Renaissance: Nondramatic Literature', p. 212.
30 Foxon, 'Greg's "Rationale" and the Editing of Pope'.
31 See, e.g., Rose, *Authors and Owners*; Johns, *Nature of the Book*.
32 Lindenbaum, 'Authors and Publishers'. See also Loewenstein, *The Author's Due*.
33 Mosley, 'Astronomical Books and Courtly Communication'; Roberts, *Dugdale and Hollar*, esp. ch. 6.
34 Robinson and Wallis, *Book Subscription Lists*; Clapp, 'Beginnings of Subscription Publication'.
35 See Davis, 'Beyond the Market'; Scott-Warren, *Sir John Harington and the Book as Gift*; Kerrigan, 'The Editor as Reader'.

4 Types of Edition

1   Serjeantson, *Generall Learning*. See Spiller, *'Concerning Natural Experimental Philosophie'*; Hunter, 'Ancients, Moderns, Philologists and Scientists'.
2   See Marotti, *Manuscript, Print and the English Renaissance Lyric*, p. 135 and passim.

Notes to pp. 38–47

3 The putative edition by Edward G. McGee, in three volumes and 1,864 pages, was advertised in *The Periodical*, Spring 1972, p. 9.
4 See Clark, *Brief Lives*, vol. 2, pp. 317–32 and passim. The edition of the *Lives* which Kate Bennett is currently preparing will largely adopt this approach, though she is omitting the Hobbes life, which she believes should be separately edited. On the other hand, she will include certain short lives from the Wood and Rawlinson MSS. See further below, p. 85.
5 See Foucault, 'What is an Author?', esp. pp. 103–4, 107.
6 McLaverty, 'For Who So Fond as Youthful Bards of Fame?'
7 Carter, *History of Oxford University Press*, pp. 239–40.
8 See, for instance, *A Catalogue of the Mathematical Works of the Learned Mr Thomas Baker . . . with a Proposal about Printing the Same* [1683], Wing B516A. The Wood, Gough and John Johnson collections in the Bodleian contain a number of such items.
9 See Hooker et al., *Works of Dryden*.
10 Lindenbaum, 'Dividing and Conquering Milton'.
11 See Patterson, *Works of Milton*; Wolfe et al., *Complete Prose Works of Milton*.
12 Donaldson, 'Collecting Ben Jonson', pp. 25–7.
13 See Hunter, *Archives of the Scientific Revolution*, p. 7.
14 See Donaldson, 'Collecting Ben Jonson', pp. 19–20. Cf. Foucault, 'What is an Author', pp. 103–04.
15 Hunter and Davis, *Works of Boyle*, vol. 1, pp. lxxviiiff. For the continuation of this attempt, see ibid., vol. 14, pp. 359–65.
16 Ibid., vols. 13–14 passim. For the rationale, see ibid., vol. 1, pp. xc–xci, and vol. 13, pp. xii–xiv. For a supplement, see Hunter and Knight, *Unpublished Material*.
17 For details, see: www.cambridge.org/literature/features/cwbj/project/. Cf. Donaldson, 'Collecting Ben Jonson', pp. 29–30.
18 See Jardine, *Erasmus, Man of Letters*; Clough, 'Cult of Antiquity', p. 44 and passim.
19 Wotton, *Reliqui*; Sherburn, *Correspondence of Pope*, vol. 1, pp. xiff. and passim.
20 Halsband, 'Editing the Letters of Letter-writers', p. 29.
21 Rusnock, *Correspondence of Jurin*.
22 Pearce Williams, *Selected Correspondence of Faraday*; James, *Correspondence of Faraday*.
23 Cunningham, *Letters of Walpole*, title-page. For a summary, see Hazen, *Bibliography of Walpole*, pp. 75–93.
24 Birch, *Works of Boyle*, vol. 5, pp. 229ff.
25 Malcolm and Stedall, *Pell and his Correspondence with Cavendish*. For other examples, see Pears, *Correspondence of Sidney and Languet*; Isham, *Correspondence of Duppa and Isham*.
26 See Carter, *Sheep and Wool Correspondence*; Ritter et al., *Leibniz Sämtliche Schriften und Briefe*.
27 Hunter and de Mowbray, 'Editor in the Republic of Letters', p. 223.
28 See Hunter, Clericuzio and Principe, *Correspondence of Boyle*, vol. 6, pp. 362ff., and compare the relevant section of Maddison, 'A Tentative Index', pp. 180–4.
29 See Sherburn, *Correspondence of Pope*, vol. 1, pp. xi, xv–xvi. For the nineteenth century, see Millgate, *Testamentary Acts*.
30 E.g., Hall, *Correspondence of Oldenburg*, in relation to the letters of van Leeuwenhoek and Newton, though not those of Huygens.

31 See esp. Keeble and Nuttall, *Correspondence of Baxter*, vol. 1, p. viii. For the Wallis case, see Beeley and Scriba, *Correspondence of Wallis*, vol. 1, pp. 42–109 and passim, and Hunter, 'Whither Editing', p. 811.
32 See Maddison, 'Tentative Index', passim.
33 For a discussion of this matter, see Hunter, Clericuzio and Principe, *Correspondence of Boyle*, vol. 1, pp. xxxiff.
34 Chambers, 'Excuse these Impertinences', p. 25 and passim.
35 Clough, 'Cult of Antiquity', p. 35.
36 Jardine, *Erasmus, Man of Letters*, esp. ch. 6; id., 'Defamiliarising Erasmus'.
37 See Beeley and Scriba, *Correspondence of Wallis*, vol. 1, p. xli and passim.
38 Labaree et al., *Papers of Franklin*, vol. 4, pp. 125–30, 458–61 and passim.
39 Ibid., vol. 21, p. xxxiv and passim. Cf. Boyd et al., *Papers of Jefferson*, vol. 16, pp. ix–x.
40 Boyd et al., *Papers of Jefferson*, vol. 1, pp. xv–xvi; vol. 22, p. vii and passim.
41 Turnbull et al., *Correspondence of Newton*, vol. 1, pp. xxv, xxviii.
42 For instance, the document published in ibid., vol. 2, pp. 168–71, appears in Whiteside, *Mathematical Papers*, vol. 1, pp. 318–21, while that in vol. 3, pp. 54–8, appears in ibid., vol. 1, pp. 392–6.
43 See Turnbull et al., *Correspondence of Newton*, e.g. vol. 3, pp. 327–47, 355, 384–9; vol. 4, pp. 15–20. The edition of selected extracts by Hiscock, *David Gregory, Isaac Newton and their Circle*, merely underlines the need for a proper edition.
44 Josten, *Elias Ashmole*.
45 Whiteside, *Mathematical Papers*, vol. 1, pp. x, xi n. and passim; Shapiro, *Optical Papers*, esp. vol. 1, p. xii.
46 Popkin, 'Plans for Publishing'; Iliffe, 'Digitizing Isaac', p. 35 and passim.
47 See Iliffe, 'A "connected system?"' and Spargo, 'Sotheby's, Keynes and Yahuda'.
48 Jones, *Newton Manuscripts and Papers*. For the Newton Project, see: www.newtonproject.ic.ac.uk.
49 See: www.rossettiarchive.org.
50 Hartlib Papers Project, *Newsletter*, November 1989, [p. 2].
51 Braddick and Greengrass, *Letters of Sir Cheney Culpeper*; Hitchens et al., *Letters of Jan Jonston*.
52 See esp. Greengrass, 'Archive Refractions', and 'Samuel Hartlib and Scribal Communication'; *The Hartlib Papers*, 2nd edn.
53 Greengrass, 'Archive Refractions', p. 47.
54 See Hunter, 'Whither editing', pp. 816–17.
55 See Boyd et al., *Papers of Jefferson*, vol. 1, p. xxv.
56 For details see: www.bbk.ac.uk/boyle. See also Hunter et al., *The Boyle Papers*, passim.
57 See Hunter and Principe, 'Lost Papers of Boyle'.
58 See: www.livesandletters.ac.uk/wd.
59 See: www.imss.fi.it/ms72/.
60 For an example, see Greengrass, 'Archive Refractions', p. 36n.
61 For a useful bibliography, see Mullins, *Texts and Calendars*. See also Royal Commission on Historical Manuscripts, *Manuscripts and Men*, and Anderson, *Finch Manuscripts*, pp. v–xiv.
62 Harvey, *Editing Historical Records*, pp. 24–6
63 Ibid., p. 29.
64 Anderson, *Finch Manuscripts*, p. vi.

5 Presenting Texts (1) Printed

1. McLaverty, 'Concept of Authorial Intention', esp. p. 126.
2. Greg, 'Rationale of Copy-Text'. See also above, p. 4.
3. See, e.g., McLeod, *Crisis in Editing*; Wells and Taylor, *William Shakespeare: a Textual Companion*; Taylor, *Reinventing Shakespeare*; Shillingsburg, *Scholarly Editing in the Computer Age*. For a survey, see Greetham, *Textual Scholarship*.
4. See esp. McGann, *Critique of Modern Textual Criticism*. See further the comments from him cited in Greetham, '[Textual] Criticism and Deconstruction', pp. 9–10.
5. Goldberg, 'What? in a names that which we call a Rose'; Taylor and Warren, *The Division of the Kingdoms*.
6. Robbins, *Browne's Pseudodoxia Epidemica*, vol. 1, pp. v–vi and passim.
7. Faulkner et al., *Burton's Anatomy of Melancholy*, vol. 1, pp. lii–iv and passim.
8. Hill et al., *Works of Hooker*, vol. 2, pp. xlviii–l.
9. Hinman, *Printing and Proof-reading of the First Folio*, vol. 1, pp. 7, 226–7n, 243–4 and 246.
10. This suggestion appears in the (unpublished) Editorial Principles and Procedures for the Oxford Francis Bacon.
11. See the helpful comments in Rabbie, 'Editing Neo-Latin Texts', pp. 28–30.
12. Hunter and Davis, *Works of Boyle*, esp. vol. 1, pp. xcix–c.
13. Ibid., vol. 11, pp. liiiff., 367ff.
14. See Tuck, *Hobbes' Leviathan*, pp. xlvi–lvi and passim.
15. See Tricaud, *Léviathan*, pp. xxiiff. and passim; Curley, *Hobbes' Leviathan*, pp. lxiii–v and passim.
16. Koyré and Cohen, *Principia Mathematica*, passim.
17. See Hooke, *Micrographia*.
18. See: eebo.chadwyck.com/.
19. For a helpful discussion, see Gunby et al., *Works of Webster*, vol. 1, pp. 42ff.
20. See Rabbie, 'Editing Neo-Latin Texts', esp. pp. 31–3, 37–8.
21. Gunby et al., *Works of Webster*, vol. 1, esp. p. 44; Bowers, *Works of Beaumont and Fletcher*, vol. 1, p. xiv (cf. id., *Textual and Literary Criticism*, pp. 148, 185–6); Hill et al., *Works of Hooker*, vol. 1, pp. xxxvii–viii; Faulkner et al., *Burton's Anatomy of Melancholy*, vol. 1, pp. liv–v. See also Philip Gaskell, *From Writer to Reader*, esp. p. 8.
22. See Ingram, 'Ligatures of Early Printed Greek'.
23. Gunby et al., *Works of Webster*, vol. 1, pp. 46–8.
24. Todd, *Works of Behn*, passim.
25. Warrender, *De cive. English version*, p. 21.
26. See Lohne, 'Increasing Corruption of Newton's Diagrams'; Shapiro, *Optical Papers*, vol. 1, pp. xvii–xviii.
27. Hunter and Davis, *Works of Boyle*, vol. 1, pp. cxi, 1ff.
28. Ibid., vol. 5, pp. xxxiv, xli, 529ff.
29. Hill, 'English Renaissance: Nondramatic Literature', p. 216. Cf. Kiernan, *Bacon's Essayes*.
30. See Wright, *Bacon's Essays*, pp. 269–88; Vickers, *Bacon's Essays*, pp. 134–41; Arber, *A Harmony*. See also appendix 3.
31. For a photocopy of a complete copy of the addenda in the Pforzheimer collection, see British Library LR 293. d. 43. For a copy of the first edition with

the slips inserted, owned by Locke's friend, James Tyrrell, see C122.f.14. I am grateful to J.C. Walmsley for these references.
32 Nidditch, Rogers and Schuurman, *Drafts for the 'Essay'*.
33 Rees, *Instauration magna: Last Writings*, pp. xxxff., 1–34, 35–169; Butt et al., *Twickenham Edition of Pope*, vol. 4.
34 See Gaskell, *From Writer to Reader*, pp. 63ff.
35 See: sql.uleth.ca/dmorgwiki/index.php/CTP_(Canterbury_Tales_Project).
36 See Hanna, 'Application of Thought'.

6 Presenting Texts (2) Manuscripts

1 For current work on the Bacon correspondence, see: www.livesandletters.ac.uk/bacon.
2 See de la Bédoyère, *Particular Friends*, pp. 18ff. See also Hunter, *Boyle by Himself and his Friends*, pp. 84ff.
3 E.g. the letter of John Winthrop in Hunter, Clericuzio and Principe, *Correspondence of Boyle*, vol. 4, pp. 183–7.
4 See esp. Iliffe, 'A "connected system"?', esp. pp. 152ff.
5 Reiman, *Study of Modern Manuscripts*; Iliffe, 'A "connected system"?', esp. pp. 156–7; id., 'Is he like other men?'; Bennett, 'Editing Aubrey'.
6 'Center for Scholarly Editions', p. 585; Kline, *Guide to Documentary Editing*, pp. 127–8. For editions based on these principles, see Gilman, *Journals of Emerson*; Hirst, *Mark Twain's Letters*. Cf. Malcolm and Stedall, *Pell and his Correspondence with Sir Charles Cavendish*, p. 333.
7 Forbes, Murdin and Willmoth, *Correspondence of Flamsteed*, vol. 2, pp. xlii–iv.
8 See Love, *Culture and Commerce of Texts*.
9 Malcolm and Stedall, *Pell and his Correspondence with Cavendish*, p. 333.
10 See Southam, *Jane Austen's 'Sir Charles Grandison'*, passim, esp. the pages of which photo-facsimiles *are* provided. For a comparable example, see Parrish et al., *Cornell Wordsworth*, though in this case photographic reproductions are generally provided (as is a separate reading text).
11 Forbes, Murdin and Willmoth, *Correspondence of Flamsteed*, e.g. vol. 1, p. 839, vol. 2, p. 8; in these cases, the usage is also replicated.
12 See Hunnisett, *Editing Records for Publication*, p. 24; Harvey, *Editing Historical Records*, pp. 47–50, 63.
13 Romanell, *John Locke and Medicine*, p. 180 n. 13.
14 See, for instance, Sherburn, *Correspondence of Pope*, vol. 1, pp. xxvi–vii and passim; Redford, *Letters of Samuel Johnson*, vol. 1, p. xx, and passim.
15 See Louis, *Records of Early English Drama: Sussex*, pp. 29, 34–5 and passim. This is the house style of this series, and is also to be found in other volumes.
16 It is interesting that those who have done this have had problems with 'o[r]', which they have had to expand to 'our' to avoid ambiguity: see Hall, *Correspondence of Oldenburg*, vol. 1, p. xxiii.; cf. Turnbull et al., *Correspondence of Newton*, vol. 1, pp. xxx–xxxi.
17 Cf. Maxwell-Lyte, ' "U" and "V" '; Hunnisett, *Editing Records for Publication*, pp. 28ff.
18 Rabbie, 'Editing Neo-Latin Texts', esp. pp. 31–3.
19 See van Maanen et al., 'John Pell', pp. 235–6.

20 Parrish et al., *Cornell Wordsworth*, passim.
21 McGuire and Tamny, *Certain Philosophical Questions*.
22 For examples, see the Boyle workdiaries at: www.livesandletters.ac.uk/wd, or the texts available on the Newton Project website, www.newtonproject.ic.ac.uk.
23 Vander Meulen and Tanselle, 'A System of Manuscript Transcription', p. 205 and passim.
24 Wolfe, *Life and Letters of Lady Falkland*, passim.
25 See Appendix 2.
26 See *The Hartlib Papers*. For the use of contrasting type-faces, see Boyle's greatly-interpolated 'Of the Study of the Book of Nature', in Hunter and Davis, *Works of Boyle*, vol. 13, pp. 145–72, or the differentiation of three handwriting styles in Hunter et al., *A Radical's Books*.
27 Forbes, Murdin and Willmoth, *Correspondence of Flamsteed*, vol. 1, p. xxxii.
28 See Bowers, 'Transcription of Manuscripts', p. 253.
29 Fowles and Legg, *Aubrey's Monumenta Britannica*.
30 Bennett, 'Editing Aubrey', esp. pp. 286–7.

7 Modernised Texts

1 Mumford, 'Emerson behind Barbed Wire'.
2 Wilson, 'The Fruits of the MLA'; Davis, review in *Review of English Studies*, n.s. 12 (1961), 324–5, quoted in Thorpe, *Principles of Textual Criticism*, p. 169.
3 'Center for Scholarly Editions', esp. p. 585. See also CEAA, *Statement of Editorial Principles and Procedures*, and Davis, 'The CEAA'.
4 E.g., Davis, 'The CEAA', p. 74.
5 Jardine and Silverthorne, *New Organon*; Davis and Hunter, *Free Enquiry into the Vulgarly Received Notion of Nature*; Gaukroger, *The World and other Writings*. Each volume in the series contains a list of its other titles.
6 For the rationale, see Davis and Hunter, op. cit., pp. xxxv–vi.
7 Curley, *Hobbes' Leviathan*, p. lxxv.
8 Carey and Fowler, *Poems of Milton*, p. x.
9 Harth, 'The Text of Dryden's Poetry'.
10 Tanselle, 'Editing of Historical Documents', esp. pp. 20–1, 48–50. See also Bowers, *Textual and Literary Criticism*, ch. 4.
11 Smith, *Poems of Marvell*, 'Note by the General Editors'.
12 See also Lamont's edition of Baxter's *A Holy Commonwealth*, pp. vii–viii and passim.
13 Hunter and Gregory, *An Astrological Diary*; Porter, *The Earth Generated and Anatomized*.
14 Latham and Matthews, *Diary of Samuel Pepys*, vol. 1, p. lv.
15 Bowers, *Dramatic Works of Beaumont and Fletcher*, vol. 1, pp. xviiiff.

8 The Apparatus

1 Hunter, 'Whither Editing?', pp. 807–10.
2 Rees, '*Instauratio Instauratoris*', p. 47.
3 See Gibson, 'Significant Space'. See also Hunter, Clericuzio and Principe, *Correspondence of Boyle*, vol. 1, pp. xlvi–ii.

4   For examples, see de la Bédoyère, *Particular Friends*, or Forbes, Murdin and Willmoth, *Correspondence of Flamsteed*.
5   Malcolm, *Correspondence of Hobbes*, vol. 2, pp. 777–919.
6   Rees, *Philosophical Studies, c. 1611–19*, pp. 460–6.
7   Warrender, *Hobbes' De Cive* (Latin), app. C (pp. 317–24); Smith, *Poems of Marvell*, app. 3 (pp. 432–59)
8   de Beer, *Diary of John Evelyn*, vol. 2, p. 248.
9   Dear, 'Boyle in the Bag', p. 335.
10 Smith, *Poems of Marvell*, pp. 81–4.
11 See de Beer, *Correspondence of Locke*, vol. 1, p. lxvi, and passim.
12 The passage in question is in Hunter and Davis, *Works of Boyle*, vol. 14, pp. 302–4.
13 Rees, *Instauratio magna: Last Writings*, p. xcv.
14 Vickers, 'Bacon for our Time', p. 154.
15 Rees, *Instauratio magna: Last Writings*, pp. 172–3.
16 For example, see Hall, *Correspondence of Oldenburg*.
17 For instance, Newman and Principe, *Starkey's Alchemical Notebooks*. It is interesting to compare this with the more traditional method of placing the Latin and English texts on facing pages in Principe, *Aspiring Adept*, pp. 236–55, where extra spacing was needed in the Latin to balance the two.

9   Indexing/Searching

1   De Beer, *Diary of Evelyn*, vol. 6, preface.
2   Latham and Matthews, *Diary of Pepys*, vol. 11, p. ix.
3   See Frank, 'The John Ward Diaries', pp. 161, 170.
4   Hunter, Clericuzio and Principe, *Correspondence of Boyle*, vol. 2, pp. 265–6, vol. 6, p. 574.
5   *The Hartlib Papers*, 1st edn. (accompanying booklet), app. 4.
6   See Berners-Lee et al., 'The Semantic Web'.

Appendix 1   Alternative Transcription Methods

1   It is perhaps worth noting that, in this instance, I have eschewed the rather telegraphic system of notation advocated by some commentators (e.g., Bowers, 'Transcription of Manuscripts'). The amount of space saved by abbreviating 'after' to 'aft.' or 'deleted' to 'del.' is so small that it hardly seems worth bothering with, especially since it may have an alienating effect on some readers. See also Vander Meulen and Tanselle, 'A System of Manuscript Transcription'.
2   See Bowers, 'Transcription of Manuscripts', pp. 219–20.

Appendix 2   A Confusion of Brackets

1   See Labaree et al., *Papers of Franklin*, vol. 28, p. xlv and passim.
2   Hirst et al., *Mark Twain's Letters*, vol. 1, p. xxxix and passim. It is unfortunate, however, that in the edition of Emerson's journals, this symbol was used for the page numbers of the original manuscript: Gilman et al., *Emerson's Journals*, vol. 1, p. xlix.

Appendix 3   Bacon's 'Of Regiment of Health'

1. See above. See also, for instance, Melchionda, *Gli 'Essayes' di Francis Bacon*, pp. 305–6.
2. Wright, *Bacon's Essays*, pp. 269–88; Vickers, *Bacon's Essays*, app. 1 (pp. 134–41); app. 2 (pp. 142–5).
3. Arber, *A Harmony* (see pp. 56–65 for the essay reproduced here); Pitcher, *Bacon's Essays*, pp. 241–55.

Appendix 4   Hobbes' *Leviathan*, chapter 47

1. Curley, *Hobbes' Leviathan*, pp. 482–4. See also above, ch. 7. He also numbers the paragraphs.

Glossary

Note: the words defined here are mainly 'terms of art'. For definitions of more commonly used terms, see recent editions of *The Concise Oxford English Dictionary*

accidental   used to describe readings of a text mainly affecting its formal presentation, e.g. spelling, punctuation, etc.

Boolean search   search using the logical operators 'AND', 'OR' or 'NOT'. So named after the English mathematician George Boole (1815–64).

cancel   a printed insertion, either an entire leaf or a smaller piece of paper, placed in a book to replace a portion already printed.

catchword   the word, or part of a word, printed immediately below the last line of text at the foot of a page, anticipating the first word of the next page.

CEAA   Center for Editions of American Authors, succeeded in 1976 by the Center for Scholarly Editions (CSE).

collation   the practice of comparing two or more copies of a text in a systematic way. [Note: the word may also used to describe the composition of a book, especially the order of the signatures.]

compositor   a person who sets up type for printing, a typesetter.

concordance   a list of all the words used in a book or by an author.

copy text   the text used as the basis of an edition, the choice of which has been the subject of much controversy.

diplomatic   having the character of an exact and complete reproduction of a documentary text, including the original physical arrangement.

DTD   Document Type Definition, a set of definitions in a formal syntax that describe a class of SGML or XML documents in terms of constraints on the structure of those documents.

duodecimo   a book whose sheets are formed into twelve leaves each, often called 'twelvemo' from the contraction '12mo'.

edition   all the copies of a book printed at any one time or times from a single setting of type.

folio   a book whose sheets have been folded once only, so that each sheet forms two leaves, or a leaf in a book so formed.

forme   a body of type secured in a chase for printing at one impression.

gathering   one or more pairs of conjugate leaves folded together and containing pages in sequence.

hypertext   'non-sequential writing', lateral links in an electronic text.

HTML   HyperText Markup Language, a set of encoding practices used for the World Wide Web making possible the use of hypertext links.

incunabula   books printed before 1500.

issue   a distinct group of copies of an edition distinguished from the rest by intentional, slight variations in the printed matter.

ligature   two or more letters joined together, as in 'æ'.

MS   manuscript.

octavo a book in which each sheet is folded to form eight leaves or sixteen pages.
PDF Portable Document Format, a form of online publication that retains the format of the original and does not require text encoding.
quarto a size of paper made by folding a sheet twice, giving four leaves or eight pages; hence a book composed of sheets thus folded.
recto the front of a leaf; hence the right-hand side of an open book.
RTF Rich Text Format, a file format developed for cross-platform document exchange.
scriptoria places set aside for writing.
SGML Standard Generalised Markup Language, a set of standardised, generic encoding practices used in digital texts.
signature one or more letters or other signs, often with a numeral, printed below the last line of text on certain recto pages of a book to guide the forming of printed sheets into gatherings.
solidus an oblique stroke used for editorial or other purposes.
stemmata/stemmatics the lines of descent of different versions of a text, and the study of these.
substantive used to describe readings in a text which are significant, affecting an author's meaning.
TEI Text Encoding Initiative, an initiative jointly set up in Chicago and Oxford in 1987 to establish guidelines for encoding texts in SGML using a common set of tags with agreed meanings and attributes.
thorn the name of an Old English letter denoting 'th'.
tilde the sign '~' placed over a letter to indicate a contraction.
URL Uniform Resource Locator, a string of characters conforming to a standardised format, which refers to a resource on the Internet by its location.
variant version of a text or part of a text differing from that normally encountered.
verso the back of a leaf; hence the left-hand side of an open book.
XML eXtensible Markup Language, a further set of encoding practices, originally a subset of SGML.

Bibliography

Editions are placed under the names of their editors, with a cross-reference under the name of the author. In these cross-references, the name of the first editor only is given in cases where works have more than one editor.

In citations of contributions to edited volumes, full details of the volume are only given if it does not appear in the Bibliography in its own right.

Adam, Charles, and Tannery, Paul (eds), *Œuvres de Descartes* (13 vols., Paris: Léopold Cerf, 1897–1913; revised edn, Libraire Philosophique J. Vrin, Paris, 1964–74)

Allen, P.S. (ed.), *Opus Epistolarum Des. Erasmi Roterodami* (12 vols., Oxford: Clarendon Press, 1906–58)

Anderson, Sonia (ed.), *The Finch Manuscripts, vol. 5: General Correspondence 1693, Secret Service Papers 1691–3 and Naval and Military Papers to 1694*, Historical Manuscripts Commission (London: The Stationery Office, 2004)

Arber, Edward, *A Harmony of the Essays, etc., of Francis Bacon* (London: English Reprints, 1871)

Ashmole, Elias: see Gunther, R.T.; Josten, C.H.

Aubrey, John: see Clark, Andrew; Fowles, John

Austen, Jane: see Southam, Brian

Bacon, Francis: see Arber, Edward; Jardine, Lisa; Kiernan, Michael; Melchionda, Mario; Pitcher, John; Rees, Graham; Vickers, Brian; Wright, W. Aldis

Banks, Sir Joseph: see Carter, H.B.

Barker, Nicolas, 'Typography and the Meaning of Words: the Revolution in the Layout of Books in the Eighteenth Century', in Giles Barber and Bernhard Fabian (eds), *Buch und Buchhandel in Europa im achtzehnten Jahrhundert* (Hamburg: Dr Ernt Hauswedell & Co, 1981), 126–65

Barnard, John, and McKenzie, D.F. (eds), with the assistance of Maureen Bell, *The Cambridge History of the Book in Britain*, Vol. 4, 1557–1695 (Cambridge: University Press, 2002)

Baxter, Richard: see Keeble, N.H.; Lamont, William

Beal, Peter, 'Notions in Garrison: the Seventeenth-century Commonplace Book', in W. Speed Hill (ed.), *New Ways of Looking at Old Texts: Papers of the Renaissance English Text Society, 1985–91* (Binghampton, NY: Medieval & Renaissance Texts and Studies, 1993), 131–47

Beal, Peter, *In Praise of Scribes: Manuscripts and their Makers in Seventeenth-century England* (Oxford: Clarendon Press, 1998)

Beaumont and Fletcher: see Bowers, Fredson

Beeley, Philip, and Scriba, Christoph J. (eds), with the assistance of Uwe Mayer and Siegmund Probst, *The Correspondence of John Wallis* (Oxford: University Press, 2003–, in progress)

Behn, Aphra: see Todd, Janet

Bennett, H.S., *English Books & Readers, 1475–1557* (Cambridge: University Press, 1952)

Bennett, H.S., *English Books & Readers, 1558–1603* (Cambridge: University Press, 1965)

Bennett, H.S., *English Books & Readers, 1603–40* (Cambridge: University Press, 1970)

Bennett, Kate, 'Editing Aubrey', in Joe Bray, Miriam Handley and Anne C. Henry (eds), *Ma(r)king the Text: the Presentation of Meaning on the Literary Page* (Aldershot: Ashgate, 2000), 271–90

Berners-Lee, Tim, Hendler, James, and Lassila, Ora, 'The Semantic Web', *Scientific American*, 17 May 2001 [consulted online at: www.scientificamerican.com/print_version.cfm?articleID=00048144-10D2-1C]

Binns, J.W., *Intellectual Culture in Elizabethan and Jacobean England: the Latin Writings of the Age* (Leeds: Francis Cairns, 1990)

Birch, Thomas (ed.), *The Works of Robert Boyle* (5 vols., London: Andrew Millar, 1744)

Boswell, James: see Osborn, J.M.

Bourcier, Élisabeth, *Les journaux privés en Angleterre de 1600 à 1660* (Paris: Publications de la Sorbonne, 1976)

Bowers, Fredson, *Principles of Bibliographical Description* (Princeton: University Press, 1949; repr. New York: Russell & Russell, 1962)

Bowers, Fredson, *Textual and Literary Criticism* (Cambridge: University Press, 1959)

Bowers, Fredson, *Bibliography and Textual Criticism* (Oxford: Clarendon Press, 1964)

Bowers, Fredson, *Essays in Bibliography, Text and Editing* (Charlottesville: University Press of Virginia, 1975)

Bowers, Fredson, 'Transcription of Manuscripts: the Record of Variants', *Studies in Bibliography*, 29 (1976), 212–64

Bowers, Fredson (general editor), *The Dramatic Works in the Beaumont and Fletcher Canon* (10 vols., Cambridge: University Press, 1966–96)

Boyd, Julian P., Cullen, Charles T., Catanzariti, Oberg, Barbara B., et al. (eds), *The Papers of Thomas Jefferson* (Princeton: University Press, 1950–, in progress)

Boydston, Jo Ann, 'Standards for Scholarly Editing: the CEAA and the CSE', *Text*, 6 (1994), 21–33

Boyle, Robert: see Birch, Thomas; Davis, Edward B.; Harwood, John; Hunter, Michael

Braddick, M.J., and Greengrass, M. (eds), 'The Letters of Sir Cheney Culpeper (1641–1657)', in *Seventeenth-century Political and Financial Papers: Camden Miscellany XXXIIII*, Camden 5th series, vol. 7 (Cambridge: University Press for the Royal Historical Society, 1996), 105–402

Brink, C.O., *English Classical Scholarship: Historical Reflections on Bentley, Porson and Housman* (Cambridge: James Clarke, 1986)

Briquet, C-M., *Les filigranes: dictionnaire historique des marques du papier*, ed. Allan Stevenson (4 vols., reprint edition with supplementary material in vol. 1, Amsterdam: Paper Publications Society, 1968)

Broadway, Jan, *Sir William Dugdale and the Significance of County History in Early Stuart England*, Dugdale Society Occasional Papers, No. 39 (Stratford-on-Avon: Dugdale Society, 1999)

Brown, Sylvia (ed.), *Women's Writing in Stuart England* (Stroud, Gloucs.: Sutton Publishing, 1999)

Browne, Sir Thomas: see Robbins, Robin

Burkhardt, Frederick, Smith, Sydney, et al. (eds), *The Correspondence of Charles Darwin* (Cambridge: University Press, 1985–, in progress)

Burton, Robert: see Faulkner, Thomas C.
Butt, John, et al. (eds), *The Twickenham Edition of the Poems of Alexander Pope* (11 vols., London: Methuen, 1939–69)
Carey, John, and Fowler, Alastair (eds), *The Poems of John Milton*, Longman Annotated English Poets (London and Harlow: Longman, 1968)
Carter, Clarence E., *Historical Editing* (Bulletins of the National Archives, No. 7, 1952)
Carter, Harry, *A History of the Oxford University Press, Volume 1: To the Year 1780* (Oxford: Clarendon Press, 1975)
Carter, H.B. (ed.), *The Sheep and Wool Correspondence of Sir Joseph Banks, 1781–1820* (Sydney and London: Library Council of New South Wales in association with the British Museum (Natural History), 1979)
Casaubon, Meric: see Serjeantson, Richard
CEAA [Center for Editions of American Authors], *Statement of Editorial Principles and Procedures: a Working Manual for Editing Nineteenth-century American Texts* (revised edn., New York: Modern Language Association of America, 1972)
'The Center for Scholarly Editions: an Introductory Statement', *Publications of the Modern Language Association of America*, 92 (1977), 583–97
Chambers, Douglas, ' "Excuse these Impertinences". Evelyn in his Letterbooks', in Frances Harris and Michael Hunter (eds), *John Evelyn and his Milieu* (London: British Library, 2003), 21–36
Chapman, R.W., 'An Inventory of Paper, 1674', *The Library*, 4th series 7 (1926–7), 402–8
Chesterfield, Philip Dormer Stanhope, 4th Earl of, *Letters* (2nd edn., 4 vols., London: Dodsley, 1774)
Clapp, S.L.C., 'The Beginnings of Subscription Publication in the Seventeenth Century', *Modern Philology*, 29 (1931), 199–224
Clark, Andrew (ed.), *'Brief Lives', chiefly of Contemporaries, set down by John Aubrey, between the Years 1669 and 1696* (2 vols., Oxford: Clarendon Press, 1898)
Clough, C.H., 'The Cult of Antiquity: Letters and Letter Collections', in C.H. Clough (ed.), *Cultural Aspects of the Italian Renaissance: Essays in Honour of Paul Oskar Kristeller* (Manchester: University Press, 1976), 33–67
Cohen, I. Bernard, *Introduction to Newton's Principia* (Cambridge, Mass.: Harvard University Press, 1971)
Culpeper, Sir Cheney: see Braddick, M.J.
Cunningham, Peter (ed.), *The Letters of Horace Walpole, Earl of Orford* (9 vols., London: Bentley, 1857)
Curley, Edwin (ed.), Thomas Hobbes, *Leviathan, with Selected Variants from the Latin Edition of 1668* (Indianapolis: Hackett Publishing Co., 1994)
Dainard, J.A. (ed.), *Editing Correspondence* (New York: Garland, 1979)
Darwin, Charles: see Burkhardt, Frederick
Davies, Martin, 'Humanism in Script and Print in the Fifteenth Century', in Jill Kraye (ed.), *The Cambridge Companion to Renaissance Humanism* (Cambridge: University Press, 1996), 47–62
Davis, Edward B., and Hunter, Michael (eds), Robert Boyle, *A Free Enquiry into the Vulgarly Received Notion of Nature* (Cambridge: University Press, 1996)
Davis, Natalie Zemon, 'Beyond the Market: Books as Gifts in Sixteenth-century France', *Transactions of the Royal Historical Society*, 5th series 33 (1983), 69–88
Davis, Tom, 'The CEAA and Modern Textual Editing', *The Library*, 5th series 32 (1977), 61–74

Dear, Peter, 'Boyle in the Bag!' (review essay), *British Journal for the History of Science*, 35 (2002), 335–40

de Beer, E.S. (ed.), *The Diary of John Evelyn* (6 vols., Oxford: Clarendon Press, 1955)

de Beer, E.S. (ed.), *The Correspondence of John Locke* (8 vols., Oxford: Clarendon Press, 1976–89)

de la Bédoyère, Guy (ed.), *Particular Friends: the Correspondence of Samuel Pepys and John Evelyn* (Woodbridge: Boydell Press, 1997)

Descartes, René: see Adam, Charles; Gaukroger, Stephen

Donaldson, Ian, 'Collecting Ben Jonson', in Nash, *Culture of Collected Editions*, 19–31

Dryden, John: see Hooker, E.N.

Duppa, Brian: see Isham, Sir Gyles

Eisenstein, Elizabeth, *The Printing Press as an Agent of Change: Communications and Cultural Transformations in Early Modern Europe* (2 vols. Cambridge: University Press, 1979)

Emerson, R.W.: see Gilman, W.H.

Erasmus, Desiderius: see Allen, P.S.

Evelyn, John: see de Beer, E.S.; de la Bédoyère, Guy

Ezell, Margaret J.M., *The Patriarch's Wife: Literary Evidence and the History of the Family* (Chapel Hill: University of North Carolina Press, 1987)

Falkland, Elizabeth Cary, Lady: see Wolfe, Heather

Faraday, Michael: see James, Frank; Pearce Williams, L.

Faulkner, Thomas C., Kiessling, Nicholas K, and Blair, Rhonda L. (eds), Robert Burton, *The Anatomy of Melancholy*, with an Introduction and Commentary by J.M. Bamborough with Martin Dodsworth (6 vols., Oxford: Clarendon Press, 1989–2000)

Favaro, Antonio (ed.), *Le Opere di Galileo Galilei* (20 vols., Florence: G. Barbèra, 1890–1909)

Febvre, Lucien, and Martin, Henri-Jean, *The Coming of the Book: the Impact of Printing 1550–1650* (English edn., trans. David Gerrard, ed. Geoffrey Nowell-Smith and David Wootton, London: NLB, 1976, new edn., Verso, 1984; original French edition, 1958)

Finlay, Michael, *Western Writing Implements in the Age of the Quill Pen* (Wetheral, Cumbria: Plains Books, 1990)

Flamsteed, John: see Forbes, E.G.

Forbes, E.G., Murdin, Lesley, and Willmoth, Frances (eds), *The Correspondence of John Flamsteed, First Astronomer Royal* (3 vols., Bristol: Institute of Physics Publishing, 1995–2002)

Foucault, Michel, 'What is an Author?', in Paul Rabinow (ed.), *The Foucault Reader* (London: Penguin Books, 1984), 101–20

Fowles, John, and Legg, Rodney (eds), John Aubrey, *Monumenta Britannica*, Parts 1–3 (2 vols., Milborne Port: Dorset Publishing Company, 1980–2)

Foxon, David, 'Greg's "Rationale" and the Editing of Pope', *The Library,* 5th series 33 (1978), 119–24

Frank, Robert G., 'The John Ward Diaries: Mirror of Seventeenth Century Science and Medicine', *Journal of the History of Medicine*, 29 (1974), 147–79

Franklin, Benjamin: see Labaree, L.W.

Frasca-Spada, Marina, and Jardine, Nick (eds), *Books and the Sciences in History* (Cambridge: University Press, 2000)

Gaisser, Julia H., *Catullus and his Renaissance Readers* (Oxford: Clarendon Press, 1993)
Galilei, Galileo: see Favaro, Antonio
Gaskell, Philip, *A New Introduction to Bibliography* (Oxford: Clarendon Press, 1972)
Gaskell, Philip, *From Writer to Reader: Studies in Editorial Method* (Oxford: Clarendon Press, 1978)
Gaudricault, Raymond, *Filigranes et autres caractéristiques des papiers fabriqués en France au XVIIe et XVIIIe siècles* (Paris: CNRS Éditions, 1995)
Gaukroger, Stephen (ed.), René Descartes, *The World and other Writings* (Cambridge: University Press, 1998)
Gibson, Jonathan, 'Significant Space in Manuscript Letters', *The Seventeenth Century*, 12 (1997), 1–10.
Gilman, William H., Orth, Ralph H., et al. (eds), *The Journals and Miscellaneous Notebooks of Ralph Waldo Emerson* (16 vols., Cambridge, Mass: Belknapp Press, 1960–82)
Goldberg, Jonathan, ' "What? in a names that which we call a Rose", the Desired Texts of *Romeo and Juliet*', in McLeod, *Crisis in Editing*, 173–201
Goldie, Mark (ed.), *John Locke: Selected Correspondence* (Oxford: University Press, 2002)
Grafton, Anthony, *Joseph Scaliger: a Study in the History of Classical Scholarship. I: Textual Criticism and Exegesis* (Oxford: Clarendon Press, 1983)
Grafton, Anthony, *The Footnote: a Curious History* (London: Faber & Faber, 1997)
Greengrass, Mark, 'Samuel Hartlib and Scribal Publication', *Acta Comeniana*, 12 (1997), 47–62
Greengrass, Mark, 'Archive Refractions: Hartlib's Papers and the Workings of an Intelligencer', in Hunter, *Archives of the Scientific Revolution*, 35–47
Greetham, D.C., '[Textual] Criticism and Deconstruction', *Studies in Bibliography*, 44 (1991), 1–30
Greetham, D.C., *Textual Scholarship: an Introduction* (New York: Garland Publishing, 1994)
Greetham, D.C. (ed.), *Scholarly Editing: a Guide to Research* (New York: Modern Language Association of America, 1995)
Greetham, D.C., *Theories of the Text* (Oxford: University Press, 1999)
Greg, W.W., *Collected Papers*, ed. J.C. Maxwell (Oxford: Clarendon Press, 1966)
Greg, W.W., *A Companion to Arber*, ed. I.G. Philip (Oxford: Clarendon Press, 1967)
Greg, W.W., 'The Rationale of Copy-Text', *Studies in Bibliography*, 3 (1950–1), 19–36, reprinted in his *Collected Papers*, 374–91, and in Ronald Gottesman and Scott Bennett (eds), *Art and Error: Modern Textual Editing* (London: Methuen, 1970), 17–36
Gregory, David: see Hiscock, W.G.
Gunby, David, Carnegie, David, Hammond, Anthony, DelVecchio, Doreen, and Jackson, M.P. (eds), *The Works of John Webster* (Cambridge: University Press, 1995–, in progress)
Gunther, R.T. (ed.), *The Diary and Will of Elias Ashmole, Edited and Extended from the Original Manuscripts* (Oxford: Old Ashmolean Reprints no. 2, 1927)
Gunther, R.T. (ed.), *Early Science in Oxford* (14 vols., Oxford: privately printed, 1923–45)
Hall, A. Rupert, 'Pitfalls in the Editing of Newton's Papers', *History of Science*, 40 (2002), 407–24

Hall, A.R., and Hall, M.B. (eds), *The Correspondence of Henry Oldenburg* (13 vols., Madison, Milwaukee and London: University of Wisconsin Press, Mansell and Taylor & Francis, 1965–86)

Halsband, Robert, 'Editing the Letters of Letter-writers', *Studies in Bibliography*, 11 (1958), 25–37, reprinted in Ronald Gottesman and Scott Bennett (eds), *Art and Error: Modern Textual Editing* (London: Methuen, 1970), 124–39

Handlin, Oscar, et al. (eds), *Harvard Guide to American History* (Cambridge, Mass.: Harvard University Press, 1954); revised edn., ed. Frank Freidel (2 vols., Cambridge, Mass: Belknapp Press, 1974)

Hanna, Ralph, 'The Application of Thought to Textual Criticism in All Modes – With Apologies to A.E. Housman', *Studies in Bibliography*, 53 (2002), 163–72

Harth, Phillip, 'The Text of Dryden's Poetry', *Huntington Library Quarterly*, 63 (2000), 227–44

The Hartlib Papers on CD-Rom, 1st edn. (Ann Arbor: University Microfilms International, 1995)

The Hartlib Papers on CD-Rom. A Complete Text and Image Database, 2nd edn. (Sheffield: HROnline, 2002)

Hartlib Papers Project, *Newsletter* (10 issues, November 1989 to February 1996)

Harvey, P.D.A., *Editing Historical Records* (London: British Library, 2001)

Harwood, John T. (ed.), *The Early Essays and Ethics of Robert Boyle* (Carbondale and Edwardsville: Southern Illinois University Press, 1991)

Hazen, A.T., *A Bibliography of Horace Walpole* (New Haven: Yale University Press, 1948)

Heawood, Edward, 'Sources of Early English Paper Supply', *The Library*, 2nd series 10 (1929–30), 282–307, 427–54

Heawood, Edward, 'Paper Used in England after 1600', *The Library*, 2nd series 11 (1930–1), 263–99, 466–98

Heawood, Edward, 'Further Notes on Paper Used in England after 1600', *The Library*, 3rd series 2 (1947), 119–49

Heawood, Edward, *Watermarks, Mainly of the Seventeenth and Eighteenth Centuries* (Hilversum, 1950; repr., Amsterdam: Paper Publications Society, 1970 and 1986)

Herford, C.H., Simpson, Percy, and Simpson, Evelyn (eds), *Ben Jonson* (11 vols., Oxford: Clarendon Press, 1925–52)

Hervey, Lord Francis (ed.), *Suffolk in the XVIIth Century. The Breviary of Suffolk by Robert Reyce* (London: John Murray, 1902)

Higgins-Biddle, J.C. (ed.), John Locke, *The Reasonableness of Christianity as Delivered in the Scriptures* (Oxford: Clarendon Press, 1999)

Hill, W. Speed (general editor), *The Folger Library Edition of the Works of Richard Hooker* (Cambridge, Mass.: The Belknapp Press of Harvard University Press, 1977–, in progress)

Hill, W. Speed, 'English Renaissance: Nondramatic Literature', in Greetham, D.C. (ed.), *Scholarly Editing: a Guide to Research* (New York: Modern Language Association of America, 1995), 204–30

Hinman, Charlton, *The Printing and Proof-Reading of the First Folio of Shakespeare* (2 vols., Oxford: Clarendon Press, 1963)

Hirst, R.H., et al. (eds), *Mark Twain's Letters* (Berkeley and Los Angeles: University of California Press, 1988–, in progress)

Hiscock, W.G. (ed.), *David Gregory, Isaac Newton and their Circle. Extracts from David Gregory's Memoranda, 1677–1708* (Oxford: for the Editor, 1937)

Hitchens, W.J., Matuszewski, Adam, and Young, John (eds), *The Letters of Jan Jonston to Samuel Hartlib* (Warsaw: wydawnictwo, 2000)

Hobbes, Thomas: see Curley, Edwin; Malcolm, Noel; Tricaud, François; Tuck, Richard; Warrender, Howard

Hobbs, Mary, *Early Seventeenth-century Verse Miscellany Manuscripts* (Aldershot: Scolar Press, 1992)

Hobbs, William: see Porter, Roy

Hockey, Susan, *Electronic Texts in the Humanities: Principles and Practice* (Oxford: University Press, 2000)

Hooke, Robert, *Micrographia* (1665) (CD-ROM from Octavo, 1998: www.octavo.com/editions/hkemic/index.html)

Hooker, Edward N., Swedenberg, H.T. jr., Dearing, V.A., and Roper, Alan (eds), *The Works of John Dryden* (Berkeley and Los Angeles: University of California Press, 1956–, in progress)

Hooker, Richard: see Hill, W. Speed

Hunnisett, R.F., *Editing Records for Publication*, Archives and the User, No. 4 (British Records Association, 1977)

Hunter, Lynette, and Hutton, Sarah (eds), *Women, Science and Medicine 1500–1700* (Stroud, Gloucs: Sutton Publishing Ltd., 1997)

Hunter, Michael, 'The Impact of Print', *The Book Collector*, 28 (1979), 335–52

Hunter, Michael, 'Ancients, Moderns, Philologists and Scientists', *Annals of Science*, 39 (1982), 187–92, reprinted in id., *Science and the Shape of Orthodoxy* (Woodbridge: Boydell Press, 1995), 215–22

Hunter, Michael, 'How to Edit a Seventeenth-century Manuscript: Principles and Practice', *The Seventeenth Century*, 10 (1995), 277–310

Hunter, Michael, 'The Reluctant Philanthropist: Robert Boyle and the "Communication of Secrets and Receits in Physick" ', in O.P. Grell and Andrew Cunningham (eds), *Religio Medici: Medicine and Religion in Seventeenth-century England* (Aldershot: Ashgate, 1997), 247–72, reprinted in Michael Hunter, *Robert Boyle (1627–91): Scrupulosity and Science* (Woodbridge: Boydell Press, 2000), 202–22

Hunter, Michael, 'Whither Editing?' (review essay), *Studies in History and Philosophy of Science*, 34 (2003), 805–20

Hunter, Michael (ed.), *Robert Boyle by Himself and his Friends* (London: William Pickering, 1994)

Hunter, Michael (ed.), *Archives of the Scientific Revolution: the Formation and Exchange of Ideas in Seventeenth-century Europe* (Woodbridge: Boydell Press, 1998)

Hunter, Michael (with contributions by Davis, Edward B., Knight, Harriet, Littleton, Charles, and Principe, Lawrence M.), *The Boyle Papers: Understanding the Manuscripts of Robert Boyle* (Aldershot: Ashgate, forthcoming 2006)

Hunter, Michael, Clericuzio, Antonio and Principe, Lawrence M. (eds), *The Correspondence of Robert Boyle* (6 vols., London: Pickering & Chatto, 2001)

Hunter, Michael, and Davis, Edward B. (eds), *The Works of Robert Boyle* (14 vols., London: Pickering & Chatto, 1999–2000)

Hunter, Michael, and Gregory, Annabel (eds), *An Astrological Diary of the Seventeenth Century: Samuel Jeake of Rye 1652–99* (Oxford: Clarendon Press, 1988)

Hunter, Michael, and Knight, Harriet (eds), *Unpublished Material Relating to Robert Boyle's 'Memoirs for the Natural History of Human Blood'*, Robert Boyle Project

Occasional Papers, No. 2 (London: Robert Boyle Project, 2005; available as PDF at: www.bbk.ac.uk/boyle)

Hunter, Michael, and Littleton, Charles, 'The Work-diaries of Robert Boyle: a Newly-discovered Source and its Internet Publication', *Notes and Records of the Royal Society*, 55 (2001), 373–90

Hunter, Michael, Mandelbrote, Giles, Ovenden, Richard and Smith, Nigel (eds), *A Radical's Books. The Library Catalogue of Samuel Jeake of Rye 1623–90* (Woodbridge: D.S. Brewer, 1999)

Hunter, Michael, and de Mowbray, Malcolm, 'The Editor in the Republic of Letters' (review essay), *British Journal for the History of Science*, 30 (1997), 221–5

Hunter, Michael, and Principe, Lawrence M., 'The Lost Papers of Robert Boyle', *Annals of Science*, 60 (2003), 269–311

Huygens, Christiaan: see Korteweg, D.J.

Iliffe, Rob, ' "Is he like other men?" The meaning of the *Principia Mathematica* and the Author as Idol', in Gerald Maclean (ed.), *Culture and Society in the Stuart Restoration: Literature, Drama, History* (Cambridge: University Press, 1995), 159–76

Iliffe, Rob, 'A "connected system"? The Snare of a Beautiful Hand and the Unity of Newton's Archive', in Hunter, *Archives of the Scientific Revolution*, 137–57

Iliffe, Rob, 'Digitizing Isaac: the Newton Edition and an Electronic Edition of Newton's Papers', in James E. Force and Sarah Hutton (eds), *Newton and Newtonianism: New Studies* (Dordrecht: Kluwer Academic Publishers, 2004), 23–38

Ingram, William H., 'The Ligatures of Early Printed Greek', *Greek, Roman & Byzantine Studies*, 7 (1966), 371–89

Isham, Sir Gyles (ed.), *The Correspondence of Bishop Brian Duppa and Sir Justinian Isham 1650–1660* (Lamport: Northamptonshire Record Society, vol. 17, 1955 for 1951)

James, Frank (ed.), *The Correspondence of Michael Faraday* (London: Institution of Electrical Engineers, 1991–, in progress)

Jardine, Lisa, *Erasmus, Man of Letters* (Princeton: University Press, 1993)

Jardine, Lisa, 'Defamiliarising Erasmus: Unstitching P.S. Allen's Edition of the Letters' (available online at: www.livesandletters.ac.uk, reference ERA/2002/03/001)

Jardine, Lisa, and Silverthorne, Michael (eds), Francis Bacon, *The New Organon* (Cambridge: University Press, 2000)

Jeake, Samuel: see Hunter, Michael

Jefferson, Thomas: see Boyd, Julian P.

Johns, Adrian, *The Nature of the Book: Print and Knowledge in the Making* (Chicago: University Press, 1998)

Johnson, Charles, and Jenkinson, Hilary, *English Court Hand, AD 1066 to 1500. Illustrated Chiefly from the Public Records. Part 1: Text* (Oxford: Clarendon Press, 1915)

Johnson, Samuel: see McAdam, E.L.; Redford, Bruce

Jones, Peter (ed.), *Sir Isaac Newton: a Catalogue of Manuscripts and Papers Collected and Published on Microfilm by Chadwyck-Healey* (microfilm edition, Cambridge: Chadwyck-Healey, 1991)

Jonson, Ben: see Herford, C.H.

Jonston, Jan: see Hitchens, W.J.

Josten, C.H. (ed.), *Elias Ashmole (1617–92): His Autobiographical and Historical Notes, his Correspondence and Other Contemporary Sources Relating to his Life and Work* (5 vols., Oxford: Clarendon Press, 1966)

Jurin, James: see Rushnock, Andrea

Keeble, N.H., and Nuttall, G.F., *Calendar of the Correspondence of Richard Baxter* (2 vols., Oxford: Clarendon Press, 1991)

Kennedy, A.J., *The Internet: the Rough Guide* (4th edn., London: Penguin, 1998)

Kenny, E.J., *The Classical Text: Aspects of Editing in the Age of the Printed Book* (Berkeley and Los Angeles: University of California Press, 1974)

Kerrigan, John, 'The Editor as Reader: Constructing Renaissance Texts', in James, Raven, Helen, Small and Naomi Tadmor (eds), *The Practice and Representation of Reading in England* (Cambridge: University Press, 1996), 102–24

Kiernan, Michael (ed.), Sir Francis Bacon, *The Essayes or Counsels, Civill and Morall* (Oxford: Clarendon Press, 1985)

Kline, Mary-Jo, *A Guide to Documentary Editing* (2nd edn., Baltimore: Johns Hopkins Press, 1998; 1st edn., 1987)

Korteweg, D.J., et al. (eds), *Oeuvres Complètes de Christiaan Huygens* (22 vols., The Hague: Martin Nijhoff, 1888–1950)

Koyré, Alexandre, and Cohen, I.B. (eds), *Isaac Newton's Philosophia Naturalis Principia Mathematica* (2 vols., Cambridge: University Press, 1972)

Kümmel, W.G., *The New Testament: the History of the Investigation of its Problems*, trans. S.M. Gilmour and H.C. Kee (London: SCM Press, 1973)

Labaree, L.W., Willcox, William B., Lopez, Claude A., Oberg, Barbara B., Cohn, Ellen R. et al. (eds), *The Papers of Benjamin Franklin* (New Haven.: Yale University Press, 1959–, in progress)

Lamont, William (ed.), Richard Baxter, *A Holy Commonwealth* (Cambridge: University Press, 1994)

Laslett, Peter (ed.), John Locke, *Two Treatises of Government. A Critical Edition with Introduction and Apparatus Criticus* (2nd edn., Cambridge: University Press, 1967)

Latham, Robert, and Matthews, William (eds) *The Diary of Samuel Pepys* (11 vols., London: G. Bell & Sons, 1970–83)

Leibniz, G.W.: see Ritter, Paul

Levere, Trevor H. (ed.), *Editing Texts in the History of Science and Medicine* (New York: Garland, 1982)

Lewis, W.S. (ed.), *The Yale Edition of Horace Walpole's Correspondence* (48 vols., New Haven: Yale University Press, 1937–83)

Lindenbaum, Peter, 'Authors and Publishers in the Late Seventeenth Century: New Evidence on their Relations', *The Library*, 6th series 17 (1995), 250–68

Lindenbaum, Peter, 'Dividing and Conquering Milton', in Nash, *Culture of Collected Editions*, 32–48

Locke, John: see de Beer, E.S.; Goldie, Mark; Higgins-Biddle, J.A.; Laslett, Peter; Nidditch, P.H.

Loewenstein, Joseph, *The Author's Due: Printing and the Prehistory of Copyright* (Chicago: University of Chicago Press, 2002)

Lohne, J.A., 'The Increasing Corruption of Newton's Diagrams', *History of Science*, 6 (1967), 69–89

Long, P., *A Summary Catalogue of the Lovelace Collection of the Papers of John Locke in the Bodleian Library* (Oxford: Bodleian Library, 1959)

Lord, G.F. de, et al. (eds), *Poems on Affairs of State: Augustan Satirical Verse 1660–1714* (7 vols., New Haven: Yale University Press, 1963–75)

Louis, Cameron (ed.), *Records of Early English Drama: Sussex* (Toronto: University of Toronto Press, 2000)

Love, Harold, *The Culture and Commerce of Texts: Scribal Publication in Seventeenth-century England* (new edn., Amherst: University of Massachusetts Press, 1998; originally published as *Scribal Publication in Seventeenth Century England*, Oxford: Clarendon Press, 1993)

Maanen, Jan van, Jesseph, Douglas, Hunter, Michael, Stedall, Jacqueline, and Malcolm, Noel, 'John Pell (1611–85): Mathematical Utopian' (Review Symposium), *Metascience*, 15 (2006), 217–49.

Maas, Paul, *Textual Criticism*, trans. Barbara Flower (Oxford: Clarendon Press, 1958)

Maddison, R.E.W., 'A Tentative Index of the Correspondence of the Honourable Robert Boyle, F.R.S.', *Notes and Records of the Royal Society*, 13 (1958), 128–201

Malcolm, Noel (ed.), *The Correspondence of Thomas Hobbes*, The Clarendon Edition of the Works of Thomas Hobbes, vols. 6–7 (2 vols., Oxford: Clarendon Press, 1994)

Malcolm, Noel, and Stedall, Jacqueline, *John Pell (1611–85) and his Correspondence with Sir Charles Cavendish* (Oxford: University Press, 2005)

Marotti, Arthur F., *Manuscript, Print and the English Renaissance Lyric* (Ithaca: Cornell University Press, 1995)

Martin, Henri-Jean, *The History and Power of Writing*, English trans. by Lydia Cochrane (Chicago: University of Chicago Press, 1994; original French edition, 1988)

Marvell, Andrew: see Smith, Nigel

Matthews, William, *British Diaries: an Annotated Bibliography* (Berkeley and Los Angeles: University of California Press, 1950; reprinted 1984)

Maxwell-Lyte, H., ' "U" and "V": a Note on Palaeography', *Bulletin of the Institute of Historical Research*, 2 (1925), 63–5

McAdam, E.L., Bate, W.J., et al. (eds), *The Yale Edition of the Works of Samuel Johnson* (New Haven: Yale University Press, 1958–, in progress)

McCarren, Vincent, and Moffat, Douglas (eds), *A Guide to Editing Middle English* (Ann Arbor: University of Michigan Press, 1998)

McGann, Jerome, *A Critique of Modern Textual Criticism* (Chicago: University of Chicago Press, 1983)

McGann, Jerome, 'The Monks and the Giants: Textual and Bibliographical Studies and the Interpretation of Literary Works', in id. (ed.), *Textual Criticism and Literary Interpretation* (Chicago: University of Chicago Press, 1985), 180–99

McGann, Jerome J., *Radiant Textuality: Literature after the World Wide Web* (New York and Basingstoke: Palgrave, 2001)

McGann, Jerome J., 'The Rationale of Hypertext', in Sutherland, *Electronic Text*, 19–46, reprinted in McGann, *Radiant Textuality*, 53–74

McGuire, J.E., and Tamny, Martin (eds), *Certain Philosophical Questions: Newton's Trinity Notebook* (Cambridge: University Press, 1983)

McKenzie, D.F., *The Cambridge University Press 1696–1712: a Bibliographical Study* (2 vols., Cambridge: University Press, 1966)

McKenzie, D.F., 'Printers of the Mind: Some Notes on Bibliographical Theories and Printing-House Practices', *Studies in Bibliography*, 22 (1969), 1–75, reprinted in McKenzie, *Making Meaning*, 12–85

McKenzie, D.F., 'Typography and Meaning: the Case of William Congreve', in Giles Barber and Bernhard Fabian (eds), *Buch und Buchhandel in Europa in achtzehnten Jahrhundert* (Hamburg: Dr Ernt Hauswedell & Co., 1981), 81–125, reprinted in McKenzie, *Making Meaning*, 198–236

McKenzie, D.F., *Bibliography and the Sociology of Texts* (London: British Library, 1986)

McKenzie, D.F., 'Speech-Manuscript-Print', in Dave Oliphant and Robin Bradford (eds), *New Directions in Textual Studies* (Austin: Harry Ransom Humanities Research Center, 1990), 87–109, reprinted in *Making Meaning*, 237–58

McKenzie, D.F., *Making Meaning*, ed. P.D. McDonald and M.F. Suarez (Amherst: University of Massachusetts Press, 2002)

McKerrow, R.B., 'Some Notes on the Letters *i, j, u* and *v* in Sixteenth-century Printing', *The Library*, 3rd series 1 (1910), 239–59

McKerrow, R.B., *An Introduction to Bibliography for Literary Students* (Oxford: Clarendon Press, 1927; 2nd impression, 1928)

McKerrow, R.B., *Prolegomena for the Oxford Shakespeare: a Study in Editorial Method* (Oxford: Clarendon Press, 1939)

McKitterick, David, *Print, Manuscript and the Search for Order, 1450–1830* (Cambridge: University Press, 2003)

McLaverty, James, 'The Concept of Authorial Intention in Textual Criticism', *The Library*, 6th series 6 (1984), 121–38

McLaverty, James, ' "For Who So Fond as Youthful Bards of Fame?" Pope's *Works* of 1717', in Nash, *Culture of Collected Editions*, 49–68

McLeod, Randall (ed.), *Crisis in Editing: Texts of the English Renaissance* (New York: AMS Press, 1994)

Melchionda, Mario (ed.), *Gli 'Essayes' di Francis Bacon. Studio Introduttivo, Testo Critico e Commento* (Florence: Leo S. Olschki, 1979)

Metzger, B.M., *The Text of the New Testament. Its Transmission, Corruption and Restoration* (3rd edn., Oxford: Clarendon Press, 1992; new edn., with B.D. Ehrman, 2005)

Millgate, Michael, *Testamentary Acts: Browning, Tennyson, James, Hardy* (Oxford: Clarendon Press, 1992)

Milton, John: see Carey, John; Patterson, F.A.; Wolfe, D.M.

Milton, J.R., Review article on Nidditch and Rogers (eds), John Locke, *Drafts for the Essay Concerning Human Understanding, Locke Newletter*, 22 (1991), 125–39

Moore, J.K., *Primary Materials Relating to Copy and Print in English Books of the Sixteenth and Seventeenth Centuries* (Oxford: Oxford Bibliographical Society, Occasional Publication No. 24, 1992)

Mosley, Adam, 'Astronomical Books and Courtly Communication', in Marina Frasca-Spada and Nick Jardine (eds), *Books and the Sciences in History* (Cambridge: University Press, 2000), 114–31

Moxon, Joseph, *Mechanick Exercises on the Whole Art of Printing* (1683–4), ed. Herbert Davis and Harry Carter (London: Oxford University Press, 1958)

Mullins, E.L.C., *Texts and Calendars: an Analytical Guide to Serial Publications* (2 vols., London: Royal Historical Society, 1958, 1983)

Mumford, Lewis, 'Emerson behind Barbed Wire', *New York Review of Books*, 10, no. 1 (18 Jan. 1968), 3–5

Nash, Andrew (ed.), *The Culture of Collected Editions* (Basingstoke: Palgrave Macmillan, 2003)

Nash, Paul W., 'The Abandoning of the Long "s" in Britain in 1800', *Journal of the Printing History Society*, n.s. 3 (2001), 3–19

Needham, Paul, 'Concepts of Paper Study', in Daniel W. Mosser, Michael Saffle and Ernest W. Sullivan II (eds), *Puzzles in Paper: Concepts in Historical Watermarks* (Delaware: Oak Knoll Press, and London: British Library, 2000), 1–36

Newman, William R., and Principe, Lawrence M., George Starkey, *Alchemical Laboratory Notebooks and Correspondence* (Chicago: University of Chicago Press, 2004)

Newton, Isaac: see Koyré, Alexandre; McGuire, J.E.; Shapiro, Alan; Turnbull, H.W.

Nidditch, P.H. (ed.), John Locke, *An Essay concerning Human Understanding* (Oxford: Clarendon Press, 1975; abbreviated paperback reprint, 1979)

Nidditch, P.H., Rogers, G.A.J., and Schuurman, Paul (eds), John Locke, *Drafts for the 'Essay concerning Human Understanding', and other Philosophical Writings* (Oxford: Clarendon Press, 1990–, in progress)

Oldenburg, Henry: see Hall, A.R., and Hall, M.B.

Orgel, Stephen, 'What is a Text', *Research Opportunities in Renaissance Drama*, 24 (1981), 3–6

Osselton, N.E., 'Spelling-Book Rules and the Capitalisation of Nouns in the Seventeenth and Eighteenth Centuries', in Mary-Jo Arn and Hanneke Wirtjes, with Hans Jansen (eds), *Historical & Editorial Studies in Medieval & Early Modern English for Johan Gerritsen* (Groningen: Wolters-Noordhoff, 1985), 49–61

Parrish, Stephen (general editor), *The Cornell Wordsworth* (Ithaca: Cornell University Press, 1975–, in progress)

Patterson, F.A. (ed.), *The Works of John Milton* (18 vols., New York: Columbia University Press, 1931–8)

Pearce Williams, L. (ed.), *The Selected Correspondence of Michael Faraday* (2 vols., Cambridge: University Press, 1971)

Pears, S.A. (ed.), *The Correspondence of Sir Philip Sidney and Hubert Languet* (London: William Pickering, 1845; repr. Farnborough: Gregg International, 1971)

Pebworth, Ted-Larry, 'Towards a Taxonomy of Watermarks', in Daniel W. Mosser, Michael Saffle and Ernest W. Sullivan II (eds), *Puzzles in Paper: Concepts in Historical Watermarks* (Delaware: Oak Knoll Press, and London: British Library, 2000), 229–42

Pell, John: see Malcolm, Noel

Pepys, Samuel: see Latham, Robert

Petroski, Henry, *The Pencil: a History of Design and Circumstance* (New York: A.A. Knopf, 1989; London: Faber & Faber, 1990)

Petti, Anthony G., *English Literary Hands from Chaucer to Dryden* (London: Edward Arnold, 1977)

Pfeiffer, Robert H., *Introduction to the Old Testament* (New York: Harper and Brothers, 1948)

Pfeiffer, Rudolph, *History of Classical Scholarship from 1300 to 1850* (Oxford: Clarendon Press, 1976)

Pitcher, John (ed.), Francis Bacon, *The Essays* (Harmondsworth: Penguin, 1985)

Pollard, Graham, 'Notes on the Size of the Sheet', *The Library*, 4th series 22 (1942), 105–37

Poole, H.E., 'The Printing of William Holder's "Principles of Harmony"', *Proceedings of the Royal Musical Association*, 101 (1974–5), 31–43

Pope, Alexander: see Butt, John; Sherburn, George

Popkin, Richard H., 'Plans for Publishing Newton's Religious and Alchemical Manuscripts, 1982–98', in James E. Force and Sarah Hutton (eds), *Newton and Newtonianism: New Studies* (Dordrecht: Kluwer Academic Publishers, 2004), 15–22

Porter, Roy (ed.), William Hobbs, *The Earth Generated and Anatomized* (Ithaca: Cornell University Press, and London: British Museum (Natural History), 1981)

Preston, Jean F., and Yeandle, Laetitia, *English Handwriting 1400–1650: an Introductory Manual* (Binghampton, NY: Medieval and Renaissance Texts and Studies, 1992)

Principe, Lawrence M., *The Aspiring Adept: Robert Boyle and his Alchemical Quest* (Princeton: University Press, 1998)

Rabbie, Edwin, 'Editing Neo-Latin Texts', *Editio*, 10 (1996), 25–48

Redford, Bruce (ed.), *The Letters of Samuel Johnson* (The Hyde Edition) (5 vols., Princeton: University Press; Oxford: Clarendon Press, 1992–4)

Rees, Graham, '*Instauratio Instauratoris*: Towards a New Edition of the Works of Francis Bacon', *Nouvelles de la République des Lettres*, 7 (1987), 37–48

Rees, Graham (ed.), Francis Bacon, *Philosophical Studies c. 1611–19*, The Oxford Francis Bacon, vol. 6 (Oxford: Clarendon Press, 1996)

Rees, Graham (ed.), Francis Bacon, *The Instauratio Magna: Last Writings*, The Oxford Francis Bacon, vol. 13 (Oxford: Clarendon Press, 2000)

Rees, Graham, with Wakely, Maria (eds), Francis Bacon, *The Instauratio Magna Part II: Novum organum and Associated Texts*, The Oxford Francis Bacon, vol. 11 (Oxford: Clarendon Press, 2004)

Reiman, Donald H., *The Study of Modern Manuscripts: Public, Confidential and Private* (Baltimore: The Johns Hopkins Press, 1993)

'Report on Editing Historical Documents', *Bulletin of the Institute of Historical Research*, 1 (1923), 6–25

'Report on Editing Modern Historical Documents', *Bulletin of the Institute of Historical Research*, 3 (1925), 13–26

Reyce, Robert: see Hervey, Lord Francis

Reynolds, L.D., and Wilson, N.G., *Scribes and Scholars: a Guide to the Transmission of Greek and Latin Literature* (3rd edn., Oxford: Clarendon Press, 1991)

Rhodes, Neil, and Sawday, Jonathan (eds), *The Renaissance Computer: Knowledge Technology in the First Age of Print* (London: Routledge, 2000)

Ritter, Paul, Müller, Karl, Heinekamp, Albert, Breger, Herbert, Schepers, Heinrich, et al. (eds), *Gottfried Wilhelm Leibniz, Sämtliche Schriften und Briefe* (7 series, Darmstadt: Otto Reichl Verlag; Leipzig: K.F. Koehler Verlag; Berlin: Akademie Verlag, 1923–, in progress)

Robbins, Robin (ed.), *Sir Thomas Browne's Pseudodoxia Epidemica* (2 vols., Oxford: Clarendon Press, 1981)

Roberts, Marion [with Vander Meulen, David], *Dugdale and Hollar: History Illustrated* (Newark: University of Delaware Press, 2002)

Robinson, F.J.G., and Wallis, P.J., *Book Subscription Lists: a Revised Guide* (Newcastle upon Tyne: Book Subscription Lists Project, 1975)

Robinson, P.M.W., 'New Directions in Critical Editing', in Kathryn Sutherland (ed.), *Electronic Text: Investigations in Method and Theory* (Oxford: Clarendon Press, 1997), 145–71

Romanell, Patrick, *John Locke and Medicine: a New Key to Locke* (New York: Prometheus Books, 1984)

Rose, Mark, *Authors and Owners: the Invention of Copyright* (Cambridge, Mass.: Harvard University Press, 1993)
Royal Commission on Historical Manuscripts, *Manuscripts and Men* (London: Her Majesty's Stationery Office, 1969)
Rusnock, Andrea (ed.), *The Correspondence of James Jurin (1684–1750)* (Amsterdam: Rodopi, 1996)
Salmon, Vivian, 'Orthography and Punctuation', in Roger Lass (ed.), *The Cambridge History of the English Language, vol. 3: 1476–1776* (Cambridge: University Press, 1999), 13–55
Scott-Warren, Jason, *Sir John Harington and the Book as Gift* (Oxford: University Press, 2001)
Scragg, D.G., *A History of English Spelling* (Manchester: University Press, 1974)
Serjeantson, Richard (ed.), Meric Casaubon, *Generall Learning* (Cambridge: Renaissance Texts from Manuscripts, No. 2, 1999)
Shapiro, Alan E., 'Beyond the Dating Game: Watermark Clusters and the Composition of Newton's *Opticks*', in P.M. Harman and A.E. Shapiro (eds), *The Investigation of Difficult Things: Essays on Newton and the History of the Exact Sciences* (Cambridge: University Press, 1992), 181–227
Shapiro, Alan E. (ed), *The Optical Papers of Isaac Newton* (Cambridge: University Press, 1984–, in progress)
Sharpe, Kevin, *Reading Revolutions: the Politics of Reading in Early Modern England* (New Haven and London: Yale University Press, 2000)
Sherburn, George (ed.), *The Correspondence of Alexander Pope*, 5 vols. (Oxford: Clarendon Press, 1956)
Shillingsburg, Peter L., *Scholarly Editing in the Computer Age: Theory and Practice* (3rd edn., Ann Arbor: University of Michigan Press, 1996; 1st published 1985; 1st trade edn., 1986)
Sidney, Sir Philip: see Pears, S.A.
Smith, John, *The Printer's Grammar* (London, 1755, reprinted London: Gregg Press, 1965)
Smith, Nigel (ed.), *The Poems of Andrew Marvell*, Longman Annotated English Poets (London: Pearson/Longman, 2003)
Southam, Brian (ed.), *Jane Austen's 'Sir Charles Grandison'* (Oxford: Clarendon Press, 1980)
Spargo, Peter, 'Sotheby's, Keynes and Yahuda – the 1936 Sale of Newton's Manuscripts', in P.M. Harman and A.E. Shapiro (eds), *The Investigation of Difficult Things: Essays on Newton and the History of the Exact Sciences* (Cambridge: University Press, 1992), 115–34
Spiller, Michael R.G., *'Concerning Natural Experimental Philosophie': Meric Casaubon and the Royal Society* (The Hague: Martin Nijhoff, 1980)
Stallybrass, Peter, Chartier, Roger, Mowery, J. Franklin, and Wolfe, Heather, 'Hamlet's Tables and the Technologies of Writing in Renaissance England', *Shakespeare Quarterly*, 55 (2004), 379–419
Starkey, George: see Newman, William R.
Steinberg, S.H., *Five Hundred Years of Printing* (2nd edn., Harmondsworth: Penguin Books, 1961)
Stevens, Michael E., and Burg, Steven B., *Editing Historical Documents: a Handbook of Practice* (Walnut Creek, Ca.: AltaMira Press, 1997)
Sutherland, Kathryn (ed.), *Electronic Text: Investigations in Method and Theory* (Oxford: Clarendon Press, 1997)

Swift, Jonathan: see Williams, Harold
Tanselle, G. Thomas, 'The Editorial Problem of Final Authorial Intention', *Studies in Bibliography*, 29 (1976), 167–211, reprinted in his *Textual Criticism and Scholarly Editing*, 27–71
Tanselle, G. Thomas, 'The Editing of Historical Documents', *Studies in Bibliography*, 31 (1978), 1–56, reprinted in his *Textual Criticism and Scholarly Editing*, 218–73
Tanselle, G. Thomas, 'Classical, Biblical and Medieval Textual Criticism and Modern Editing', *Studies in Bibliography*, 36 (1983), 21–68, reprinted in his *Textual Criticism and Scholarly Editing*, 274–321
Tanselle, G. Thomas, *A Rationale of Textual Criticism* (Philadelphia: University of Pennsylvania Press, 1989)
Tanselle, G. Thomas, *Textual Criticism and Scholarly Editing* (Charlottesville: University Press of Virginia, 1990)
Tanselle, G. Thomas, 'Editing without a Copy-Text', *Studies in Bibliography*, 47 (1994), 1–22
Tanselle, G. Thomas, 'Textual Criticism at the Millenium', *Studies in Bibliography*, 54 (2001), 1–80
Taylor, Gary, *Reinventing Shakespeare: a Cultural History from the Restoration to the Present* (London: Hogarth Press, 1990)
Taylor, Gary, and Warren, Michael (eds), *The Division of the Kingdoms: Shakespeare's Two Versions of 'King Lear'* (Oxford: Clarendon Press, 1983)
Thomas, Keith, 'The Meaning of Literacy in Early Modern England', in Gerd Baumann (ed.), *The Written Word: Literacy in Transition* (Oxford: Clarendon Press, 1986), 97–131
Thorpe, James, *Principles of Textual Criticism* (San Marino: Huntington Library, 1972)
Todd, Janet (ed.), *The Works of Aphra Behn* (7 vols., London: William Pickering, 1992–6)
Tricaud, François (ed.), Thomas Hobbes, *Léviathan* (Paris: Editions Sirey, 1971)
Tuck, Richard (ed.), Thomas Hobbes, *Leviathan* (revised student edn., Cambridge: University Press, 1996; originally published 1991)
Turnbull, H.W., Scott, J.F., Hall, A.R., and Tilling, Laura (eds), *The Correspondence of Isaac Newton* (7 vols., Cambridge: University Press, 1959–77)
Twain, Mark: see Hirst, R.H.
Vander Meulen, David L., and Tanselle, G. Thomas, 'A System of Manuscript Transcription', *Studies in Bibliography*, 52 (1999), 201–12
Vickers, Brian, 'Bacon for our Time' (review essay), *Early Science and Medicine*, 9 (2004), 144–62
Vickers, Brian (ed.), Francis Bacon, *The Essays or Counsels Civil and Moral* (Oxford: University Press, 1999)
Wakely, Maria, and Rees, Graham, 'Folios Fit for a King: James I, John Bill and the King's Printers, 1616–20', *Huntington Library Quarterly*, 68 (2005), 467–95
Wallis, John: see Beeley, Philip
Walpole, Horace: see Cunningham, Peter; Lewis, W.S.
Warrender, Howard (ed.), Thomas Hobbes, *De Cive. The English Version*, Clarendon Edition of the Philosophical Works of Thomas Hobbes, vol. 3 (Oxford: Clarendon Press, 1983)
Warrender, Howard (ed.), Thomas Hobbes, *De Cive. The Latin Version*, Clarendon Edition of the Philosophical Works of Thomas Hobbes, vol. 2 (Oxford: Clarendon Press, 1983)
Webster, John: see Gunby, David

Wells, Stanley, and Taylor, Gary, with John Jowett and William Montgomery, *William Shakespeare: a Textual Companion* (Oxford: Clarendon Press, 1987)

West, M.L., *Textual Criticism and Editorial Technique applicable to Greek and Latin Texts* (Stuttgart: B.G. Teubner, 1973)

Whiteside, D.T., *The Mathematical Papers of Isaac Newton* (8 vols., Cambridge: University Press, 1967–81)

Williams, Harold (ed.), *The Correspondence of Jonathan Swift*, 5 vols. (Oxford: Clarendon Press, 1963)

Wilson, Edmund, 'The Fruits of the MLA', *New York Review of Books*, 11, no. 5 (26 Sept. 1968), 7–10, no. 8 (10 Oct. 1968), 6–14

Wilson, F.P., *Shakespeare and the New Bibliography*, revised and edited by Helen Gardner (Oxford: Clarendon Press, 1970)

Wolfe, D.M. (general editor), *The Complete Prose Works of John Milton* (8 vols., New Haven: Yale University Press, 1953–82)

Wolfe, Heather (ed.), Elizabeth Cary, Lady Falkland, *Life and Letters* (Cambridge: Renaissance Texts from Manuscript, No. 4, 2001)

Woolf, Daniel, *The Social Circulation of the Past: English Historical Culture 1500–1730* (Oxford: University Press, 2003)

Wordsworth, William: see Parrish, Stephen

Wotton, Sir Henry, *Reliquiæ Wottonianæ*, ed. Izaak Walton (London, 1651)

Woudhuysen, H.R., *Sir Philip Sidney and the Circulation of Manuscripts 1558–1640* (Oxford: Clarendon Press, 1996)

Woudhuysen, H.R., 'Writing-Tables and Table Books', *British Library Journal*, 2004 (accessed electronically as *eBLJ* 2004), article 3

Wright, W. Aldis (ed.), *Bacon's Essays and Colours of Good and Evil* (3rd edn., Cambridge and London: Macmillan, 1865)

Index

abbreviations: *see* contractions
accidentals and their treatment   4, 33–4, 59, 96, 121–2, 145
   see also capitalisation, italicisation, punctuation, spelling
administrative and legal records   17, 56–7
Alberti, Leon Battista   24
Allen, P.S.   49
Allix, Pierre   137
Ames, Joseph   30
ampersand, treatment of   78
angle brackets: *see* brackets
anglicana: *see* court hand
annotation, placing of   97, 98–9
   rationale of   96–9
anthologies, role of   37–8, 90
antiquarianism   21–2, 35, 38, 56
apparatus in scholarly editions   13, 64, 87, 89, 92–101
Arber, Edward   69, 121
archives   13, 19, 46, 48, 52–6, 93
   completeness of   55
   exploitation of   46, 52–6
archives, electronic   42, 52, 54
Aristotle   39
arrow-heads, use of   82, 117, 120
Ashmole, Elias   50–1, 56
astrology   19, 38, 51
Aubrey, John   38, 74, 85
Austen, Jane   75
author, rights of   34
   role of   29, 31–2, 33–5
authorial intention   29, 58–61, 65, 68–9, 71, 72, 78, 79, 82, 85
authorship, attitudes to   21, 37–8
Avery, William   104

Bacon, Francis   6, 91, 96, 100
   attitude to accidentals   34, 96
   correspondence   72
   Essays   22, 28, 69, 121–6
   Historia densi & rari   70
   New Organon   88, 94
   Oxford Francis Bacon   40, 41, 99, 100, 140
Bacon, Robert   135
Baker, Thomas   138
Banks, Sir Joseph   45
Barret, Hanna   124
Bateson, F.W.   89
Baxter, Richard   48
Beale, John   123
Beaumont, Francis   91
Beeley, Philip   48
Behn, Aphra   66
Bekker, Immanuel   39
Bennett, Kate   x, 74, 85, 138
Bentley, Richard   3
Berlin, Max Planck Institute for the History of Science   56
Berners-Lee, Tim   108
Bible, editing of   3, 22
biographical guides   95–6, 97
Birch, Thomas   42, 45
Black, Jeremy   x
black letter type   32, 67
Bodleian Library: *see* Oxford
book sizes: *see* format
booksellers   34–5
Boole, George   145
Boolean searches   105, 145
Bourdelot academy   107
Bowers, Fredson   3–4, 5, 59–60, 91
Boyd, Julian   49

163

Index

Boyle, Robert   6, 103–4, 106, 109
  amanuenses   109, 135
  Correspondence   6, 46, 48, 84, 96, 101, 103–4, 107, 117, 118, 120
  Experimenta et Observationes Physicæ   63, 109–17
  Free Inquiry into the . . . Notion of Nature   88–9
  Invitation to Free Communication   68
  letters 45: *see also Correspondence*
  'Inquiries touching *Mines*'   68
  notebooks   109
  workdiaries   6, 12, 55, 81, 142
  Works   6, 41, 42, 48, 55, 62–3, 67, 68, 84, 94, 98, 99, 101, 103–4, 109, 117, 118, 120
Boyle Papers   54–5, 62–3
Boyle website   12
brackets   31
  angle   82, 118–20
  editorial use of   65, 66, 79, 81, 82, 83, 109, 109–17, 118–20
  half square   82, 118
  square   5, 66, 83, 118–20
  see also arrow-heads
Brahe, Tycho   35
British Library   54
British Records Association   5
Broadway, Jan   x, 12, 135
Broghill, Roger Boyle, Baron   106
Brown, Sylvia   118, 120
Browne, Sir Thomas   60–1
Burkhardt, Frederick   110, 115
Burnet, Gilbert   48
Burton, Robert, *Anatomy of Melancholy*   61, 65, 68
  Clarendon Press edition of   61, 65

Calendar of State Papers   56
Calendar of Treasury Books   56
calendaring   46, 52, 54–7
Calhoun, John C.   49
Cambridge, University of   52
Cambridge University Press   26
  'Texts in the History of Philosophy'   87, 88, 89
  'Texts in the History of Political Thought'   86, 91

  see also Jonson, Ben
cancels   28, 63, 145
Canterbury Tales Project   9, 12, 70–1
Capell, Edward   3, 30
capitalisation   8, 31–2, 33–4, 96
  editorial treatment of   82, 88–90, 91
  see also accidentals
Carter, Clarence E.   5
Casaubon, Meric   37
catchwords   33, 66, 84, 145
Cavendish, Sir Charles   45, 110, 114
CD-ROM, use of   12, 53–4, 64
Celsus   123, 124, 126
Center for Editions of American Authors (CEAA)   4, 59, 87, 110–11, 145
Center for Scholarly Editions (CSE)   4, 74, 110–11, 145
Centre for Editing Lives and Letters   x, 12
Chadwick-Healey (publishers)   52
Chambers, Douglas   48
Charles II   63
Chaucer, Geoffrey   39
  Canterbury Tales   9, 70–1
  see also Canterbury Tales Project
Chesterfield, Philip Dormer Stanhope, 4th Earl of   25
Cicero, M.T.   43
Clarendon Press: *see* Burton, Robert, Hobbes, Thomas
classical texts, editing of   3, 22–3, 132
clear text editorial method   110, 115–16
Clericuzio, Antonio   6
Cohen, I. Bernard   64
collation, role of   9, 28, 53–5, 62–3, 68, 71, 72, 145
  computer collation   9
collected editions   25, 38–42
Columbia: *see* Milton, John
Commercium epistolicum   49
commonplace books   20
completeness: *see* correspondence, editions of
composition, process of   16–17, 73–5, 78–9, 92–3, 96

compositors, role of   14, 26–8, 30–2, 33–4, 59, 66, 77, 86, 87–90, 137
computers, editorial use of   8–12
  see also electronic editions
concordances, use of   107, 145
Conference on Editorial Problems, Toronto   6, 59–60
conjectural identification, and indexing   107
contractions and abbreviations   8, 16, 30, 137
  editorial treatment of   74–7, 91, 109–17, 122, 133
copy text
  theory of   4, 29, 33, 59, 60–1
  treatment of   60–1, 62, 65–8, 72, 93
Copyright Act (1710)   34
Cornell: *see* Wordsworth
corrections: *see* cancels, errata, stop-press corrections
correspondence
  annotation of   97–8
  apparatus to   93, 94–6, 99–100
  and archival survival   46, 93
  artificiality of genre   46
  definition of   43–5, 47–50, 54, 56
  editions of   13, 36, 43–4, 77
  ordering of   44–6, 93
  overlap between editions   46–7
  see also epistolary form, essay-epistles, letters
court hand   15–16
crayon, use of   15
'Crisis in Editing' (1988 conference)   59–60
Crooke, Andrew   127
CSE: *see* Center for Scholarly Editing
Culpeper, Sir Cheney   54
Cunningham, Peter   44
Curley, Edwin   64, 127

Darwin, Charles   110, 115
databases, creation and use of   9, 46–7, 53
Davis, Edward B.   6, 89
Davis, Herbert   87–8
Davis, Richard   67

Dear, Peter   98
de Beer, Esmond   43, 97, 99, 101, 102, 105, 107
deletions: *see* manuscripts
DelVecchio, Doreen   66
demy: *see* paper sizes
Descartes, René   6, 43, 88
devotional manuscripts   19
diagrams, editorial treatment of   67–8
diaries   20, 51, 96, 97
Dictionary of National Biography   97
  see also Oxford University Press
digitisation   8–12, 46
  see also electronic editions
diplomatic editions   80, 87, 145
  see also manuscripts, transcription of
documentary editing: *see* editing
Domesday Book   75–6
Donne, John   18
Dryden, John   40, 89
  'California' Dryden   40
Dugdale, Sir William   21, 35
duodecimo: *see* formats

Early English Books Online   12, 36, 64
early modern period, distinctiveness of   6–8
  see also hand-press period
editing, documentary   4–5, 6, 90
  in history of science   5–6
  literary   3–4, 6, 59–61
editions
  arrangement of   41, 51
  boundaries of   38, 41–2, 47–51, 56
  introductory material   92–5
  selective   37, 43–4
  see also correspondence, *Works*
editor, role of   1, 13, 36, 56, 58–60, 61–3, 70–1, 74, 78, 81, 82, 85, 92, 94, 104–5
electronic editions   9, 12, 42–3, 44, 51–4, 55–7, 58, 64, 70–1
  and correspondence   46, 47
  and indexing   105–8
  and manuscript texts   78, 80–1, 84–5

electronic editions (*continued*)
  presentation of apparatus 92, 95, 97–8, 99, 100–1
  presentation of facsimiles 9–10, 12, 52–3, 84–5
  and revised texts 69–71, 121
  see also hypertext links, use of
electronic mail 10
Elizabeth, Queen 129, 131
emendation, silent, legitimacy of 64–5
Emerson, Ralph Waldo 87, 118, 120, 143
epistles, dedicatory 48
epistolary form, use of 47–9
Erasmus, Desiderius 43, 49
errata 28, 65
essay-epistles 48
Evelyn, John 48, 60, 72
  Diary 97, 102, 103, 107

facsimiles, use of 40, 54–5, 64, 66–7, 67, 73, 75, 94, 141
  see also electronic editions
Falkland, Elizabeth Cary, Lady 81
Faraday, Michael 44
Farley, Abraham 75–6
Fiesole 24
fixity and print 24–5
Flamsteed, John, *Correspondence* 50, 74, 75, 83, 93
Fletcher, John 91
Florence
  Biblioteca Nazionale Centrale 56
  Istituto e Museo di Storia della Scienza 56
Folger, Henry Clay 62
Folger Library x, 19, 62
  see also Hooker, Richard
foliation, editorial presentation of 84
  see also pagination
folio: *see* formats
foolscap: *see* paper sizes
footnotes, authorial, treatment of 66
  see also annotation
formats (duodecimo, folio, octavo, quarto) 25, 27, 145–6
Foucault, Michel 39

Fowles, John 85
Franklin, Benjamin 49–50
  The Papers of 49–50, 119

Galilei, Galileo 6, 56
Gaskell, Philip 25–6
Gilman, W.H. 118
Glanvill, Joseph 60–1
glossary, editorial use of 95–6, 132
Goldie, Mark 43
Greek 66–7, 99
Greengrass, Mark 54
Greg, Hugh 109, 135
Greg, W.W. 3–4, 59–60, 118, 120
Gregory XIII, Pope 45
Gregory, David 50
Griesbach, Johann Jakob 3
Guillemets 32
Gunther, R.T. 51

Halsband, Robert 43
Hamilton, Alexander 49
Hammond, Anthony 66
Hammond, Paul 89–90
hand-press period 7–8, 25–6
handwriting 8, 14–17, 20, 29–30, 51, 84
  see also manuscripts, transcription of
Harth, Phillip 89–90
Hartlib, Samuel 9, 52–4, 68, 82
Hartlib Papers 9, 52–4, 82, 107–8
Hartlib Papers Project 9, 12, 52–4, 107–8
Harvey, P.D.A. 5, 56
Haviland, John 124
Henry VIII 129, 131
Herford, C.H. 42, 65
HiDES/Microcosm 11
Higgins-Biddle, J.C. 118, 120
Hill, W. Speed 61
history of science, editing in: *see* editing
Hobbes, Thomas 6, 38
  Clarendon edition of 40, 63, 98
  Correspondence of 96, 98, 110, 114
  De cive 67, 96, 98
  Leviathan 22, 63–4, 89, 91, 127–31
Hobbs, Mary 21
Hobbs, William, of Weymouth 91

Index

Hooke, Robert 46, 64
Hooker, Richard 39–40, 61, 62
  Folger Library edition of 40, 61, 65
Hooper, Humfrey 122
Housman, A.E. 3
HTML, use of 11, 145
Hunnisett, R.F. 5
Huygens, Christiaan 6, 43, 138
hypertext links, use of 10, 12, 64, 80, 92, 97–8, 99, 100–1, 102, 107, 121

illustrations, treatment of 67–8
imperial: *see* paper sizes
incunabula 32, 144
indexes 13, 102–8
  indexing packages 105
  of semantic content 108
  subdivisions 103–4, 106–7
  subject entries 104–5
ink 15–16, 73
ink, printing 26
insertions: *see* manuscripts
Institute of Historical Research 5, 6
Internet 11–12, 105
inverted commas, use of 32
italic
  hands 15
  type 8, 26, 32, 33–4: editorial treatment of 67, 82, 88, 89–90, 91, 127
  see also accidentals

James, Frank 44
Jardine, Lisa 88
Jeake, Samuel, of Rye 19, 91
Jefferson, Thomas, *Papers of* 49–50
Johnson, Samuel 40
  Yale edition of 40
Jonson, Ben 39, 41, 42, 65
  Cambridge Ben Jonson 42–3
Jonston, Jan 54
Josten, C.H. 50–1, 56
Jurin, James 44

Keeble, Neil 48
Kiernan, Michael 69, 121
Kline, Mary-Jo 5, 118
Koyré, Alexandre 64

Lachmann, Karl 3
Lambarde, William 21
Latham, Robert 103
Latin
  editions 25, 39, 62, 63
  editorial treatment of 65, 78, 87–8, 99, 100–1
Leeuwenhoek, Antoni van 138
Legg, Rodney 85
Leibniz, G.W. 6, 45
letter-forms (ff, i/j, u/v, long 's', thorn, w) 7, 16–17, 30–1
  editorial treatment of 65–6, 73, 75, 77–8, 122, 133
letters 18, 20, 43–9, 73
  dating of 45–6, 95
  format of 18, 84, 95
  survival of 46, 93
  see also correspondence
ligatures, use of 75, 145
line-breaks, editorial treatment of 66, 84
literary editing: *see* editing
Littleton, Charles x, 12
Lizardière, Monsieur 107
Locke, John 6, 76
  correspondence 43–4, 99, 101
  drafts for *Essay* 76, 80, 132–3
  Essay 69
  manuscripts 19, 132–3
  Reasonableness of Christianity 118
Longman Annotated English Poets 86, 89–91, 98

Maber, Richard x
machine-press period 7, 26
Maddison, R.E.W. 48
Malcolm, Noel 45, 63, 74, 96, 98, 110, 114
Malone Society reprints 118, 120
manuscripts
  characteristics of 7–8, 13, 14–20, 21, 73, 85
  circulation of 7, 13, 20–3
  damage to 15, 83–4, 118, 120
  deletions in 16–7, 73, 74, 78–81, 109–17, 133
  editions of 36–7, 87
  genres of 20–1

168 *Index*

manuscripts (*continued*)
  insertions in   17, 75, 78–9, 81–2, 109–17
  as private   20, 73–4, 76
  'publication' of   22, 25, 74
  transcription of   1, 73–84, 109–17, 132–3
  transmission of   21–2, 56, 72–3, 74, 85
  see also composition, process of; print, relationship to manuscript
markup language, use of   9–12, 67
  see also SGML, XML
Marotti, Arthur   21
Marvell, Andrew   96, 98
McGann, Jerome   4, 52
McGee, Edward G.   138
McGuire, J.E.   80, 110, 112
McKenzie, D.F.   4, 22, 26, 60
McKerrow, R.B.   3, 59
McLaverty, James   59
medical recipes, collections of   21, 109
Medici, Cosimo de'   24
memoranda: *see* notebooks
microfilm, use of   54–5
Miles, Henry   42
Milton, John   40, 41
  'Columbia' Milton   41
  poems   74, 89
modernised texts   13, 81, 86–91, 113, 127–31
Money, David   99
Morison, S.E.   134
Mosaic   11
Moxon, Joseph   30, 32
Mumford, Lewis   87, 91

National Historical Publications and Records Commission   5, 49
Netscape   11
newsletters, scribal   22
Newton, Sir Isaac   6, 16, 18, 46, 50, 51–2, 68, 74, 76, 138
  annotations to books   52
  correspondence   46, 50, 138
  handwriting   16, 51
  manuscripts   16, 18, 72, 74
  Opticks   91
  Principia   64, 91
  Trinity notebook   80, 110, 112
Newton Project   51–2, 142
Nidditch, Peter   x, 69, 70, 80, 132–3
notebooks   19, 73, 109
Nuttall, Geoffrey   48

octavo: *see* formats
Oldenburg, Henry   109
online publication   12
  see also electronic editions
oral transmission   14, 20
Oxford
  Bodleian Library   19, 51, 137, 138
  Oxford University Press (Clarendon Press)   38, 40, 132: *Concise Oxford English Dictionary*   95; *Oxford Dictionary of National Biography*   97; Oxford Francis Bacon: *see* Bacon, Francis; *Oxford Shakespeare*   60;
  see also Burton, Robert, Hobbes, Thomas

page-breaks, editorial treatment of   66, 84–5, 122
pagination   33
  editorial treatment of   66, 84–5
paper   17–20, 94
  availability of   20
  booklets of   19
  cost of   20
  re-use of   20
  sheets   18, 25–8
  see also watermarks
paper sizes (demy, foolscap, imperial, octavo, pot)   18–20, 25, 145–6
  see also format
papermaking   17–18
'Papers' as genre   5, 49–52
parchment   17
Pascal, Blaise   132
PDF, use of   12, 146
Pearce Williams, L.   44
Pell, John   45, 110, 114
pen, use of   15–16, 75
pencil, use of   15, 73, 75
Pepys, Samuel, *Diary* of   91
Perkins, William   39

Perseus Project   11
Peter, St   128, 130
Pforzheimer collection   140
Pickering & Chatto   66, 67
Pitcher, John   121
Pitt, Moses   67
Pliny the Younger   43
Plot, Robert   137
poetry   21, 37–8, 74, 91
  annotation of   98
Pope, Alexander   34, 39, 43, 45, 70
  Twickenham edition of   70
Portsmouth Papers   56
postmarks   95
pot: *see* paper sizes
presentation copies   22, 63
Principe, Lawrence M.   6
print
  and dissemination   24–5
  and 'fixity'   24–5
  impact of   7, 9, 24–5, 35, 43
  relationship to manuscript texts
    14, 27–8, 29–30, 33, 35, 42, 61,
    62–3, 68, 70, 76
  role of   24–35
  and standardisation   24, 31–2
printed books, defects of   28
  as gifts   35
  manuscript corrections to   28, 123
  market for   25, 34–5
  new editions and reissues   28–9
  presentation of   7–8, 13, 29–33, 60,
    64, 67, 94
  range of   25
printing house practice   4, 24,
    25–9
printing, multiple   27–8
printing, speed of   24
Prior, Matthew   34
proofs and proof-reading   27–8, 30,
    61, 102
public/private distinction: *see*
    manuscripts, as private
punctuation   8, 31–2, 33–4, 96
  editorial treatment of   82–3,
    88–90, 91, 127, 133
  see also accidentals

quarto: *see* formats

Ramus, Peter   30
RDF (Resource Description
    Framework)   108
readers, early modern
  role of   20–1, 35
readers, modern
  needs of   2, 13, 37, 57, 58–60, 71,
    76, 78–9, 80, 86–91, 92, 102,
    106, 107–8, 133
recipes   83
  collections of   20–1, 109–17
Record Commissioners   76
record type   76
Rees, Graham   x, 88, 94, 100
Reiman, Donald   74
Reliquiae Wottonianae   43, 49
Renaissance
  editing   3, 39
  letter collections   43, 49
  scripts   15
Restoration, church settlement   40
revised texts, presentation of   13, 37,
    68–70, 72–3, 79, 121–6
  see also variants
Reyce, Robert   21–2
Richardson, Samuel   70
Robbins, Robin   60–1
Rogers, John   x, 70, 132
Rome, Colosseum   97
Rossetti Archive   52
Rossetti, Dante Gabriel   52
Rowbottom, Margaret   68
Royal Commission on Historical
    Manuscripts   56
Royal Society   54–5, 109
RTF files   11, 146
rubrication   7
running heads   33
Rusnock, Andrea   44
Rye, Sussex   19

's', long: *see* letter-forms
Scaliger, Joseph   3
scanning, use of   64
schools, texts for   90
Schuurman, Paul   70
Scriba, Christoph   48
scribal publication   22, 25, 74
  see also manuscripts, circulation of

scriptoria 22, 53, 146
seals 18, 95
secretary hand 15–16
semantic web 108
Serjeantson, Richard 37
SGML, use of 10, 58, 67, 71, 82, 83, 146
Shakespeare
  editing of 1, 3, 6, 60, 62
  First Folio 62
Shakespearean and Jacobean texts, editions of 65, 77–8
Shapiro, Alan 51
Sheffield, University of 9, 52, 132
Shillingsburg, Peter 60
Sidney, Sir Philip 21
signatures 33, 146
Silverthorne, Michael 88
Simpson, Percy and Evelyn 42, 65
Smith, John 32
Smith, Nigel x, 96, 98
Sotheby's 52
Southam, Brian 75
Speght, Thomas 39
spelling 31–2, 33–4, 96
  editorial treatment of 82, 86, 88–9, 91, 127, 133
  variants 106
  see also accidentals
spelling reformers 31
Spenser, Edmund 34
Spiller, Michael 37
standardisation: see printing
Starkey, George 143
stemmata, study of 3, 21–2, 71, 72, 93, 146
Stillingfleet, Edward 60
stop-press corrections 28, 62–3
strike-through, use of 79, 81, 109, 112
Studies in Bibliography 4
subscription publishing 22, 35
substantives 4, 59, 121, 146
  see also accidentals
superscripts, use of 16, 30
  editorial treatment of 75–7, 91
symbols, treatment of 83

Tamny, Martin 80, 110, 112
Tanselle, G. Thomas 5, 90, 134
Telnet 10–11
Text 4
Text Encoding Initiative (TEI) 10, 71, 146
thorn 16, 75–8, 137, 146
  see also letter-forms
tilde 16, 30, 77, 122, 146
  see also contractions and abbreviations
title-pages 32–3, 66–7, 84
Tourneur, Zacharie 132
Toynbee, Mrs Paget 44
translations 99–101
  presentation of 100–1
Tricaud, François 63–4
Tuck, Richard 63, 91
tunes 10
Twain, Mark, *Letters* 119
type-facsimile, use of 67, 74–6, 81, 85
typesetting 26
  cost of 22
Tyrell, James 141
Tyson, Edward 137

URI (Uniform Resource Indicator) 108
users: see readers, modern

variants 146
  recording of 96, 98, 121–2
  treatment of 68–71, 72–3, 87, 91, 143
  see also revised texts
Verdi, Guiseppe, *Don Carlos* 60
verse miscellanies 21, 22, 37–8
Vickers, Brian 98, 100, 121
Virginia, University of 52

Wagner, Richard, *Tannhäuser* 60
Wakely, Maria 88
Wallis, John 39–40, 47–8, 49
Walmsley, J.C. x, 141
Walpole, Horace 44, 45
  Yale edition of 45
Walton, Izaak 43
Ward, John 19, 106

Warrender, Howard   67, 98
watermarks   17–18, 95
Webster, John   66
Wellington Papers   56
Whitaker, Richard   124
Whiteside, D.T.   51
Wiggins, Alison   x, 12
Willmoth, Frances   74
Wilson, Edmund   87
Wilson, Woodrow   49
Winthrop, John   141
Wolf, Friedrich August   3
Wolfe, Heather   x, 81
women   20–1, 136
Wood, Anthony   38
woodblocks   68
Word (Microsoft)   76
word searches, use of   9, 102, 105–6, 107
Wordsworth, William   79
  Cornell Wordsworth   79, 141
  Works, editions of   13, 36, 37–43
    appendices   96
    boundaries of   41–2
    introductory material   92–3
    see also editions
World Wide Web   10
Wortley Montagu, Lady Mary   43
Wotton, Sir Henry   43
Woudhuysen, Henry   21
Wright, John   44
Wright, W.A.   28, 121
writing-tables   14

XML, use of   11, 67, 71, 146

Yale: *see* Johnson, Samuel; Walpole, Horace